About the Author

Junior Tay is a FIDE Candidate Master and an ICCF Senior International Master. He is a former National Rapid Chess Champion and represented Singapore in the 1995 Asian Team Championship. A frequent opening surveys contributor to *New In Chess Yearbook*, he lives in Balestier, Singapore with his wife, WFM Yip Fong Ling, and their dog, Scottie.

Contents

Junior Tay

The Benko Gambit

move by move

EVERYMAN CHESS

First published in 2014 by Gloucester Publishers Limited, Northburgh House,
10 Northburgh Street, London EC1V 0AT

British Library Cataloguing-in-Publication Data
A catalogue record for this book is available from the British Library.

ISBN: 978 1 78194 157 7

Distributed in North America by The Globe Pequot Press, P.O Box 480,
246 Goose Lane, Guilford, CT 06437-0480.

All other sales enquiries should be directed to Everyman Chess, Northburgh House,
10 Northburgh Street, London EC1V 0AT
tel: 020 7253 7887 fax: 020 7490 3708
email: info@everymanchess.com; website: www.everymanchess.com

Everyman Chess Series
Chief advisor: Byron Jacobs
Commissioning editor: John Emms
Assistant editor: Richard Palliser

Typeset and edited by First Rank Publishing, Brighton.
Cover design by Horatio M

Series Foreword

Move by Move is a series of opening books which uses a question-and-answer format. One of our main aims of the series is to replicate – as much as possible – lessons between chess teachers and students.

All the way through, readers will be challenged to answer searching questions and to complete exercises, to test their skills in chess openings and indeed in other key aspects of the game. It's our firm belief that practising your skills like this is an excellent way to study chess openings, and to study chess in general.

Many thanks go to all those who have been kind enough to offer inspiration, advice and assistance in the creation of *Move by Move*. We're really excited by this series and hope that readers will share our enthusiasm.

John Emms,
Everyman Chess

Bibliography

Books

A Strategic Chess Opening Repertoire for White, John Watson (Gambit 2012)
Attack with Black, Valery Aveskulov (Gambit 2013)
Beating the Fianchetto Defences, Efstratios Grivas (Gambit 2006)
Dangerous Weapons: The Benoni and Benko, Richard Palliser, John Emms, Chris Ward & Gawain Jones (Everyman 2008)
Play the Benko Gambit, Nicolai Pedersen (Everyman 2011)
Playing 1.d4 – The Indian Defences, Lars Schandorff (Quality Chess 2011)
Squeezing the Gambits, Kiril Georgiev (Chess Stars 2010)
The Alterman Gambit Guide – Black Gambits 1, Boris Alterman (Quality Chess 2011)
The Benko Gambit, Pal Benko (RHM 1974)
The Benko Gambit, Byron Jacobs & Andrew Kinsman (Batsford 1999)
The Dynamic Benko Gambit, Sergey Kasparov (New in Chess 2012)
The Kaufman Repertoire for Black and White, Larry Kaufman (New in Chess 2012)

Other Resources

ChessBase Magazine
Chesspublishing.com
Chessvibes.com
Chess Informant
Correspondence Database 2013
Houdini 3
Mega Database 2013
MegaCorr 4
New in Chess Yearbook
The Week in Chess

Introduction

What is the Benko Gambit?

This book is about the Benko Gambit which has served me well for the past 14 years in correspondence chess and over-the-board play. The Benko Gambit (or if you prefer the Eastern European version, the Volga Gambit) arises after the moves 1 d4 ♞f6 2 c4 c5 3 d5 b5.

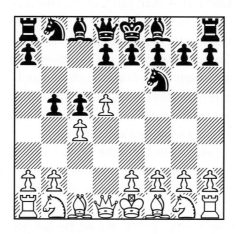

It is named after the American Grandmaster and former World Championship Candidate Pal Benko who popularized the opening by playing it almost without exception whenever the opportunity presented itself, and against all kinds of opposition. Benko published his games and commentary in *Chess Life and Review* frequently and according to his book, *The Benko Gambit* (RHM 1973), he had "as much as announced publicly that anyone can play against me with an extra pawn within a few moves of the opening."

Why play the Benko Gambit?

1) For the price of a pawn (sometimes even two), Black obtains tremendous queenside pressure and puts White on the defensive early in the game. This may give Black an early psychological edge. In the final round of both the 2003 and the 2009 Cairnhill Open (Singapore), I won two games relatively quickly against a former National Champion and National Master. The first was a Benko Gambit Declined and the second time round, my opponent gave a huge sigh after 1 d4 ♞f6 2 c4 c5, played the insipid 3 e3 to avoid the Benko Gambit and allowed me to equalise very quickly.

2) Black's motifs in the Benko are quite clear cut: pile as much pressure as possible on the queenside, try to find ideal squares for the knights in the vicinity of White (usually b4, c4 and d3), and at the right time, undermine White's centre. Many a time at amateur level, White's pieces are reduced to the first three ranks trying to cope with Black's threats. At club level it is far easier to attack than to defend and thus easier for White to make mistakes early on in the Benko Gambit.

3) When I started playing correspondence chess in the late 90s, I wanted to look for a black opening which computer engines did not assess well. The Benko Gambit was the perfect weapon for me as the engines frequently assessed that White was winning or clearly better in Benko middlegames and endgames which are tenable or even good for Black. These days, the engines view positional factors such as space and initiative more favourably than in the past and are better at assessing compensation for material. GM Larry Kaufman, the co-developer of the powerful *Komodo* chess engine, concurred, stating: "I would even say 'much better' rather than just 'better'. This was not gradual, it pretty much happened with *Rybka 2.3* and *Rybka 3*, and all later programs are similar in this respect."

My Benko passed muster in correspondence play. One of my first high-level CC games was against the Russian Correspondence Chess Champion Sergey Romanov and I fought him to a draw. In 12 Benko Gambit games I was unbeaten and the only one time I played against it with white at correspondence, I got beaten like a drum. The point I want to make is that it is still playable even at master level correspondence chess, even if opponents have months to analyse with so many resources at hand.

4) The Benko has been played by many of the world's leading players such as Garry Kasparov, Magnus Carlsen, Viswanathan Anand, Veselin Topalov, Vassily Ivanchuk and Fabiano Caruana to name just a few. Two particular incidents stand out for me with respect to the Benko Gambit:

i. In the final round of the 1986 Dubai Olympiad, the Soviets needed to blank Poland 4-0 to overcome Hungary's lead and so claim the gold medals. It was at this juncture that Garry Kasparov resorted to the Benko Gambit and won a tense game against Wlodzimierz Schmidt to help secure the top spot for USSR.

ii. Viswanathan Anand shockingly lost the first game of the 2001 FIDE Knockout World Cup to an internet qualifier, the French IM Olivier Touzanne. In a must-win second game, he essayed the Benko Gambit to win in 23 moves and even the score (eventually winning the match on tiebreak).

5) See for yourself the fundamental concepts of the Benko Gambit as applied convincingly by the man himself, Grandmaster Pal Benko, during his heyday.

Firstly, a forceful demonstration of queenside pressure.

A.Segal-P.Benko
Sao Paulo 1973

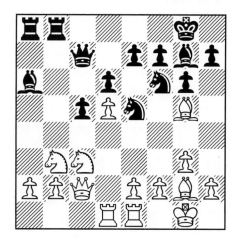

A typical set-up for Black, placing the king's rook on b8 to exert pressure down the b-file.

17 ♗c1 ♘fd7

Getting ready to unleash the dark-squared bishop's power over White's queenside.

18 h3 ♘c4

Pressing the b2 soft spot. Sometimes Black also has ...♘a3 tricks after going ...♘c4.

19 ♔h2 ♕b6

Exerting even more pressure on the b-file.

20 ♘e4 ♕b4

Preparing ...♕a4 to weaken White on the a-file as well.

21 ♘ed2 ♕a4 22 ♘xc4 ♗xc4 23 ♗g5

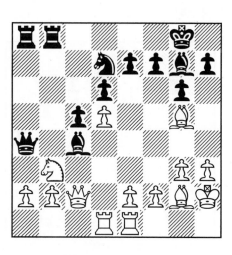

23...♖xb3!

A combination to win back the gambited pawn as well as exchange a couple of pieces.

24 axb3 ♗xb3 25 ♕d2 ♗xd1 26 ♖xd1 ♘f6

After winning the pawn back, Black usually retains his positional advantage and this is a good example.

27 ♗f4? ♖b8

Hitting the weakness.

28 ♖b1 h5 29 ♗g5 ♗xg5 30 ♕xg5 ♘f6 31 ♕e3 ♖b7

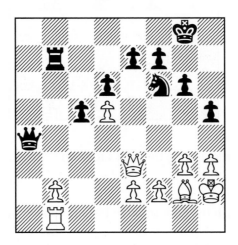

The e7-pawn is usually easier to defend than White's isolani on b2.

32 ♖c1

White gives up the b2-pawn which would have fallen sooner or later, since Black has ...c5-c4-c3 looming. Indeed, after 32 ♕c3 ♕a2 33 ♕c1 ♖b8 Black can start rolling the c-pawn down the board.

32...♕b3 33 ♖c3 ♕xb2 34 ♖a3 ♔g7

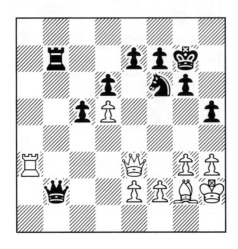

White has zero counterplay and resigned in 14 more moves.

Next, a demonstration of how Benko undermined White's centre and then took over that sector with some powerful piece play.

R.Gross-P.Benko
Aspen Open 1968

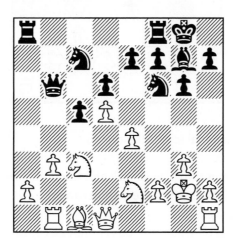

14...e6!

Black decided to undermine the white centre with the idea of eradicating it thanks to pressure from the h1-a8 diagonal.

15 dxe6 fxe6 16 ♗e3 ♛c6!

Exerting more pressure on the centre, with the aim of advancing the d-pawn to stress it yet further.

17 ♛d2?

In Benko's own *The Benko Gambit*, he wrote that "White underestimated the danger from Black's advancing mobile centre."

17...d5!

Black already has a huge advantage here, whether White gives up or tries to hold the centre.

18 exd5 exd5 19 ♗f4 d4!

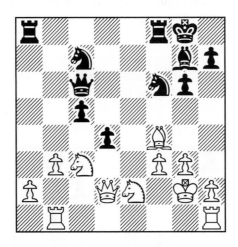

Opening up the long diagonal for Black's queen.

20 ♘a4 ♘fd5

Now the king's rook comes into play as well and the centralized knights do their part to wreck White's kingside structure, since the bishop cannot move away.

21 ♖hf1 ♘e6 22 ♖f2 d3 23 ♘g1

23 ♕xd3 is met by 23...♖xf4! when the rook cannot be captured because of the potential queen fork.

23...♘exf4+ 24 gxf4 ♘xf4+ 25 ♔h1 ♗d4 26 ♖ff1 ♘e2 0-1

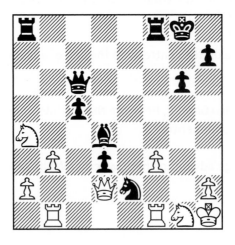

White resigned due to the insurmountable threats.

On this note, we start the book proper. I do hope you will enjoy the examples and commentary from this, my very first chess book, as I have attempted to include, to the best of my knowledge, examples which are currently theoretically relevant, as well as some of my own games, in particular my correspondence games which always require months of analysis.

Acknowledgements

I would especially like to thank the following for their help in making this work possible:

IMs Goh Wei Ming, Lim Yee Weng and Miodrag Perunovic for their help in assessing positions and providing key advice.

IM Erik Kislik for generously sharing his superb Benko Gambit theory and taking the time to analyse some key positions.

CM Olimpiu Urcan for his persistent reminders that I needed to graduate from writing articles to authoring a book, as well as for ideas on writing this book.

GM John Emms, a very patient chief editor who has to deal with my constant edits and updates.

Assistant Editor, IM Richard Palliser for his meticulous proofreading and editing (even working at the book on Christmas Day!).

Most of all, I want to thank my wife, WFM Yip Fong Ling, for her constant encouragement, full support and valuable 'time-off' to write my first chess book, a cherished ambition of mine.

Junior Tay,
February 2014,
Balestier, Singapore

Chapter One
The King Takes a Stroll

1 d4 ♘f6 2 c4 c5 3 d5 b5 4 cxb5 a6 5 bxa6 g6 6 ♘c3 ♗xa6 7 e4 ♗xf1 8 ♔xf1

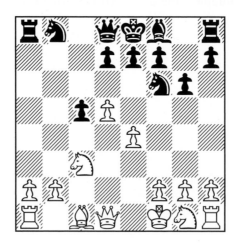

In the chapter, we'll examine the most topical line in the Benko Gambit Accepted where White accepts the gambit pawn and castles artificially. This is the most natural line where White digests the gambit pawn and plays to shore up his queenside while consolidating his extra pawn. In 2012, the reputation of the Benko Gambit took a beating when Benko Gambit expert Viorel Bologan sustained losses against both the world no.1 Magnus Carlsen and the American no.1 Hikaru Nakamura in this variation at Biel. In both cases, White kept his pawn advantage and nursed it all the way into the endgame. Hence, this line is extremely important from a theoretical viewpoint.

The First Few Moves
Let's go through the first few moves of this variation.

1 d4 ♘f6 2 c4 c5 3 d5 b5

This constitutes the Benko Gambit. Black opens up the b-file for his rook and tries to prise the c4-pawn away from its defence of the d5-pawn.

4 cxb5

White accepts the gambit pawn.

4...a6

Black offers to exchange White's extra pawn to open up the a-file as well and to develop his queen bishop swiftly.

5 bxa6

In for a penny, in for a pound. White accepts the challenge and goes one clean pawn up.

5...g6

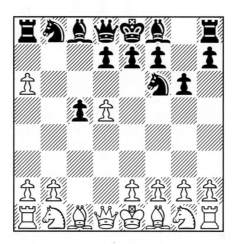

Question: Why not recapture the pawn immediately with 5...♗xa6?

Answer: This requires a brief explanation. Against 5...♗xa6, White has done well tradition-ally with 6 g3 d6 7 ♗g2 g6 8 b3! ♗g7 9 ♗b2 when Black's dark-squared bishop is well con-tested by the bishop on b2 (in my database involving players rated 2200 and above, White has scored a very respectable 64% in this line), and the white queenside pawn structure has been bolstered to boot. In Chapter 2: Flummoxing the Fianchetto Variation, you will see the great lengths White takes there to establish his bishop on b2 in order to shore up the queenside.

Question: So why does 5...g6 make a difference?

Answer: After 5...g6, if White plays 6 b3, Black can improvise with 6...♘xa6! when the knight can stir up trouble with an eventual ...♘b4 hitting a2 and d5.

6 ♘c3

White develops the knight on its natural square and shores up b2 as well. White also lends support to the d5-pawn as well as the e2-e4 central push.

6...♗xa6

Black takes over the a6-f1 diagonal immediately and also helps clear the back rank to allow the king's rook to move to the b-file faster. Remember, Black has gambited a pawn and therefore has to play for swift development before White can consolidate his queenside and realize his extra pawn.

7 e4

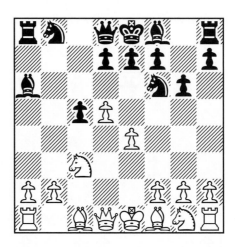

> *Question:* Is this good? Doesn't White lose the right to castle and
> have to waste one more move getting the king to the g-file?

Answer: White indeed has to 'lose' a move by having the king move again to g1 or g2 (after g2-g3). However, there are several factors that are favourable for him:

1) If Black exchanges the bishop on a6 for the one on f1, his light-squared bishop has been exchanged for a piece which didn't have to make a move.

2) White has put his central pawns on light squares, which, in a sense, gives his light-squared bishop less scope. Hence, the exchange makes sense.

3) In some variations, White might even leave the rook on h1 to play for a kingside attack with h2-h4-h5.

7...♗xf1

Denying White castling rights while giving the black knight and perhaps later the queen or a rook the a6-square to operate from.

8 ♔xf1 d6

Putting a stop to e4-e5, which would give White very strong central presence.

We've arrived at our first divide and must consider a number of ideas for both sides.

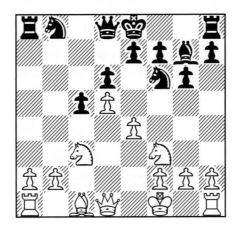

A) 12 ♕e2 and a2-a4

After the standard moves **9 g3 ♗g7 10 ♔g2 0-0 11 ♘f3 ♘bd7**, currently the vogue continuation in the Benko Gambit is 12 a4 or 12 ♕e2 followed by 13 a4 with the omission of both the once standard h2-h3 (to deny Black's knight's access to g4) and ♖fe1 (this rook will instead head for the queenside). This can be attributed to its successful use by the new world champion Magnus Carlsen and the mercurial American GM Hikaru Nakamura. In Haugen-Gonzalez, we examine how Black can try to neutralize the a4/♖a3/♘b5 bind.

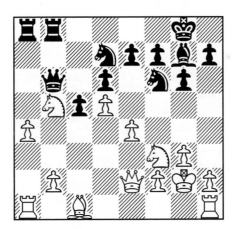

As previously mentioned, White used to play h2-h3 to snuff out ...♘g4-e5. Nowadays, White often forgoes this as ...♘g4-e5 tends to lose a move once White sidesteps with ♘f3-d2 and plays to kick the knight from e5. Black must be careful as Jovanovic-Stojanovski will demonstrate how the tempo loss can prove fatal for Black if he reacts even a little inaccurately.

With Black suffering in 'draw or lose' mode, in recent months we have seen him attempt to take the bull by the horns and hit White quickly with an early ...e7-e6 in the spirit of the Blumenfeld Gambit, blowing up the centre before White can consolidate his queenside completely. Jayakumar-Leon Hoyos and Zilka-Guidarelli are two such examples, but White is still in the driver's seat from a theoretical perspective, provided he does not let Black's central pawn mass run riot. Note that in Game 3, I've also included a brief coverage of early ...♕a5 lines – a Magnus Carlsen brevity with 6...♗g7 and 8...♕a5 as well as some analysis to GM Aveshkulov's novel 7....♕a5 concept (which contain ideas similar to the 11...♘a6 line advocated in Game 5), which he designed to stymie the ♕e2/a2-a4 plan.

Game 1
A.Haugen-B.Gonzalez
Correspondence 2010

---

1 d4 ♘f6 2 c4 c5 3 d5 b5 4 cxb5 a6 5 bxa6 g6 6 ♘c3 ♗xa6 7 e4 ♗xf1 8 ♔xf1 d6 9 g3

Preparing to move the king to the safer g-file.

9...♗g7 10 ♔g2 0-0

The black king also makes its exit from the centre and the f8-rook is activated.

11 ♘f3

The natural square for the knight, which can aid the e4-e5 push or sometimes make its way to the juicy c4-square via d2.

11...♘bd7

Clearing the back rank for the rooks while preventing the e4-e5 advance. This knight sometimes can make its way to b6 to put pressure on d5 and c4 or aid in the exchange of a pair of knights after a future ...♘g4-e5.

12 a4!

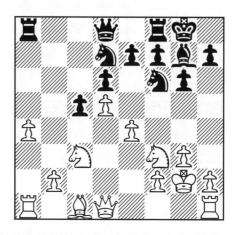

Question: Isn't this foolhardy? Black is setting up his forces to aim at the white queenside, so why is White pushing a pawn in a sector where he's supposed to be weaker?

Answer: In the past, White used to concentrate on defending the queenside, with moves such as ♖e1-e2-c2, and trying to effect an e4-e5 break. However, in the past two to three years, Chinese Grandmasters have discovered that by setting up with a4, ♖a3, b2-b3 and ♘b5 as quickly as possible, White can put a stop to Black's queenside intentions. He can then concentrate on his space advantage in the centre or on creating an outside passed a-pawn (after advancing b2-b4 and exchanging the pawn for Black's c5-pawn).

12...♕b6

Clearing the back rank for the rooks and putting pressure on the b-file. The queen usually finds its way to b7 to put pressure on the h1-a8 diagonal coupled with ...e7-e6 or sometimes ...f7-f5. Other times, it moves to a6 to take over or at least contest the f1-a6 diagonal.

> **Question:** What about 12...♖a6 with the idea of ...♕a8 and
> ...♖fb8, putting massive pressure on the white queenside?

Answer: I'm not inclined to recommend this variation as White gets to consolidate the queenside very swiftly: for example, 13 ♕c2 ♕a8 14 ♖a3 ♕b7 (after 14...e6?! 15 dxe6 fxe6 16 ♖e1 ♘g4 17 ♘b5 ♕b7 18 ♗f4 d5 19 exd5 exd5 20 ♗d6 Black is in serious trouble, R.Leitao-M.Leon Hoyos, Istanbul Olympiad 2012, while 14...♖b8 runs into 15 ♘b5 when Black must cover c7: 15...♘e8 16 ♗d2 ♘b6 17 ♖ha1 and White retains a slight pull) 15 ♘b5 ♖fa8 16 ♗d2 and White has a nice queenside bind.

13 ♕e2

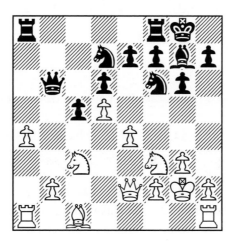

This move:
1) Releases the need for the knight on c3 to hold the e-pawn and so sets up ♘c3-b5.
2) Overprotects the b2-pawn and so frees up the dark-squared bishop.
C3 Prepares a future e4-e5 break.

In my online blitz games against master level players, I noticed a recent trend towards 13 ♕c2. A good counter is 13...♕b4! 14 ♗d2 ♖fb8 15 ♖hb1 (or 15 ♖ab1 ♕b3 16 ♖hc1 ♕xc2

17 ♖xc2 ♖b4 18 ♖e1 ♘e8 19 e5?! ♘xe5 20 ♘xe5 ♗xe5 21 f4 ♗f6 22 ♘e4 ♖bxa4 23 ♘xf6+ ♘xf6 24 ♖xe7 ♘xd5 25 ♖d7 ♖4a6 with winning chances for Black, P.Issakson-Bj.Thorfinnsson, Revkjavik 2013) 15...♕b3 16 ♕xb3 ♖xb3 17 a5 ♘e8 18 ♗e1 ♖ab8 19 ♘a4 ♘c7 and Black was holding up well in J.Sarkar-M.Turov, New Delhi 2010.

13...♖fb8

Intensifying the pressure on the b-file. Black has more or less achieved his ideal opening set-up.

14 ♘b5

This knight foray shields the b2-pawn from the queen and rook battery. Later Hikaru Nakamura came up with a nice way to connect his rooks with a pseudo pawn return in the shape of 14 ♗d2!.

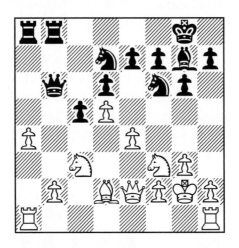

> **Question:** Can Black take the pawn on b2 or is it poisoned?

Answer: The pawn is toxic. After 14...♕xb2?? 15 ♖hb1 ♕c2 16 ♘e1 the Black queen goes back into the box.

After 14...♘e8 15 ♖hb1 ♘c7 16 ♘d1 ♕a6 17 ♕xa6 ♖xa6 18 a5 f5! 19 exf5 ♘xd5?! (Black does better with 19...gxf5! 20 ♘h4 ♖f8 21 ♘e3 f4 22 gxf4 ♘f6 23 ♘ef5 ♘fxd5 when he has good chances to hold) 20 fxg6 hxg6 21 ♖a4 Nakamura managed to realize his extra pawn in a protracted endgame, H.Nakamura-V.Bologan, Biel 2012.

14...♘e8

Black frees up the long diagonal for the dark-squared bishop and also prepares to contest the strong knight on b5 by exchanging it via ...♘c7.

15 ♗g5

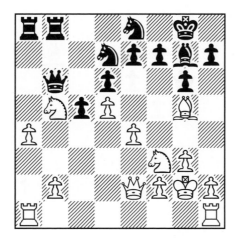

Taking advantage of the loose e7-pawn to gain a move.

15...♖b7!

Answer: Black intends to sacrifice the e-pawn to intensify the pressure on the queenside. Moreover, after capturing on e7 the bishop will find itself having difficulty escaping once Black plays ...h7-h6, cutting off the g5-square and ♗h4 will run into ...g6-g5, trapping the bishop again.

Answer: Yes, it's a possible transposition.

15...♕d8 was what the Moldovan Grandmaster Viorel Bologan played against Magnus Carlsen. However, moving the queen back to the defence of the pawn allowed the Norwegian genius to consolidate his queenside. Moreover, the queenside is the area of focus for Black and to remove an attacker from there diminishes the pressure on the white queenside pawns. Following 16 ♖a3 ♘b6 17 b3 ♕d7 18 ♖a2 White had just the sort of slight but durable edge which is deadly in the hands of the world no.1, M.Carlsen-V.Bologan, Biel 2012. White's queenside pawns are secure and he can now concentrate on action in the centre or kingside. Later, Bologan took excessive risks and lost.

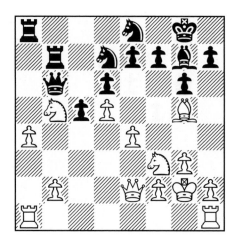

16 ♗xe7

> **Question:** Since the bishop is likely to get trapped after 16 ♗xe7, can't
> White just ignore the pawn and carry on with his ♖a3 and b2-b3 plan?

Answer: Yes, he could. In fact this occurred in another correspondence game: 16 ♖a3 h6 17
♗e3 ♘c7 18 ♘xc7 ♕xc7 19 b3 ♘f6 20 ♘d2 ♖b4 21 ♕d3 ♘g4 22 ♘c4 ♘xe3+ 23 ♕xe3 ♗d4
24 ♕d3 ♕b7 25 a5 ♖a6 26 ♖b1 ♕b5!, A.Lobanov-K.Gierth, correspondence 2011. White's
pieces are tied to defending his a- and b-pawns which have been firmly blockaded and it is
difficult for him to start active operations in the centre or on the queenside.

16...h6

As previously mentioned, cutting off the escape route for the e7-bishop.

17 ♖a3

Aside from getting the rook out of the way of the g7-bishop, White also prepares for the
possible sacrifice of the dark-squared bishop if it gets trapped on h4. The rook on a3 can
aid in a potential kingside attack.

In a recent game, White attempted to sacrifice the bishop a different way, but the activity of Black's pieces in the centre more than called the sacrifice into question: 17 ♘d2 ♕a6
18 ♘c4?! (the superior 18 ♖he1! ♘b6 19 ♗xd6 ♘xa4 20 b3 ♗xa1 21 ♖xa1 ♕xb5 22 ♕xb5
♖xb5 23 ♖xa4 ♖xa4 24 bxa4 ♖a5 25 ♗e7 ♖xa4 26 ♗xc5 ♘f6 results in equality; also possible here is 18...♘b8 19 ♗h4 g5 20 ♗xg5 hxg5 21 ♘f3 ♘d7 22 ♘xg5 with a murky position
where I'm going with 'unclear') 18...♘b6 19 ♗xd6 ♘xc4 20 ♕xc4 ♘xd6 21 ♕xc5 ♘xe4 22
♕b4 ♘f6 23 ♖hd1 ♖d7 24 ♘c3 ♖ad8 25 ♖ac1 ♕a8! and White's three pawns (soon to be
two) were no match for Black's activity in A.Diermair-D.Milanovic, Bad Gleichenberg 2013.

The critical continuation is 17 g4!.

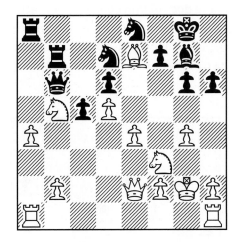

Here the American IM Erik Kislik has analysed 17...f6 18 ♖a3! (total mayhem will occur after 18 ♘h4 ♔f7 19 ♖a3 ♔xe7 20 ♘xg6+ ♔f7 21 ♘h4 ♘e5 22 ♘f5 ♗f8 23 h4! ♘c7 24 ♘xc7 ♕xc7 25 g5! ♔e8 26 ♖g3! ♖ab8 27 gxh6 ♕h7 28 ♖b1 ♔d8 and White has the better chances in this complex position) 18...♖b8 19 ♘h4 ♔f7 20 e5! fxe5 21 ♕d3 ♔xe7 22 ♕xg6 ♔d8 23 ♘f5 ♗f8 24 h4 ♖xa4 (after 24...♕a5 25 ♘fxd6 ♗xd6 26 ♘xd6 ♘xd6 27 ♕xd6+ ♖d7 28 ♕xh6 White's passed pawns are stronger than Black's sorry-looking knight, V.Lifanov-V.Tunyik, correspondence 2011) 25 ♖xa4 ♕xb5 26 ♖ha1 ♕xb2 27 h5! with a strong attack for White.

Returning to 17 ♖a3:

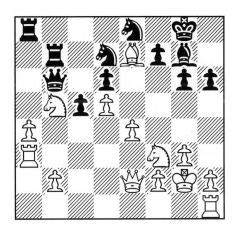

17...♘e5!?

A brave idea to exchange off the knight on f3 so White no longer can sacrifice it on g5 after the bishop retreats to h4.

> **Question:** Why not 17...♘b8, trapping the bishop?

Answer: It is possible, but White does obtain good compensation for the piece after 18 ♗h4 g5 19 ♗xg5 hxg5 20 ♘xg5. White has four pawns for the piece and chances for a kingside pawn storm attack. However, Black does have a superb bishop on g7 and his knight can return to aid the defence via d7 and f6. Chances seem about equal in this variation.

18 ♘xe5 ♗xe5 19 ♗h4

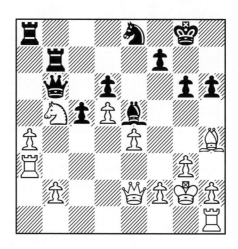

19...♘c7!

Immediately putting pressure on the pride of White's queenside blockade, the knight on b5.

> ***Question:*** Why not 19...g5, trapping the bishop?

Answer: 19...g5? is countered by the powerful 20 f4! ♗f6 21 fxg5 hxg5 22 ♗xg5! ♗xg5 23 ♕g4. White regains the piece with three extra pawns and the black king is extremely exposed.

20 f4

Preventing ...g6-g5 once and for all.

20...♗g7 21 ♖ha1

Lending support to the a3-rook. It is often a good idea to double the rooks behind a passed pawn.

21...♖e8!

Black is two pawns down, but has fantastic compensation. This is in essence a Modern Benoni where Black has very well-placed pieces. The h4-bishop doesn't have much scope and it is difficult for White to guard so much territory with Black keeping the tension in the centre and on the queenside. Black also sets up the possibility of ...♘xd5, with the e-pawn pinned from recapturing.

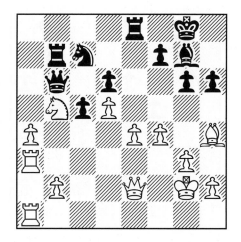

22 ♖b3!

Tempting Black to capture on d5 as well as preparing ♘d4 (with a discovered attack on the black queen), heading to the juicy c6-square.

22...♕a6!

Moving the queen away from the rook and instead of taking advantage of d5 being pinned, Black prevents the knight from moving.

After 22...♘xd5 23 ♖d3! ♗d4 24 ♖e1 ♘b4 25 ♖d2 Black has to exchange off his beloved dark-squared bishop or his d6-pawn will be too exposed.

23 ♕c4

Avoiding any ...♘xd5 tricks. Now, though, Black utilizes the pin on the queen to regain one of his sacrificed pawns.

After 23 ♖aa3 Black can sacrifice the exchange with 23...♘xd5! 24 ♖d3 ♖xb5! 25 axb5 ♕xb5 26 ♖d2 c4 27 ♖c2 ♘b6, obtaining very good compensation.

23...♘xb5 24 ♖xb5 ♖eb8

The b2-pawn comes under severe pressure.

Not 24...♗xb2? 25 ♖a2 ♗g7 26 ♖xc5! when White is winning, but 24...♖xb5 was possible, and if 25 ♕xb5 ♕xb5 26 axb5 ♖xe4 27 ♖a6 ♖b4 28 ♖xd6 ♖xb5 with good drawing chances for Black.

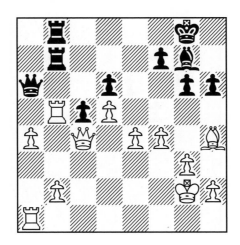

25 ♖a3

Question: Can't White simply defend the b2-pawn with 25 ♖a2 and play b2-b3 to finally remove the pawn from the g7-bishop's glare?

Answer: 25 ♖a2 is met by 25...♖a8! when the pins on a4 and b5 force White to return the pawn after 26 ♖a3 ♗xb2 27 ♖ab3 ♗d4.

25...♗xb2 26 ♖ab3

Now after 26 ♖a2! ♗g7 27 ♕e2 ♖e8 Black has enough pressure to reach an equal position: 28 ♖xb7 (after 28 ♖c2 ♖xb5 29 ♕xb5 ♕xb5 30 axb5 ♖xe4 31 b6 ♖b4 32 ♗d8 c4 33 ♗c7 c3 34 ♔f3 f5 it is likely that the b6-pawn will be traded for the one on c3, leading to an eventual draw) 28...♕xb7 29 ♕b5 ♕xb5 30 axb5 ♖xe4 31 ♖a6 ♖b4 32 ♖xd6 ♖xb5 33 ♖c6 c4 34 d6 ♖d5 35 ♗e7 ♖d2+ 36 ♔f3 f5 37 ♖xc4 ♗d4 38 g4 ♔f7 39 gxf5 gxf5 40 h4 ♔e6 41 h5 ♗b6 42 ♗f8 ♖d3+ 43 ♔e2 ♖h3 44 ♖c6 ♗d4 45 d7+ ♔xd7 46 ♖xh6 ♔e8 47 ♗d6 ♔f7 48 ♖h7+ ♔g8 49 ♖b7 ♖xh5 and a draw beckons.

26...♗d4

White cannot do much with his extra pawn due to the impasse on the queenside.

27 g4

Freeing the bishop. After the tricky 27 e5 dxe5 28 ♗f6 ♖xb5 29 ♗xe5 Black gets out of trouble with 29...♕a5! 30 ♖xb5 ♕d2+ 31 ♔h3 ♖e8! 32 ♖xc5! ♗xc5 33 ♕xc5 ♕d1 34 ♕c6! and here he should settle for a perpetual check with 34...♕h5+ 35 ♔g2 ♕e2+ 36 ♔g1 (after 36 ♔h3?? ♖xe5!! 37 fxe5 ♕f1+ 38 ♔h4 ♕f5 and White cannot stop mate) 36...♕e1+.

27...♖e8!

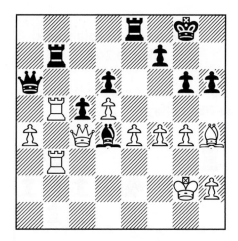

Now Black switches target and asks White's doubled rooks what they are doing on the b-file.

28 ♕c2 ♖c7!

With the idea of pushing his own passed pawn.

29 ♖b1

After 29 a5 c4 30 ♖3b4 c3 Black is not worse despite the pawn deficit.

29...♕a8!

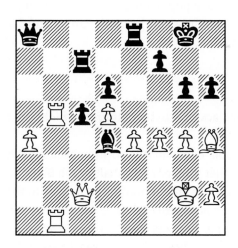

Introducing the possibility of ...♖a7 and ...f7-f5.

30 f5 gxf5 31 gxf5 ♖a7 ½-½

White has no good way of taking advantage of the exposed black king: for example, after 32 ♔h1 ♖xa4 33 f6 ♔h7! 34 e5+ ♔h8 35 exd6 ♕xd5+ 36 ♕g2 ♕xg2+ 37 ♔xg2 ♔h7 38 ♖b7 ♔g6 39 d7 ♖d8 Black is at least equal.

Game 2
B.Jovanovic-S.Stojanovski
Skopje 2013

1 d4 ♘f6 2 c4 c5 3 d5 b5 4 cxb5 a6 5 bxa6 ♗xa6 6 ♘c3 d6 7 e4 ♗xf1 8 ♔xf1 g6 9 ♘f3 ♘bd7 10 g3 ♗g7 11 ♔g2 0-0 12 a4 ♕b6 13 ♖a3!?

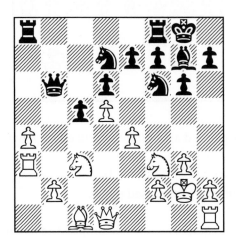

This rook lift is becoming one popular idea these days. In my Internet blitz games this year with IMs and GMs on playchess.com, I mostly ran into 13 ♖a3 (or 13 ♕c2 and 14 ♖a3) after either 12...♕b6 or 12...♖a6.

13...♖fb8

> *Question:* Can Black play to try planting a knight on d3 with 13...c4?

Answer: It is extremely double-edged in this position because White obtains a very swift central breakthrough. Another problem is that although Black has seized the d3-square, he loses control over d4 and a white knight might find its way to the c6 outpost. GM Suat Atalik analysed the following powerful exchange sacrifice for White: 14 ♕e2 ♖fc8 15 ♖d1 ♘c5 (or 15...♘g4 16 ♘b5 ♘ge5 17 ♘xe5 ♘xe5 18 ♗e3 ♕b7 19 ♗d4 with a nice advantage) 16 e5 ♘e8 17 ♕xc4 dxe5 18 ♕e2 ♘d6 19 ♘xe5 ♗xe5 20 ♕xe5 ♘c4 21 ♕xe7 ♘xa3 22 bxa3 ♕b3 23 ♗e3! ♕xc3 24 ♗d4 ♕b3 25 ♕e5 f6 26 ♕xf6 ♕xd5+ 27 f3 ♘e6 28 ♕h8+ ♔f7 29 ♕xh7+ ♔e8 30 ♕xg6+ ♔d7 31 ♕h7+ ♔e8 32 ♗f6 with a crushing game for White.
14 ♕c2

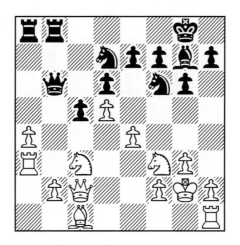

14...♘g4?

Question: Isn't it good to take advantage of the omission of h2-h3 to plonk one knight on e5 with an eye on d3 and c4?

Answer: Not when White can push back the knight on e5 with tempi: 14...♘e8 15 h4! (there is also a trend towards this h-pawn push in recent years, the point being to weaken the black kingside before committing the white king's rook to the centre or queenside) 15...h5 16 ♘b5 ♘c7 17 ♘xc7 ♕xc7 18 b3! (White has almost totally consolidated and Black must play extremely actively to prevent a total bind; 18 ♖e3 c4 was his idea) 18...c4! (now or never; in S.Atalik-S.Kasparov, Serbian Team Championship 2012, White managed to slowly but surely gain the advantage after 18...♖b7 19 ♗d2 ♕b8 20 ♖b1 ♖aa7 21 a5 ♖c7 22 ♖a4 ♕c8 23 ♖c4 ♘b8 24 b4!, with a great game for White, although Sergey Kasparov put up so much resistance that the game was eventually drawn) 19 ♕xc4 (19 ♗e3!? c3 20 ♘d4 ♕c5 21 ♘b5 ♕b4 22 ♖aa1 ♘c5 23 ♗xc5 dxc5! was pointed out by Atalik, while after 19 bxc4?! ♖b4! Black takes over the initiative) 19...♕xc4 20 bxc4 ♘b6 21 ♗g5 ♘xc4 22 ♖a2 ♖b2 23 ♖xb2 ♗xb2 24 ♗xe7 f6 25 ♖b1 ♖xa4 26 ♗xd6 ♘xd6 27 ♖xb2 ♘xe4 28 ♘g1 g5! 29 hxg5 fxg5 30 ♘h3 g4 31 ♘f4 ♖d4 32 ♘xh5 ♖xd5 33 ♘f4 ♖d2 and White cannot make headway.
15 ♘b5 ♘ge5 16 ♘d2!

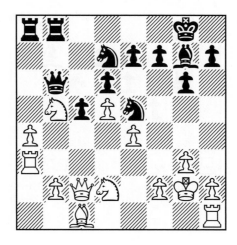

Rendering the ...♘g4-e5 idea superfluous. The black knights are stepping on each other's toes and this gives White the chance to build a strong centre and secure his queenside firmly.

16...♛b7

Hoping to chip away later at the white centre.

17 f4 ♘g4 18 h3 ♘gf6 19 ♘c4 ♘b6 20 b3

White has achieved his ideal queenside structure. Black has no real counterplay and soon succumbed.

20...♘fd7 21 ♗d2 ♘xc4?

Very bad. This allows the a- rook to be activated along the rank and also further strengthens the white centre. I suspect that by now Black was too demoralized to put up any fight.

22 bxc4 ♘b6 23 ♖b1 ♖a6 24 a5 ♘d7 25 ♖ab3

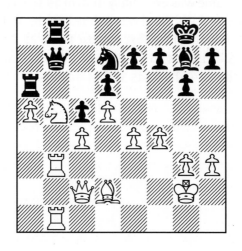

The rest is just a mopping up exercise for White.

25...♕c8 26 ♘a3 ♖ba8 27 ♖b7 ♖6a7 28 ♕b3 h5 29 ♕b5 ♔h7 30 ♘c2 ♗f6 31 ♘e1 h4 32 g4 ♗g7 33 ♘f3 ♘f6 34 ♘g5+ 1-0

<table><tr><td>Game 3</td></tr><tr><td>A.Jayakumar-M.Leon Hoyos</td></tr><tr><td>Las Vegas 2013</td></tr></table>

1 d4 ♘f6 2 c4 c5 3 d5 b5 4 cxb5 a6 5 bxa6 g6 6 ♘c3 ♗xa6

The World Champion Magnus Carlsen mixed around the move order against Boris Gelfand with 6...♗g7 7 e4 0-0 8 ♘f3 ♕a5 9 ♗d3?! (9 ♗d2 is more circumspect) 9...♘xd5! 10 exd5 ♗xc3 11 bxc3? ♕xc3+ and won easily in 23 moves; B.Gelfand-M.Carlsen, Zurich (rapid) 2014.

7 e4 ♗xf1

GM Aveshkulov, in his 2013 Kindle edition of *Attack with Black*, analysed 7...♕a5 instead as a viable alternative to avoid the 12 a4 system. This variation is still in its infancy but a couple of lines caught my eye:

a) White can try for an ultra-sharp exchange sacrifice after 8 ♗xa6 ♘xa6 9 e5 ♘e4 10 ♘ge2 ♗g7 11 0-0 ♘xc3 12 ♘xc3 ♗xe5 13 ♖e1 d6 14 ♖xe5!? (Aveshkulov analysed 14 ♗h6 ♘c7 15 ♖xe5 dxe5 16 ♕f3 and concluded Black has "adequate defensive resources") 14...dxe5 15 ♗h6 with strong attacking chances for the exchange. I prefer White here though *Houdini*'s take was that 'White is very slightly better' after cranking in deep analysis mode for a few hours.

b) White can try to reach a standard a2-a4 line with 8 ♗d2 ♗xf1 9 ♔xf1 d6 10 g3 ♗g7 11 ♔g2 0-0 12 ♘f3 ♘a6! (An analogous concept to Tin Jingyao's plan in Game 5) 13 a4 ♕b6 14 ♕e2 ♘c7 (covering b5) 15 ♖ab1! with a slight edge for White. White plans b2-b3 while Black can play for a ...♕a6 trade or an ...e7-e6 break.

8 ♔xf1 d6 9 ♘f3 ♘bd7 10 g3 ♗g7 11 ♔g2 0-0 12 a4 ♕b6 13 ♕e2 e6?!

Erik Kislik, who watched this game live at the venue, remarked that "this was a one-off gamble by Leon Hoyos". Usually, in the cut-throat American Opens, the pros have to score heavily in the early rounds to be in contention for the big money prizes, which explains the risk that the Mexican GM is taking. The advantage for him is that his opponent is now out of his theoretical preparation and has to make committal decisions at an early stage of the game. The ...e7-e6 break aims to whittle away at White's centre and if White exchanges the pawns, Black obtains an f-file to play down.

Instead, 13...♕b7 transposes to Zilkas-Guidarelli – see the next game.

14 dxe6

White chooses to give up part of his central space to play against the black centre. Safest is for White to just keep the position closed and slowly nurse his extra pawn advantage: 14 ♖d1 exd5 15 exd5 ♖fe8 16 ♕c4! and White is simply going to play ♖b1, b2-b3 and ♘b5 to solidify the queenside.

14...fxe6 15 ♖d1 d5 16 exd5 exd5

Black has obtained a centre pawn structure more commonly associated with the Blumenfeld Gambit.

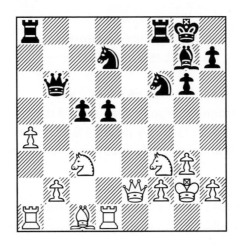

17 ♗f4?!

Hoyos's dare works as White blinks first. The Mexican's mobile centre coupled with threats on the long diagonal now begins to take shape. The way to refute Black's overly ambitious set-up is 17 a5! ♕c6 18 ♕b5 ♘b8 (if 18...♕e6 19 a6 with good winning chances and 18...♕xb5 19 ♘xb5 would make it even harder for Black to block White's a-pawn from promotion) 19 ♕b3! c4 20 ♕b4 ♘a6 (or 20...♘bd7 21 ♗f4) 21 ♕b6 ♕d7 22 ♗f4 and White is calling the shots.

17...d4

Black increases his central spatial advantage and gradually takes over the long light-square diagonal.

18 ♘b5?!

Better is 18 ♕c4+!? ♔h8 19 ♘b5 ♘h5 20 ♗d6 ♖xf3 21 ♕d5! (or 21 ♔xf3 ♕c6+ 22 ♔e2 ♖e8+ 23 ♔d2 ♕f3 24 ♔c2 ♘b6 25 ♕d3 ♕xf2+ 26 ♖d2 ♕f6 with counterplay) 21...♖af8 22 ♗xf8 ♖xf8 23 ♕xd7 ♘f6 24 ♕c7 ♕e6 25 ♘xd4 cxd4 26 ♖xd4 ♘d5 27 ♕c5 ♖f5 with chances for both sides.

18...♘d5

Centralizing the knight as well as applying more pressure down the f-file. White's bishop is hence evicted.

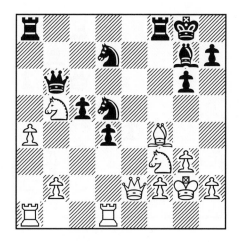

19 ♗g5

Trying to prevent the black queen from reaching f6 to prevent the accumulation of black heavy pieces on the f-file. Jayakumar had to fight hard to stay in the game:

a) After 19 ♗d6 ♖f6 20 ♖e1 ♕c6 (or 20...♖xd6 21 ♘xd6 ♕xd6 22 ♕e6+ ♕xe6 23 ♖xe6 and Black has the better endgame) 21 a5 ♗f8 22 ♕c4 ♔h8! 23 ♔g1 ♘5b6! 24 axb6 ♕xf3 25 ♗f4 ♖xa1 26 ♖xa1 g5 27 ♗xg5 ♕xf2+ 28 ♔h1 ♖xb6 29 ♖f1 ♕xb2 Black's winning chances are minimal due to the exposed nature of his king.

b) 19 ♕c4 is too late as 19...♕e6! threatens to win the queen with a discovered check after ...♘f4 or ...♘e3. Black switches his attention totally to the kingside where weaknesses abound and White is already defenceless against the mounting pressure.

19...♖ae8

Gaining a tempo on the queen and adding another piece to the eventual kingside assault.

20 ♕d3 ♕c6

Seizing the long diagonal as well as threatening ...♘e3+. Even stronger was 20...h6! clearing f6 for the queen. After this move, White is simply lost as his king cannot hope to survive the force of the heavy pieces: 21 ♗d2 ♕f6 22 ♖f1 c4! 23 ♕a3 ♖e2 with a winning attack for Black.

21 ♔g1 h6 22 ♗d2

Alternatively, 22 ♘fxd4 cxd4 23 ♘xd4 ♕a8 24 ♘b5 ♔h8 25 ♗c1 (if 25 ♕xd5 ♖e1+!) 25...♖f5 and Black is winning.

22...♕f6

Finally, the queen reaches the desired square and White is defenceless against the accumulation of force.

23 ♔g2 c4! 24 ♕a3

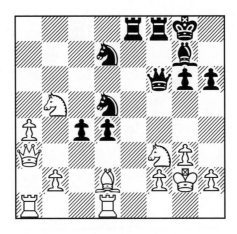

Exercise: How can Black terminate the contest quickly?

Answer: **24...♘e3+!!**

Cutting off the white queen from the defence of the kingside.

25 fxe3 ♕xf3+ 26 ♔g1 ♕f2+ 27 ♔h1 ♘e5 0-1

Game 4
S.Zilka-L.Guidarelli
Meissen 2013

1 d4 ♘f6 2 c4 c5 3 d5 b5 4 cxb5 a6 5 bxa6 ♗xa6 6 ♘c3 d6 7 e4 ♗xf1 8 ♔xf1 g6 9 ♘f3 ♗g7 10 g3 0-0 11 ♔g2 ♘bd7 12 a4 ♕b8!?

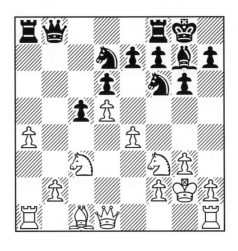

Question: What is the main difference between
this move and the more commonly played 12...♕b6?

Answer: In the 12...♕b6 line, Black has the option of shifting the queen to a6 and also protects the a5-square.

13 ♕e2 ♕b7

Black's plan is use the queen's placement to crack open the long light-square diagonal.

14 ♗d2 e6?!

Question: What is White's best move after 14...♖fb8 15 ♘b5 ♘e8?

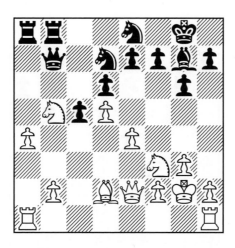

Answer: White should trade Black's strong bishop with 16 ♗c3!. This is one of the salient strategic aims of the a4, ♕e2 and ♘b5 set-up (the others being to solidify the centre with ♖a2 or ♖a3, b2-b3 and possibly ♘d2-c4).

15 dxe6

After 15 ♕b5 ♖fb8 16 dxe6 fxe6 17 ♖hd1 ♕a6 18 ♕xa6 ♖xa6 19 ♖a2 Black has decent pressure for his pawn minus.

15...fxe6 16 ♖he1?!

White decides on a policy of restraint. However, more drastic measures are required in order to stop Black's central pawn mass from expanding like an umbrella.

Erik Kislik suggested playing actively to prevent Black from allowing the centre pawns to march unimpeded and after his 16 ♘g5! Black seems to be worse. This is a good illustration of how accurately White must play, especially when Black has obtained a Blumenfeld-type of position, which allows him to play on the kingside (the half-open f-file), in the centre (the pawn mass) and on the queenside (the a- and b-files). Here Black might try:

a) 16...♖fe8 17 ♘b5 (after 17 ♖he1 h6 18 ♘f3 d5 19 h3 d4 20 ♘b5 ♕c6 21 b3 e5 Black has good play on the f-file) 17...♕c6 18 f3! ♘f8 19 ♖hd1 h6 20 ♘xd6! ♕xd6 21 e5 ♕c6 22 exf6 ♗xf6 23 ♘e4 and the position is structurally hopeless for Black.

b) 16...♖ae8 17 a5 d5 (not 17...♕xb2?? 18 ♖hb1 ♕c2 19 ♖a2 and the queen is trapped, while after 17...♕c6 18 a6 h6 19 ♘f3 ♖b8 20 ♗f4 ♖b6 21 a7 d5 22 ♗c7! ♖b4 23 ♗b8! ♕a8 24 ♗d6 ♖c8 25 e5 White is for choice) 18 a6 ♕c6 19 a7 c4 20 ♗e3 ♘e5 21 ♖a5! and Black's initiative has fizzled out.

16...d5 17 ♔g1?!

Better is 17 exd5 exd5 18 a5 ♖a6 19 ♕b5 ♕a8! (after 19...♖b8 20 ♕xb7 ♖xb7 21 ♖a2 White should have an edge) 20 ♖e7 d4 and all three results are possible: for example, 21 ♕d3! dxc3 22 ♗xc3 ♖f7 23 ♖ae1 ♖a7 24 ♖xf7 ♔xf7 25 ♕e2 ♔g8 26 ♕e6+ ♔h8 with dynamic equality. White is not worse because of his strong a-pawn and very well-placed pieces.

17...c4!

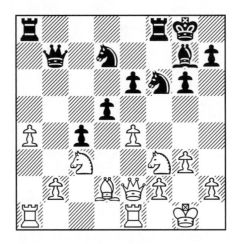

Giving Black's knight access to c5 where it hits three vital squares in b3, d3 and especially e4. Instead, 17...d4 18 ♘b5 ♘xe4 19 ♖a3! ♘df6 20 ♗f4 allows White to consolidate.

18 ♗f4

Trying to stop ...♘c5 as 19 ♗d6 forks both knight and rook, but that's not the end of the story. Instead, after 18 exd5 exd5 19 ♕e6+ ♔h8 20 ♗e3 ♖a6 21 ♕h3 h5! Black still has a strong initiative with ideas of ...♘g4 and ...♘e5, but not 21...♕xb2? 22 ♗d4!.

18...♘c5!!

An awesome exchange sacrifice, played in order to mobilize the central pawn mass and to remove a defender of the kingside.

19 ♗d6 ♘fxe4 20 ♘xe4 ♘xe4 21 ♗xf8 ♖xf8

Black is exchange down, but just look at the sheer difference in the quality of the pieces, not forgetting too Black's very strong pawn centre.

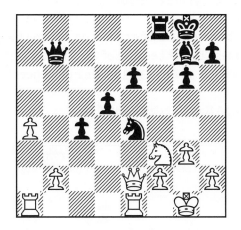

22 ♖eb1

White rationalizes that he should use this rook to protect b2 as the a1-rook can help with the a-pawn's advance. However, there is now the matter of the weak f2-square which Black can immediately take advantage of.

22...g5!

Aiming to boot the knight from f3.

23 h3

Amazingly, *Houdini* finds a way for White to escape from the onslaught by letting Black do exactly what he wants to: 23 a5! g4 24 ♘h4 ♖xf2 25 ♕xg4 ♕c6 (alternatively, 25...♔f7 26 a6 ♕a7 27 ♔h1 ♗f6 28 ♕h5+ ♔g7 29 ♕g4+ ♔f7 30 ♕h5+ with a draw, while trying to set up a discovered check with 25...♕a7 fails to 26 ♕xe6+ ♖f7+ 27 ♔h1 ♘f2+ 28 ♔g2 d4 29 ♘f5 when White will win) 26 ♖f1 ♖xb2 27 a6 ♕b6+ 28 ♔h1 ♘f2+ 29 ♖xf2 ♕xf2 30 ♕xe6+ ♔h8 31 ♕e8+ ♗f8 32 ♕e5+ ♗g7 33 ♕e8+ and it's perpetual check.

23...h5

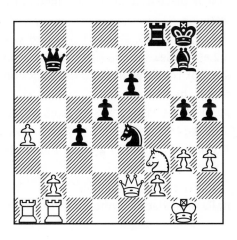

Adding support to the ...g5-g4 breakthrough.

24 ♖f1

Either b2 or f2 cannot be defended. After 24 a5 g4 25 hxg4 hxg4 26 ♘h4 ♖xf2 27 ♕xg4 ♕a7 28 ♔h1 (28 ♕xe6+ doesn't work because of 28...♖f7+ 29 ♔h1 ♘xg3+) 28...♖f6 29 ♖f1 ♘f2+ 30 ♖xf2 ♕xf2 31 a6 ♕xb2 32 ♖e1 c3 33 a7 ♕a2 there goes White's hope and joy (the a-pawn).

24...♕xb2 25 ♕xb2 ♗xb2 26 ♖a2 ♖xf3 27 ♖xb2 ♖a3

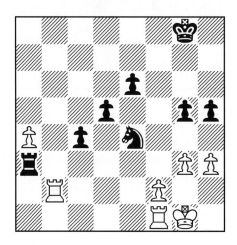

Exercise: White has one last chance of saving the game.
There's only one weak piece in the black camp and White
can try to exploit the fact. What's White's best move here?

28 ♖fb1?

Answer: The black king is a weak piece as it can be confined to the back rank by White's rooks, so 28 ♖b7! was correct:

a) 28...c3 29 ♖c1 d4 30 ♖d7 ♘d2 (or 30...♖xa4 31 ♖b1 ♖a8 32 ♖bb7 with perpetual check on the seventh rank) 31 ♔g2 e5 32 ♖e1 ♘c4 33 ♖b1 ♘b2 34 ♖e1 and Black has to keep using his knight to prevent the rook from getting into the attack on his king. After 34...♘d3 35 ♖b1 ♘b2 Black has to accept the truce.

b) 28...♘d2 29 ♖c1 ♖xa4 30 g4! h4 31 ♖e7 ♔f8 32 ♖xe6 ♔f7 33 ♖d6 d4 34 ♔g2 d3 35 ♖e1 ♖a7 36 ♖ee6 ♘b3 37 ♖h6 ♔g7 38 ♖dg6+ ♔f7 39 ♖c6 ♔e8 40 ♖xc4 d2 41 ♖c8+ ♔d7 42 ♖g8 ♖c7 43 ♖g7+ ♔c8 44 ♖g8+ ♔d7 (44...♔b7? 45 ♖d6 and White is winning) 45 ♖g7+ ♔c8 with equality.

28...♔f7!

Now that the king is totally safe, Black's humongous central pawn mass will call the shots.

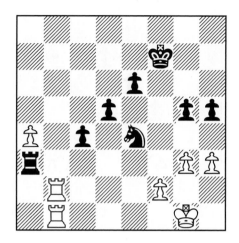

29 ♖b7+ ♔f6 30 ♖1b4 g4 31 hxg4 hxg4 32 ♖b8 ♖a1+ 33 ♔g2 ♖a2 34 ♖b2 ♖xb2!

Black finds the fastest way to end the game, not even pausing to digest the a-pawn.

35 ♖xb2 c3 36 ♖e2 ♘c5 37 ♔f1 d4 38 ♖c2 ♘xa4 39 ♔e2 ♔e5 40 ♖a2 ♘b2 41 f4+ ♔e4 42 ♖a1 d3+ 43 ♔f2 c2 44 ♖c1 d2 45 ♖xc2 d1♕ 46 ♖e2+ ♔d5 47 ♖e5+ ♔d4 48 ♖xe6 ♘d3+ 49 ♔g2 ♕f3+ 50 ♔h2 ♕f2+ 51 ♔h1 ♕f1+ 52 ♔h2 ♕h3+ 53 ♔g1 ♕xg3+ 54 ♔f1 ♕f2# 0-1

B) 11...♘a6!?

As the variations in Line A showed, White currently has the upper hand theoretically speaking. Hence, I would like to introduce an interesting sideline which is designed to cross the Kaufman-endorsed a2-a4 and ♕e2 plan. Black avoids the standard development of the queen's knight so that he can play it instead to a6 and sink it on b4 if White plays 12 a4.

Singapore's top junior player and 2013 National Rapid Champion, FM Tin Jingyao, displayed virtuoso understanding of the nuances of this line in our next game.

> ### Game 5
> ### Huynh Lam Binh Nguyen-Tin Jingyao
> Thailand 2013

1 d4 ♘f6 2 c4 c5 3 d5 b5 4 cxb5 a6 5 bxa6 ♗xa6 6 ♘c3 d6 7 e4 ♗xf1 8 ♔xf1 g6 9 g3 ♗g7 10 ♔g2 0-0 11 ♘f3 ♘a6!?

With this, if White plays 12 a4, the b4-square will be owned by a black knight.

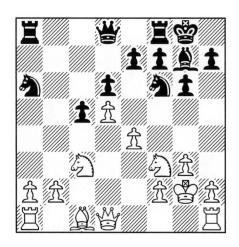

12 ♕e2

After 12 a4 ♘b4 13 ♕e2 ♕d7!? 14 ♘b5 ♖fb8 Black has an easier time compared to the 11...♘bd7 12 a4 lines.

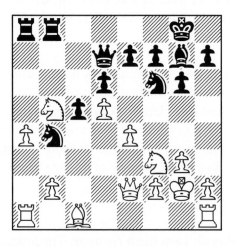

Question: Why is that so?

Answer: Firstly, in the 11...♘bd7 12 a4 line, usually when White has consolidated the queenside after a2-a4 and ♘b5, he can concentrate on playing b2-b4 to trade off his backward b-pawn for Black's strong c5-pawn, leaving him with an outside passed queenside pawn. However, the pesky knight on b4 makes it much harder for him to carry out such a plan. Secondly, White will find it more difficult to play for the e4-e5 break as the b4-knight is putting pressure on d5.

White did managed to get in e4-e5 after 12 ♖b1 ♘c7 (also playable is 12...♘d7 13 ♗f4

♕b6 14 ♕d2 ♖fb8 15 ♖he1 c4! 16 ♗e3 ♘ac5 17 ♗d4 ♗xd4 18 ♕xd4 ♘d3 and Black's activity compensates for his pawn deficit, R.Franke-C.Blocker, Detroit 1983) 13 ♖e1 ♕d7 14 e5, but Black has sufficient counterplay with 14...♘g4 15 ♗f4 ♖fd8 16 exd6 exd6 17 h3 ♘f6 18 ♕d3 ♖db8 19 ♗e2 ♘h5 20 ♗d2 ♗xc3 21 ♗xc3 ♕b5 when White has to trade queens or lose the d5-pawn. White was a shade better after 22 ♖d1 ♕xd3 23 ♖xd3 ♘b5 24 b3 ♘xc3 25 ♖xc3 ♘f6, but Black drew with relative ease in Z.Szczepanski-P.Schuster, correspondence 2010.

Instead, the sensible 12 ♖e1 ♘d7 13 ♗f4 ♕b6 14 ♕d2 was met by the committal 14...c4!?, reaching a position similar to Franke-Blocker above. Here White decided to sacrifice the exchange with 15 ♖e2 ♘ac5 16 ♗h6 (if 16 ♖b1 ♘d3 with good play for Black) 16...♘b3 17 axb3 ♖xa1 18 ♗xg7 ♔xg7 19 bxc4 with approximate equality though Black's position is the easier to play, D.Livecchi-Z.Ljubisavljevic, Agrigento 2009.

12...♕a5

Active play with the queen. Although it may be subjected to ♗d2 or ♘c4 hits, it will soon find its way to a6 where it usually belongs anyway.

As an alternative, 12...♕b6 13 ♗g5 ♕b7!? 14 ♖ab1 ♘c7 should be further explored.

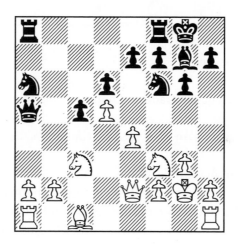

13 ♘d2

White prepares to stick the knight on c4, but Black has no problems dealing with it there. The one problem I have in this line is that Black is unable to avoid the draw if White wants to force it after 13 e5 dxe5 14 ♘xe5 ♘b4 15 ♖d1 ♕c7 16 a3 ♘bxd5 17 ♘xd5 ♘xd5 18 ♖xd5 e6 19 ♖d7 ♕xe5 20 ♕xe5 ♗xe5 21 ♖b7 ♖fb8 22 ♖xb8+ ♖xb8 with an equal position.

Instead, 13 ♗g5 ♘c7 with ...♖fb8 to follow gives Black a satisfactory game.

13...♘c7

This discourages White from playing e4-e5 as d5 will hang. Also Black prepares to shift the queen to a6.

14 ♘c4 ♕a6 15 ♖d1

White prepares to play e4-e5, but Black has no problems parrying it.

After 15 a4 Black carries on with standard development via 15...♖fb8 16 ♖a3 ♘d7 17 ♖e1 ♘b6 18 ♘xb6 ♖xb6 19 ♗g5 ♕xe2 20 ♖xe2 ♔f8 when he has equal chances already. Here 21 ♘d1 ♖b4 22 a5 ♘b5 23 ♖a2 ♘d4 24 ♖e1 ♘c2 25 ♖e2 ♘d4 26 ♖e1 ♘c2 27 ♖e2 ♘d4 was agreed drawn in S.Terzic-G.Trkulja, Neum 2008.

15...♘d7

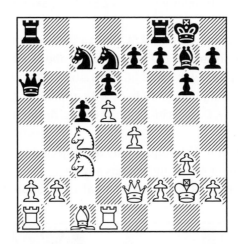

Black already has an easy game.

16 ♘e3

White decides to allow a queen trade and hopes to hold the fort with his extra pawn.

Question: What is Black's plan after 16 ♗d2, completing development for White?

Answer: Black should attempt to trade off the knight on c3 with 16...♘b5! and if White does not agree to the exchange, Black can simply plant the knight on the juicy d4-square. Usually in the Benko the white knights are the linchpins that fend off Black's attempts to put excruciating pressure on the queenside pawns. After 17 ♘xb5 ♕xb5 the position is easier to play for Black and natural moves like ...♖fb8 and ...♘b6 will follow.

16...♕xe2 17 ♘xe2 ♖fb8 18 ♖d2 ♖b4!

Black starts to exert pressure along the fourth rank while deterring ♘c4 and a2-a4.

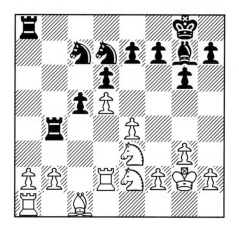

19 f3 ♘b6

My impression is that this knight left d7 a bit too early, but this move is entirely playable.

> ***Question:*** Can you find a more aggressive idea for Black to turn the screws on White?

Answer: Perhaps stronger is 19...♘b5! when White is already hard pressed to find a proper continuation: for example, 20 ♔f2 ♘e5 and Black is enjoying himself or 20 a3 ♖b3 21 ♘c4 ♖a4 (21...♘d4!? 22 ♘xd4 cxd4!?, freeing up c5 for the black knight, might be even stronger) 22 ♖c2 ♘e5 23 ♘xe5 ♗xe5 with a typical Benko queenside squeeze.
20 ♘c3

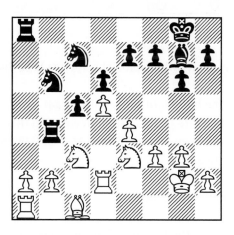

20...♘b5

After this the game peters out to equality, as Black, although having a comfortable position, could not persuade White to weaken his pawn structure.

Question: After 20...♘c4 21 ♘xc4 ♖xc4 22 a4 what would you recommend for Black?

Answer: Undermining White's centre with 22...f5! comes into serious consideration (22...♗xc3 23 bxc3 f5 leads to the same line), and after 23 a5 fxe4 24 fxe4 ♗xc3 25 bxc3 ♖xe4 White must play carefully to hold.

21 ♘xb5 ♖xb5 22 ♖c2!

White's defensive chances lie in his ability to keep his queenside compact.

22...e6!?

An attempt to play for the win by undermining the white centre. However, this break weakens the d6-pawn.

Black can weaken the queenside pawns with 22...♖ba5, but after 23 a3 ♖b5 24 ♖a2 ♖a4 White can simply parry with 25 b4! ♗d4 26 ♗d2 cxb4 27 axb4 ♗xe3 28 ♗xe3 ♘c4 29 ♗d4 ♖bxb4 30 ♖xa4 ♖xa4 leading to equality.

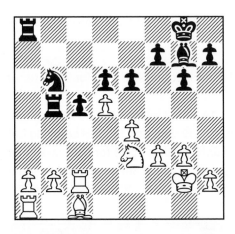

Exercise: How can White exploit the downside to Black's 22...e6?

Answer: White can deflect the b6-knight away with 23 a4! ♖xa4 (or 23...♖ba5 24 ♘c4 ♘xc4 25 ♖xc4 and White keeps his extra pawn, although winning this position will not be at all easy) 24 ♖xa4 ♘xa4, so that he can attack d6 with 25 ♘c4 ♗f8 26 dxe6 fxe6 27 ♖d2 when he has taken over the initiative.

23 dxe6?!

This allows Black to mobilize his centre.

23...fxe6 24 f4

Preparing to clamp down on the bishop if Black intends ...d6-d5.

24...♖a4!

The point is not just to hit e4, but also to control the c4-square.

25 ♔f3 d5 26 e5

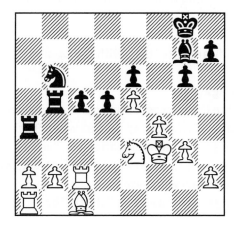

26...c4!?

An ambitious try, planning to mobilize both the c- and d-pawns.

Also deserving consideration was 26...d4!? 27 ♘d1 ♗f8 28 ♘f2 ♘d5 with strong compensation for Black.

27 ♘g4

White wants to play his knight to f2 to stem the advance of the d-pawn.

Houdini demonstrated that White can emerge with a playable position after 27 ♘d1 d4 28 ♗e3! (definitely not a 'human' move) 28...dxe3 29 ♘c3 ♖ba5 30 ♘xa4 ♖xa4 31 ♔xe3 g5! 32 fxg5 ♗xe5 33 ♖e2 ♘d5+ 34 ♔f3 ♗d4 35 ♖xe6 ♗xb2 36 ♖d1 ♖a3+ 37 ♔f2 c3 38 ♖xd5 c2 39 ♖d8+ ♔f7 40 ♖ed6 with a draw by perpetual check if Black promotes the c-pawn. If Black instead holds the seventh rank with 40...♖a7 White can still draw after 41 ♖8d7+ ♖xd7 42 ♖xd7+ ♔e6 43 ♖c7 c1♕ 44 ♖xc1 ♗xc1 45 h4 ♔f5 46 a4 ♗d2 47 ♔f3 ♗e1 since Black has no way of improving his position.

27...d4 28 ♘f2 d3 29 ♖d2 ♗f8

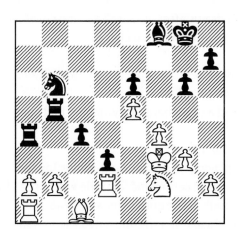

It is obvious that Black is doing well here. However, solid defence by White stopped him from gaining the full point.

30 ♘e4 ♘d5 31 ♘c3!

Black is forced to simplify and after that, with the c4- and d3-pawns fixed, it is hard to try for more.

31...♘xc3 32 bxc3 ♔f7 33 ♖g2 ♗a3

While I was watching the live telecast of this game, I considered 33...♖b3!?, hoping for 34 axb3?! ♖xa1 35 ♗b2 ♖f1+ 36 ♔f2 ♖d1 37 b4 ♗e7 when Black can try for more. However, this is met by no-nonsense 34 ♔e4, although after 34...♖xc3 35 ♗b2 ♖c2 36 ♖xc2 dxc2 37 ♔d4 ♗a3 38 ♗xa3 ♖xa3 39 ♔xc4 ♖xa2 40 ♖c1 g5! 41 fxg5 ♔g6 42 ♔b3 ♖a7 43 h4 ♔f5 44 ♖xc2 ♔xe5 Black should still draw with ease.

34 ♗xa3 ♖xa3 35 ♖c1 ♔e7 36 ♔e4 ♔d7 37 g4 ♖d5 38 ♖b2

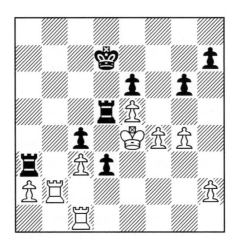

38...♖a7?!

Black is on the verge of overpressing in his determination to try for more.

Even 38...♔c6 39 ♖cb1! draws after 39...♖xc3 40 ♖b6+ ♔c7 41 ♖xe6 ♖d7 42 ♖a6 d2 43 e6 d1♕ 44 ♖a7+ ♔c6 45 ♖a6+ with perpetual check.

39 ♖f1 ♔e7 40 h4 d2?!

Risky play as the d-pawn loses its support from the c-pawn.

41 ♖d1 ♖ad7 42 ♖b4 ♖c7 43 ♖b2 ½-½

Strangely, White offered a draw here just when he had chances of trying for more.

C) The Old Main Line, 12 h3

In the old line with White playing h2-h3, Liu Yang-Junior Tay sees Black delaying the standard ...♖fb8 to see if he can play in the centre and kingside with ...f7-f5 for which he is richly rewarded. Moreover, life is tough in the once standard ...♖a6 and ...♕a8 line these days, with top Benko exponent Sergey Kasparov suffering a debacle in Gandrud-Kasparov. The manner in which Gandrud made use of the d4-square as a pivot for operations is very instructive.

Game 6
Liu Yang-J.Tay
Singapore (rapid) 2013

1 d4 ♘f6 2 c4 c5 3 d5 b5 4 cxb5 a6 5 bxa6 g6 6 ♘c3 ♗xa6 7 ♘f3 d6

White can also do away with the king stroll with a knight tour via d2 to f1 to e3, but Black equalizes easily by getting his queen to a6 swiftly: for example, 7...♗g7 8 ♘d2 0-0 9 e4 ♗xf1 10 ♘xf1 ♕a5 11 ♗d2 d6 12 ♘e3 ♕a6! and Black has easy play, B.Socko-M.Leon Hoyos, Beijing (blitz) 2008. Here 12...♘bd7 13 0-0 ♕a6! is similar: 14 ♕c2 ♘e5 15 b3 ♘fd7 16 f4 ♘d3 with a strong initiative for Black in E.Bareev-G.Kasparov, Linares 1994.

After 8 ♘d2, with this move order 8...♕a5 is also good, preventing White from recapturing on f1 with his knight after 9 e4.

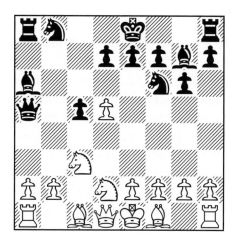

Instead, 9 g3 d6 10 ♗g2 0-0 11 0-0 ♘bd7 12 ♕c2 ♖fc8 13 ♖d1 ♖ab8 saw smooth development for Black in B.Socko-D.Andreikin, Moscow 2012.

8 e4 ♗xf1 9 ♔xf1 ♗g7 10 g3 0-0 11 ♔g2 ♘bd7 12 h3

This move is considered redundant in top-flight tournament praxis today. Thanks to Kaufman's recommendation in *The Kaufman Repertoire*, as well as the efforts of various Chinese Grandmasters, the vogue continuations nowadays are 12 ♕e2 and 12 a4, as we have already seen.

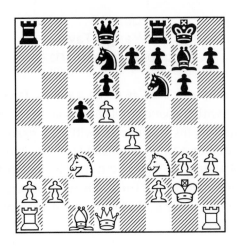

12...♕b6

This is also Topalov's and Bologan's choice in the Benko. I find this line more economical and efficient than the set-up with ...♖a6 and ...♕a8.

GM Aveskulov endorsed the line with 12...♕a5 in *Attacking with Black*. When I was playing for correspondence IM norms in ICCF events, I would avoid positions in which White can clarify the centre easily with e4-e5 as White often gets to play for two results (win or draw), while Black usually has to play well just to equalize. Here after 13 ♖e1 ♖fb8 14 e5 dxe5 15 ♘xe5 ♘xe5 16 ♖xe5 ♖b7 17 ♕f3 ♘e8 18 ♖e2 ♘d6 19 ♘e4 ♘xe4 my database shows a 70% percent success rate for White with 8 wins, 12 draws and zero losses in over-the-board play. Indeed, 20 ♕xe4 gives White a slight but definite edge. Black can also try 19...♘f5, but after 20 ♗d2 with 21 ♗c3 to follow, at best he can only hope for a draw.

13 ♖e1

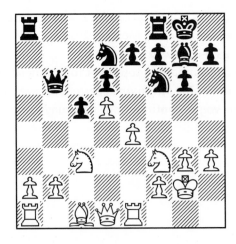

Preparing the big e4-e5 push. In some lines, White plays ♖e2 to guard the b2-pawn or even ♖e2-c2 to guard against tricks on c3.

13...♕b7!?

This move restrains e4-e5 and puts the queen on the same diagonal as the white king. However, I have another reason for delaying the ...♖fb8 sally which will be revealed by Black's 18th move.

> *Question:* Shouldn't Black just get on with the queenside pressure via 13...♖fb8?

Answer: More commonly played is, indeed, 13...♖fb8 which has been played by the Benko expert Viktor Bologan. However, White gets the slightly better game after 14 e5 dxe5 15 ♘xe5 ♘xe5 16 ♖xe5 ♕b7 17 ♕f3 h6 18 ♖e2 ♖d8 19 ♗e3, as in A.Gabrielian-V.Bologan, European Championship, Aix-les-Bains 2011, when it's too hard to play for a win with Black.

14 ♕c2

White protects the b2- and e4-pawns simultaneously. Others:

a) 14 ♖e2 ♘b6 15 ♗g5 h6 16 ♗xf6 ♗xf6 17 ♖c1 ♖a6 18 ♕d2 ♗g7 19 b3 ♖fa8 20 ♖c2 and chances are even, E.Bareev-A.Chernin, Moscow 1995.

b) If White insists on the central push 14 e5, Black hits back with 14...dxe5 15 ♘xe5 e6 16 ♘xd7 ♘xd7 17 ♔g1 c4! 18 dxe6 ♘e5 19 e7 ♖fe8 20 ♖e3 ♖xe7 and the black knight gets to wreak havoc from the d3-square.

14...♘b6

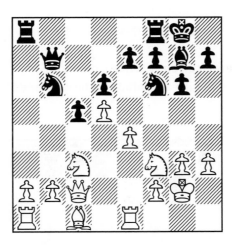

Discouraging e4-e5 while setting up ...e7-e6 which will result in an indirect hit on f3 after dxe6 fxe6.

Instead, after 14...♖fb8 15 b3 ♘b6 16 ♗b2?! (16 a4 gives White the advantage) 16...♘c4! 17 ♗c1 ♘a3 18 ♗xa3 ♖xa3 Black had good pressure in V.Gunina-T.Berlin, Beijing 2008.

15 ♗g5 ♘e8!?

The knight is heading to c7 where it eyes d5 and b5. I chose not to put the question to the bishop because of the simple 15...h6 16 ♗xf6 ♗xf6 17 a4 when Black must play very accurately to stop White from completing the ♖a3, b3 and ♘b5 bind. After 17...c4 18 ♘b5 ♘xa4 19 ♖xa4 ♕xb5 20 ♖xc4 White should draw with ease. However, a draw was practically useless as we both needed a win to make the prize list.

16 ♘d2 h6 17 ♗f4?!

It looks logical to play for a future e4-e5. However, this gives Black a tempo to gain lots of space on the kingside.

17...g5!

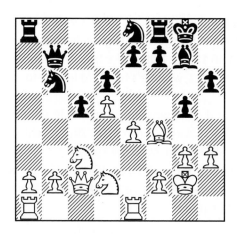

Question: Doesn't this weaken the black king?

Answer: Yes, it does. However, currently White's pieces are mostly on the queenside and not particularly well placed to take advantage of the weakened black kingside.

18 ♗e3

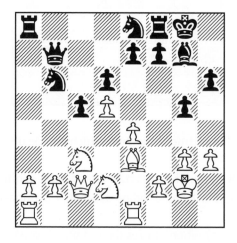

Exercise: Can you find a way to for Black to make use
of the queen on b7 to exploit White's king position?

Answer: **18...f5!**

Undermining the white pawn centre.

19 f3?!

In rapid chess, this will result in Black obtaining free play on the queenside without any harassment by White on the kingside and in the centre.

19...♘f6 20 g4?!

Trying to settle the problem of the potential threats on the kingside and Yang probably wanted to avoid complications. Better is probably to go into a dogfight after 20 a4 f4! 21 gxf4 gxf4 22 ♗xf4 ♘fxd5 23 ♗g3 ♘b4 24 ♕b3+ ♔h8 25 a5 ♘d7 26 ♘c4 ♘f6 27 ♘e3 ♘h5 with chances for both sides.

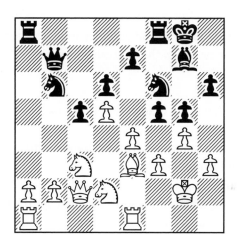

20...f4!

Ensuring that White's central or kingside play will be permanently neutralized. Now all the attention will be switched to the queenside where Black has more space than White.

Question: Why not use the f-file with 20...fxe4 21 fxe4?

Answer: Yes, it's possible, but White also has access to the f-file and the possibility of re-routing his knight to f5. Chances are about equal here.

21 ♗f2 ♘fd7 22 ♘b3?!

White hopes to reduce the queenside pressure with this as now ...c5-c4 will be met by ♘d4. However, it's now difficult to stop Black's knights from running riot. That said, even after 22 a4 ♘e5 23 b3 ♖fc8 24 ♖ab1 ♔f7! Black can set up a secondary threat with ...h6-h5.

22...♘e5 23 ♖ac1

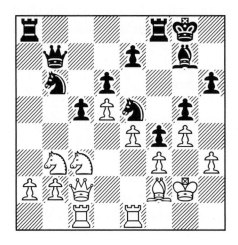

Exercise: What would you play now to accentuate
the power of the centralized knight on e5?

Answer: 23...♕a6!

The queen comes to its favourite diagonal in the Benko, eyeing the juicy d3-square.

24 ♖ed1 ♞a4!

Now the queenside simply falls apart. This exchange of the knight on a4 for the one on c3 is quite common in Benko middlegames.

25 ♞xa4 ♕xa4 26 ♖a1 ♕b5

With the idea of doubling on the a-file with control over the fourth rank after ...♖a4 and ...♖fa8. 26...♖fb8 is, of course, also natural and strong.

27 ♗e1

After 27 ♞c1 ♖fb8 28 ♖b1 ♞c4 going ...♞a3 will decide the game.

27...♖a4

Tired of being cooped up on the queenside, White makes a careless move.

28 ♗c3?? ♞c4 0-1 *(see following diagram)*

Unable to meet the threat of 29...♞e3 and with little time left on the clock, White decided to call it a day.

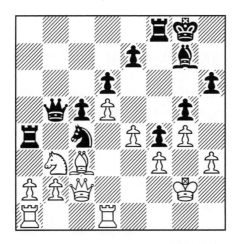

Game 7
V.Gandrud-S.Kasparov
Fagernes 2012

1 d4 ♘f6 2 c4 c5 3 d5 b5 4 cxb5 a6 5 bxa6 g6 6 ♘c3 ♗xa6 7 e4 ♗xf1 8 ♔xf1 d6 9 g3 ♗g7 10 ♔g2 0-0 11 ♘f3 ♘bd7 12 ♖e1 ♖a6

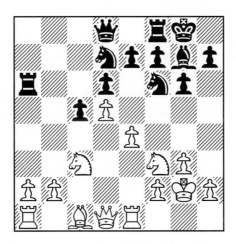

The queen's rook moves up two ranks to prepare ...♕a8 with the idea of hitting a2 as well as the long light-square diagonal via a future ...e7-e6, while also freeing up b8 for the king's rook. Moreover, on a6, the queen's rook protects the d6-pawn from the white queen after ...e6; dxe6.

13 h3

This stops the black knight from going to g4 after e4-e5.

13...♕a8 14 ♖e2

Shoring up the second rank.

14...♖b8 15 ♕c2 ♘b6

Freeing up d7 for the king's knight now that ...♘g4 is not possible.

16 ♖b1 ♘fd7 17 b3

Note that after 17 ♗g5 Black can play the pawn sacrifice 17...h6!? 18 ♗xe7 ♘c8 19 ♗h4 (if 19 ♗d8 ♕b7 with the idea of catching the bishop with ...♘a7) 19...g5 20 ♗xg5 hxg5 21 ♘xg5 with an unclear position.

17...c4!?

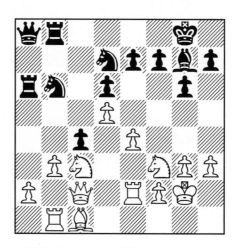

This was recommended by the player of the black pieces, one of the world's leading Benko Gambit exponents, in *The Dynamic Benko Gambit*.

Question: What is the danger associated with such a move? Surely it's a good thing to open lines on the queenside and free up a potential outpost on c5?

Answer: The big problem is that ...c5-c4 gives up a huge square on d4 for White's bishop and knight to sit on. In fact, this is what cost Sergey Kasparov the game as his continuation allowed White to transfer his knight d4 to c6.

In a world-class match-up between the two Pavels (P.Eljanov-P.Tregubov, German League 2010), Tregubov opted for the less risky 17...♖c8 18 ♗b2 ♘e5 19 ♘xe5 ♗xe5 20 h4 h5 21 ♖f1 ♗g7 22 f4 and only after White had extended himself on the kingside and in the centre did Tregubov play 22...c4.

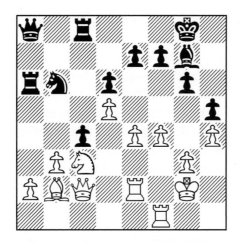

Following 23 b4 ♞a4 24 ♞xa4 ♜xa4 25 ♝xg7 ♚xg7 26 ♜f3 f6 27 ♕b2 ♕a6 28 ♜c2 Tregubov could have opted for 28...c3 as 29 ♜fxc3 ♜xc3 30 ♕xc3 ♜xa2 would lead to a draw because White's king is too exposed for his extra b-pawn to matter.

In *The Dynamic Benko Gambit*, Sergey Kasparov mentions how he escaped thanks to his opponent who "believed [his] Elo" after 17...♝xc3?! 18 ♕xc3 ♜xa2 19 ♜xa2 ♕xa2 20 ♝b2 f6 21 ♜a1. Here Sergey uncorked the resource 21...♞xd5 22 ♜xa2 ♞xc3 23 ♝xc3 ♜xb3 and eventually made it very tough for White to win in M.Pinc-S.Kasparov, Tatranske Zruby 2001.

18 ♝e3!

Another white try would be 18 b4 ♝xc3 19 ♕xc3 ♜xa2 20 ♜xa2 ♕xa2 21 ♝b2 ♞f6 (perhaps 21...f6 22 ♜a1 ♕b3 23 ♞d4 ♕xc3 24 ♝xc3 ♚f7) 22 ♜a1 ♕b3 23 ♞d2 ♕xc3 24 ♝xc3 ♞e8 (24...♞bxd5!? 25 exd5 ♞xd5 26 ♞b1 ♞xc3 27 ♞xc3 ♜xb4 might just hold, but Black definitely has to suffer here) 25 ♜a7 and Black has to defend carefully to hold this.

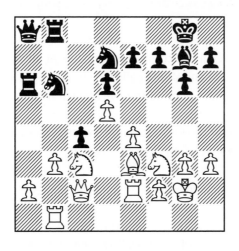

> **Exercise:** This position is already rather critical for Black. How can he bail out here?

18...cxb3?

Now Black is unable to contest the c6-square when White's knight reaches d4.

Answer: 18...♗xc3! would have given Black chances to hold: 19 ♕xc3 ♖xa2 20 ♖xa2 ♕xa2 21 ♖b2 (or 21 ♘d2 cxb3 22 ♖xb3 ♖c8 23 ♕b4 ♖c2 24 ♗xb6 ♘xb6 25 ♕xb6 ♖xd2 26 ♖f3 ♕a8 27 ♕c7 ♕e8 28 ♕b7 ♖c2 29 ♖a3 ♖c8 30 ♖a7 ♔f8 and Black is too solid to lose this) 21...♕a6 22 ♘d4 ♘e5 and the position is defensible because the timing of ...♘d7-e5 neutralizes the d4-knight's movement. Here 23 ♗h6 f6 24 bxc4 ♕xc4 25 ♕xc4 ♘exc4 26 ♖a2 ♖a8 holds the balance.

19 axb3 ♖c8

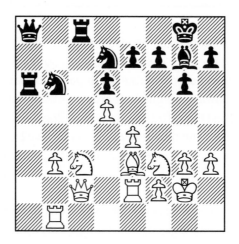

> **Question:** Which is better? Putting the bishop or knight on d4?

Answer: 20 ♗d4!

This is cleaner as now Black cannot complicate matters at all. After 20 ♘d4 e6 (20...♕b7 21 ♘c6 ♘b8 22 b4! ♖a3 23 ♘a4! and White calls the shots) 21 ♘c6 ♔h8 22 b4 sooner or later Black must sacrifice the exchange on c6 to have any survival chances.

20...♖a1?

A bad day at the office for the Benko Gambit expert. Black cannot allow the trade of the minor pieces, but even after 20...♘f6 21 ♕d3 ♘bd7 22 b4 life is tough for him.

21 ♗xg7

Removing the only obstacle to ♘d4-c6.

21...♖xb1

Even after 21...♔xg7 22 ♕b2 ♖xb1 23 ♘xb1+ ♔g8 24 ♘d4 Black is in a fix.

22 ♕xb1 ♔xg7 23 ♖a2 ♕b7 24 ♕a1 ♔g8 25 ♖a7 ♕b8 26 ♘d4

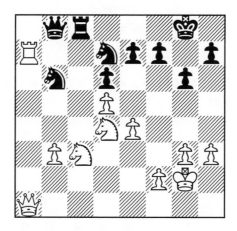

The knight makes its way to the c6 outpost and Black can no longer salvage the game.
26...♖c7 27 ♘c6 ♖xa7 28 ♕xa7 ♕xa7 29 ♘xa7 f5 30 f3 ♔f7 31 ♘c6 ♔f6 32 ♔f2 fxe4 33 fxe4 e6 34 ♔e3 h5 35 b4 exd5 36 ♘xd5+ ♘xd5+ 37 exd5 g5 38 ♔e4 h4 39 gxh4 gxh4 40 ♘d4 ♔g5 41 ♘f3+ ♔h5 42 ♔f5 ♘b6 1-0

D) 12 ♖e1

In my correspondence games, I have usually, on purpose, chosen systems which do not allow White to draw easily by removing a few choice bits with an early e4-e5 pawn break. Sabaev-Tay illustrates the problems I face with 12...♕a5, 12...♖a6 and 12...♕b6 in playing for the win after 12 ♖e1.

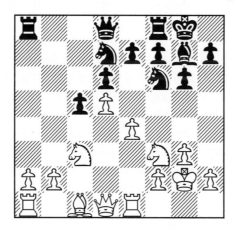

Hence, my recommendation is to play the petite queen move 12...♕c7 as demonstrated in Ulibin-Milanovic and Heiny-Sergeev. Keep in mind the following themes: ♘d1 and ♗d2-c3 to neutralize Black's dark-squared bishop, the need to be careful with ...♗xc3 followed by ...♘xa2, and Black's offer of trading off knights via ...♘a4.

Game 8
S.Sabaev-J.Tay
Correspondence 1999

1 d4 ♘f6 2 c4 c5 3 d5 b5 4 cxb5 a6 5 bxa6 ♗xa6 6 ♘c3 g6 7 e4 ♗xf1 8 ♔xf1 d6 9 g3 ♗g7 10 ♔g2 0-0 11 ♘f3 ♘bd7 12 ♖e1

Take note that I'm *not* recommending the following variation if you are aiming for a win at all costs.

12...♕a5

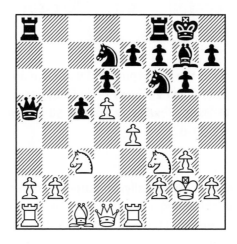

Essentially, if White wants a draw in this line, there's nothing much Black can do about it.

Another vacuum variation, which is also why I prefer not to play the move 12...♖a6, goes 13 e5 dxe5 (13...♘g4 14 ♕e2 ♕a8 15 exd6 exd6 16 ♗f4 doesn't seem very fun for Black) 14 ♘xe5 ♘xe5 15 ♖xe5 ♖d6 16 ♕f3 e6 17 dxe6 fxe6 18 ♗g5 ♕b6 19 ♗xf6 ♖xf6 20 ♕e2 ♖xf2+ 21 ♕xf2 ♗xe5 22 ♖f1 ♕c6+ 23 ♔h3 ♗g7 24 ♕f7+ ♔h8 25 ♕e7 h5 26 ♖f8+ ♗xf8 27 ♕xf8+ ♔h7 28 ♕f7+ with an easy draw for White.

I also encountered problems trying to win after 12...♕b6: for example, 13 h3 ♖fb8 14 ♖e2 ♕a6 15 ♖b1 ♘e8 16 ♗d2 ♘c7 17 b3 ♘b5 18 ♘xb5 ♖xb5 19 ♗e1 ♕b7 20 ♕c2 ♖a3 21 ♗c3 ♕a8 ½-½ R.Druon-J.Tay, correspondence 2000. White just has to exchange on g7 and line up all the major pieces on the second rank to hold firm.

13 ♗f4

The main 'vacuum variation' runs thus: 13 e5 ♘g4 14 exd6 exd6 15 ♗f4 ♖fb8 16 ♖e2 ♕a6 17 ♖c1 ♘ge5 18 ♘xe5 ♘xe5 19 ♗xe5 ♗xe5 20 b3.

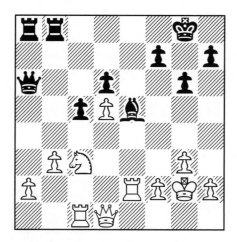

Generally, masters and grandmasters agree that Black is a little worse here, having to play well to "hold the balance with accurate play" (Jacobs and Kinsman), and with "little hope of achieving anything more" (Alterman).

13...♘g4

> ***Question:*** Why can't Black continue with the standard plan of 13...♘e8 and ...♘c7?

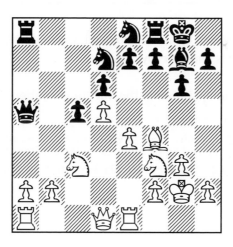

Answer: White's rook, king's knight and bishop are placed in this fashion for one clear reason. After 13...♘e8 14 e5! dxe5 15 ♘xe5 ♘xe5 16 ♗xe5 ♖a7 17 ♗xg7 ♔xg7 18 ♖e4! the idea of ♖a4 gives White a big advantage.

14 h3

There is not much point playing 14 ♘d2 as it is difficult to evict one minor piece from e5 without making excessive concessions: 14...♘ge5 15 ♗xe5 ♘xe5 16 ♕e2 ♖fb8 17 ♖ab1

♕a6! 18 ♕xa6 ♖xa6 and the e5-knight reaches the great d3-square.

14...♘ge5 15 ♘xe5 ♘xe5 16 ♕e2

After 16 ♖c1, despite pressing White for a bit, the maverick Dutch Grandmaster Van Wely had to settle for a draw in the following game. However, it is instructive to see how '6-time Loek' (coined for his streak of six consecutive Dutch titles) applied the squeeze here: 16...♘c4 17 ♕e2 ♕b4 18 a3 ♕b3 19 ♘d1 ♖a4 20 ♕c2 ♖b8 21 ♕xb3 ♖xb3 22 ♖e2 h6 23 h4 ♔h7 24 ♖cc2 ♗f6 25 ♗c1 ♗d4 26 ♘c3 ♖a5 27 ♘d1 ♖a4 ½-½, P.Van der Sterren-L.Van Wely, Breda 1997.

16...♖fb8 17 ♖ac1 c4

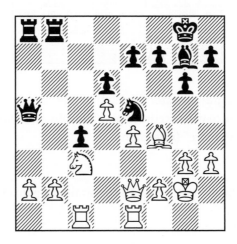

Rather committal. However, White has no good way to take advantage of the 'loose' pawn since his queenside is under heavy pressure.

18 ♗xe5 ♗xe5

We have a position roughly similar to the 'vacuum variation' and there's no way I could play for a win.

19 ♘d1! ♖c8

A last-ditch attempt to try, but to no avail. Otherwise, after 19...♕xa2 20 ♖xc4 ♖b3 21 ♕c2 ♖ab8 22 ♖e2 ♔g7 23 h4 h5 24 ♖c7 ♗f6 Black has full equality.

20 ♘e3 c3

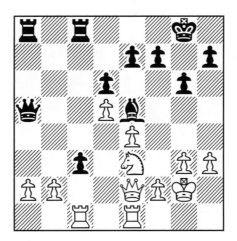

21 bxc3

> ***Exercise:*** Assess Black's options after the inferior 21 ♘c4.

Answer: There ate three candidate moves:

a) 21...♖xc4 22 ♕xc4 cxb2 23 ♖b1 ♕xa2 24 ♕xa2 ♖xa2 with a likely draw, although White must be careful to watch how Black uses the ...f7-f5 break to weaken his central pawns.

b) 21...cxb2 22 ♘xa5 bxc1♕ 23 ♖xc1 ♖xc1 24 ♘c6 ♗f6 and Black has the advantage since he can use both rooks on the a-file to tie White down.

c) 21...♕xa2?! 22 ♘xe5 cxb2 23 ♖b1 dxe5 24 ♖xb2 ♕a6 with a likely draw.

21...♕xa2 22 ♖c2 ♕b3 23 c4 ♗d4 24 ♘g4

After 24 ♖ec1 ♕b7 it is difficult to make progress.

24...h5 25 ♖d1 ½-½

The game was agreed drawn here. A possible continuation could be 25...hxg4 26 ♖xd4 gxh3+ 27 ♔xh3 ♖a1 28 ♖cd2 ♖c1 29 ♔g2 ♕b1 30 ♖d1 ♖8xc4 31 ♕xc4 ♖xc4 32 ♖xb1 ♖xd4.

It's a mystery to me why my Russian opponent (who later became an ICCF Grandmaster) would waste his white so, although this game highlights the difficulty for Black of generating decent winning chances in this line.

> ## Game 9
> ## M.Ulibin-D.Milanovic
> ## Winterthur 2012

1 d4 ♘f6 2 c4 c5 3 d5 b5 4 cxb5 a6 5 bxa6 g6 6 ♘c3 ♗xa6 7 ♘f3 d6 8 e4 ♗xf1 9 ♔xf1 ♘bd7 10 g3 ♗g7 11 ♔g2 0-0 12 ♖e1 ♕c7!?

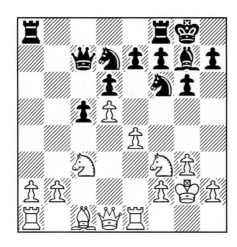

I like this little queen shift. It overprotects the e5-square against the e4-e5 break, connects the rooks and gives the queen the option of ...♕b7 or ...♕a7. The queen can also support ...c5-c4 or protect the d6-pawn after a future ...e7-e6 break. One key point is it prevents White from achieving e4-e5 easily as he does in the 12...♖a6 or ♕a5 lines.

> *Question:* Shouldn't Black take advantage of the omission of h3 to play 12...♘g4?

Answer: This is one of the main lines. However, Black is currently experiencing some problems in the variation: for example, 13 ♘d2 ♘ge5 14 ♕e2 ♘b6 15 a4! c4 16 a5 ♕c8 17 ♖a3! ♘d3 18 ♖d1 f5 19 axb6 ♖xa3 20 bxa3 ♗xc3 21 ♘xc4 fxe4 22 ♖xd3! exd3 23 ♕xd3 ♗e1 24 f3 ♕c5 25 ♗e3 was winning for White in M.Miljkovic-M.Pap, Jahorina 2012, although Black managed to later escape with a draw.

13 h3

White denies Black the g4-square for the knight.

13...♖fb8

The good, old queenside pressure.

14 ♕c2

A multipurpose move covering b2, e4 and the knight on c3.

Alternatively, White can cover the second rank with 14 ♖e2 ♖b4 15 a3 ♖b6 16 ♗e3! ♕b7 17 ♖a2 when 17...e6 18 b4 exd5 19 exd5 ♖ba6 20 bxc5 dxc5 21 ♖ab2 ♖b6 22 ♖xb6 ♕xb6 23 a4 ♕b4 24 ♕d3 ♘b6 25 d6 c4 26 ♕d1 ♖d8 27 ♗xb6 ♕xb6 28 ♘b5 ♕c6 eventually landed up as a draw in M.Gurevich-D.De Vreugt, Wijk aan Zee 2001.

14...♖b4

With the idea of putting the queen on b7 to pressure b2 and the long light-square diagonal.

Safer is 14...♖b7 15 ♖b1 c4 16 ♗e3 ♘c5 17 ♗xc5 ♕xc5 18 ♕d2 ♘d7 19 ♕e2 ♖ab8 20 ♕d2 ♘e5 (20...♕a7! would have been even better) 21 ♘xe5 ♗xe5 22 f4 ♗g7 when Black is

exerting sufficient pressure to hold the balance, K.Holm-H.Baldursson, Kecskemet 2011.
14...c4!?, ceding the d4 and c6 squares in return for d3, should also be considered.

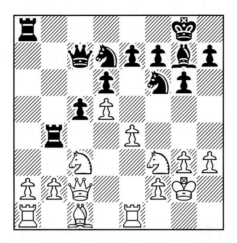

Question: Doesn't the text move allow White to
gain a tempo with a2-a3, booting the rook out of b4?

Answer: The rook will have to leave b4, but White has been provoked to weaken his queen-side, particularly the b3-square. Black hopes to make that count in the coming moves with continual heavy piece bombardment: for example, 15 a3 ♖bb7 16 a4 ♛b8.

15 ♗d2

Connecting the rooks and preparing to surround the black rook with a2-a4 and ♘b5.

15...♛b7

Putting the aforementioned pressure on b2 and the long diagonal.

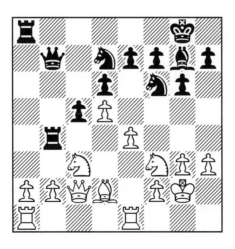

Question: What is the best way for White to defend the b2-pawn?

Answer: 16 ♘d1!

White does not weaken his pawns with b2-b3 and so can keep the rook on a1 for future operations. This knight may also find a chance to reach c4 via e3.

16...♖ba4

Gaining a tempo by hitting a2.

17 a3 ♘b6

Planning to infiltrate on c4. However, White does not give Black time to do that.

18 ♘c3?!

After the superior 18 ♗c3! ♕a6 19 ♖c1 ♖b8 20 ♘d2 White can prepare to play for f4.

18...♖4a6 19 a4

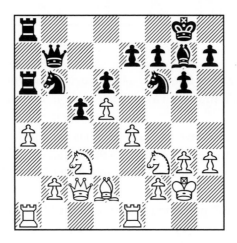

19...♘fd7

Exercise: What was wrong with 19...♘c4?

Answer: It can be met by 20 b3 ♘xd2 21 ♘xd2 when White will soon establish his ideal ♘b5 and ♘c4 blockading set-up, after which he can concentrate on central or kingside action.

20 b3

White is trying to establish a defensive fortress on the queenside, but this allows Black a 'hook' to play against.

20...c4! 21 b4!

Quite frequently in the Benko, White offers the return of the pawn by ...♗xc3 and ...♖xa2 or ...♖xa4. The crux is whether White's dark-squared bishop can then be blunted from using the long dark-square diagonal to produce dastardly kingside threats.

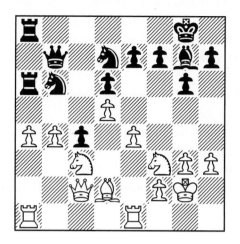

21...♗xc3 22 ♕xc3 ♘xa4?

The wrong decision, but Black probably overestimated the strength of his active knight. Black should regain his investment with 22...♖xa4!?: for instance, 23 ♗e3 ♕a6 24 ♖xa4 ♘xa4 25 ♕c2 ♕b5 26 ♗d4! (or 26 ♖b1 c3! 27 ♘d4 ♕c4 28 ♘c6 f5! 29 ♗d4 ♘b8 30 ♘xe7+ ♔f7 31 exf5 ♔xe7 32 ♕e4+ ♔d7 33 fxg6 hxg6 and there is no kill) 26...♕xb4 27 ♖b1 ♕a5 28 ♕xc4 ♘ac5 29 ♖a1 ♕d8 30 ♖xa8 ♕xa8 and even with the powerful dark-squared bishop, White cannot make headway.

23 ♕xc4 ♘b2 24 ♕f1

The only move to hold on to his extra material.

24...♘d3 25 ♖eb1!

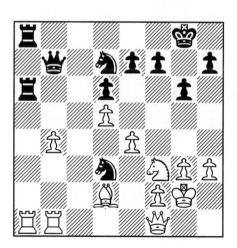

Probably at this point, Black realized that the tactics were not in his favour. Now he has to defend a pawn down and what a big b-pawn White has.

25...♘7e5

Also hopeless is 25...罩xa1 26 罩xa1 罩xa1 27 豐xa1 ②xb4 28 豐a5! (or 28 豐b1 ②c5 when 29 豐xb4?! 豐xb4 30 奧xb4 ②xe4 31 ②d4 ②f6 32 當f3 ②xd5 33 奧d2 當f8 gives Black some drawing chances, but after 29 奧xb4! ②a6 30 ②d4 豐xb4 31 豐xb4 ②xb4 32 ②c6! White will nab the e-pawn), and the game is over: 28...②d3 29 豐d8+ ②f8 30 奧h6 and it's checkmate.

26 罩xa6

It's time to cash in by trading a few lumps of wood.

26...罩xa6 27 ②xe5 ②xe5 28 奧c3!

Reminding Black that besides having to guard against the extra b-pawn, he also has to worry about back-rank mate threats.

28...②d7 29 豐c4 罩b6 30 b5

The oft-quoted expression of Aron Nimzowitsch comes to mind: "The passed pawn has a lust to expand".

30...②e5

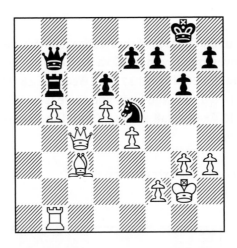

31 豐e2

Question: Is 31 奧xe5 dxe5 any good, since
White gets to create doubled e-pawns for Black?

Answer: It actually makes White's win tougher as both the reduced material and the firmly blockaded b-pawn give Black chances to hold.

31...豐a8 32 奧d4 罩b7 33 b6 豐a4 34 豐d2 f5 35 罩b4 豐a5

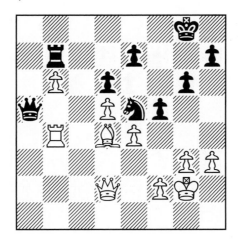

Answer: 36 ♗xe5! dxe5 37 d6!

Forcing a clean win.

37...♕c5 38 d7 ♖xd7 39 ♕xd7 ♕xb4 40 ♕d5+ ♔g7 41 ♕xe5+ ♔f7 42 ♕d5+ e6 43 ♕d7+ ♔f6 44 b7 1-0

1 d4 ♘f6 2 c4 c5 3 d5 b5 4 cxb5 a6 5 bxa6 g6 6 ♘c3 ♗xa6 7 e4 ♗xf1 8 ♔xf1 d6 9 ♘f3 ♘bd7 10 g3 ♗g7 11 ♔g2 0-0 12 ♖e1 ♕c7 13 ♖e2

White carries out the standard ♖e2-c2 manoeuvre.

13...♖fb8 14 ♖c2 ♘b6 15 ♕e2

Black now plays another standard idea in the Benko to weaken a key defender of White's central and queenside pawns.

15...♘a4!

In practical play, White will have a hard time warding off the queenside pressure without his knight on c3, which is typically used to blot out the pressure via ♘b5, by supporting a2-a4 or to sell itself for the bishop on g7 (usually after ...♗xc3, bxc3/♕xc3 and ...♖xa2).

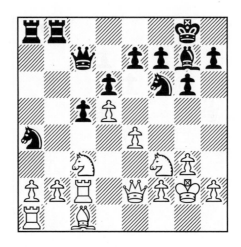

16 ♘d2

Probably White should keep the knight as a defensive piece with 16 ♘d1! ♕d7! 17 ♗d2 e6 18 dxe6 ♕xe6, with only a slight pull for Black.

16...♘xc3 17 ♖xc3

17 bxc3 is met by another Benko utility idea in 17...♖a4!, placing the rook on both the a-file and the fourth rank.

17...♘d7 18 ♖c2 ♖a4

Aside from giving Black the option to double rooks on the a- or b-file, this move also encourages White to weaken his queenside with either a2-a3 or b2-b3. Again, this is a standard Benko idea as the white pawns are more difficult to attack on their original squares.

19 a3 ♕b7 20 ♖a2

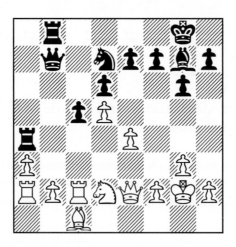

White intends to blot out the pressure with b2-b3, a3-a4 and ♗b2.

> **Question:** Black seems to have achieved as
> much as he can on the queenside. What next?

Answer: Black carries out an outflanking move which is often most effective when he has first maximized his queenside pressure.

20...f5! 21 b3 ♖aa8 22 f3 fxe4!

Of course, Black can keep the tension in the centre because of his central pressure. However, he wants to clarify matters because of his next move.

23 fxe4 ♕a6!

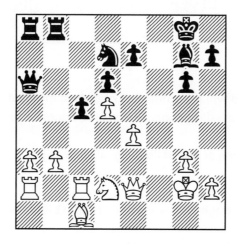

Having fixed the central structure, Black welcomes a queen trade or at least will kick the white queen off the prized a6-f1 diagonal. Now the d3-square is severely weakened and ripe for a knight invasion. Also, it helps that his queen is White's best placed piece at the point.

24 ♕xa6 ♖xa6 25 a4 ♘e5 26 ♗b2?

A better move, to prevent the following knight foray, is 26 ♗a3 and after 26...♘g4 27 ♖c1 ♗h6 28 ♖c3 ♘e3+ 29 ♔f3 ♖f8+ 30 ♔e2 ♘g4 chances are about equal.

26...♘d3

White is unable to prevent the knight fork on e1.

27 ♗xg7 ♘e1+ 28 ♔f2 ♘xc2 29 ♖xc2 ♔xg7 30 ♔e3 ♖ab6 31 ♖a2 ♔f7 32 ♔d3

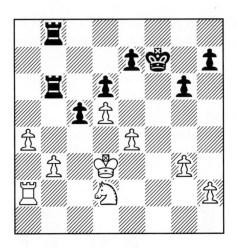

Exercise: In order to win the game, Black needs to invade down the f-file while watching out for White's dangerous a-pawn. How does he keep that pawn in check?

Answer: Bring the black king across to do the goalkeeper's job.
32...♔e8 33 ♔c3?

Question: How might White make Black's task as difficult as possible?

Answer: By prevent Black from using the f-file with 33 ♖a1 ♔d7 34 ♖f1.
33...♔d7 34 a5 ♖b4 35 ♖a3 ♔c7

Also possible is 35...♖d4 36 a6 ♔c7 37 ♖a5 with winning chances for Black.
36 ♘c4 ♖f8 37 a6 ♖f3+ 38 ♔b2 ♔b8 39 ♘a5??

White's last chance to complicate was to play 39 e5 dxe5 40 ♘xe5 ♖f2+ 41 ♔c3 ♔a8 42 ♖a5 ♖e4 43 ♘c4 ♖f3+ 44 ♔b2 ♔a7 45 ♖xc5 ♔xa6 46 ♔a3, with some drawing chances.
39...♖xe4 40 ♘c6+ ♔a8 41 ♖a5

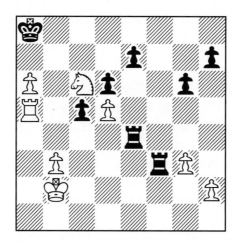

Black just has to make sure that White does not get in ♖b5-b8 and mate.

41...♖e2+ 42 ♔a3 ♖f1! 43 ♔a4 ♖b1 44 b4 ♖a1+ 45 ♔b5 ♖xa5+ 46 bxa5

Once the rook goes, the game is up.

46...♖e4 47 h3 g5 48 g4 h6 49 ♘d8 c4 50 ♔b4 ♔a7 51 ♘f7 c3+ 52 ♔xc3 ♖e3+ 53 ♔d4 ♖xh3 54 ♔e4 ♔xa6 55 ♘d8 ♔xa5 56 ♘c6+ ♔b5 57 ♘xe7 ♔c5 58 ♔f5 ♖h4 0-1

E) 10 h3

Sometimes White chooses to tuck his king away on h2 instead of g2.

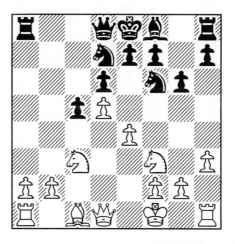

The extra move taken for it to reach there allows Black a swifter queenside initiative than in the 10 g3 and 11 ♔g2 line. In Sergeeva-Tay, White's traditional ♖e1-e2-c2 rook huddle is examined and Black employs the same e7-pawn sacrifice as in Haugen-Gonzales to speed up his attack.

As earlier discussed, White usually offers Black the chance to win back his pawn by exchanging the dark-squared bishop for the c3-knight. This is a double-edged decision, re-quiring good calculation and strong nerves as demonstrated by Black in Mastrovasilis-Georgiev.

Game 11
M.Sergeev-J.Tay
Correspondence 2002

1 d4 ♘f6 2 c4 c5 3 d5 b5 4 cxb5 a6 5 bxa6 g6 6 ♘c3 ♗xa6 7 e4 ♗xf1 8 ♔xf1 d6 9 ♘f3 ♘bd7 10 h3

White wants to castle by hand and get the king tucked away on h2 instead of g2.

Question: What are the pros of the king residing on h2?

Answer: Multipurpose:

1) With the king on h2, the chances of getting hit by a tactic on the long diagonal (usu-ally with the black queen on a8 or b7) via ...♘xd5, ...e7-e6 or ...f7-f5 are minimized.

2) It is slightly safer to launch a central breakthrough (e4-e5) with the king on h2.

10...♗g7 11 ♔g1 0-0 12 ♔h2

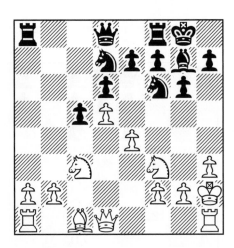

Question: What are the disadvantages of having the king here instead of on g2?

Answer: Multipurpose once again:

1) It takes an extra move for the king to get to h2.

2) White might get hit by a dark-squared tactic on the h2-b8 diagonal, as in the current game.

3) To take matters to the extreme, White's king is arguably less well placed in any endgame as it is further away from the centre.

12...♘b6

It is a matter of taste whether to play 12...♕a5 or 12...♘b6. I personally prefer the knight move as it normally goes to b6 anyway and there might be other options with the queen.

13 ♖e1 ♘fd7

Overprotecting the e5-square as well as opening the dark-squared bishop's access to the long diagonal. Black plans a future ...♘c4 or ...♘a4 with possible dark-square tactics lurking.

14 ♖e2

White begins the standard ♖e2-c2 manoeuvre.

14...♘c4 15 ♖c2 ♕a5

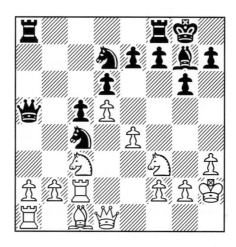

The most active square for the queen. It can head to b4 to tickle White further or to a6 to contest the light squares. Moreover, on a5 it helps create tactical chances based on ...♘xb2 tricks.

16 ♘d2!

Question: Why is White in a hurry to trade off the knight on c4? Can't White simply develop the dark-squared bishop?

Answer: After 16 ♗g5? ♘xb2 17 ♖xb2 ♗xc3 18 ♖b7 ♘f6 19 ♖xe7 ♖fe8 20 ♖xe8+ ♖xe8 21 ♖b1 ♘xe4 the second player has a great position: for instance, 22 ♕e2 ♕a4! and Black is on top.

16...♘xd2!?

Question: Doesn't it make sense for Black to keep a knight on c4 with 16...♘db6?

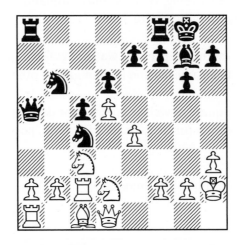

Answer: Yes, this is also a good continuation. The game might continue 17 ♕e2 ♕a6 18 ♘f3 ♖fb8 19 ♖b1 with Black having full compensation for the pawn minus.

17 ♗xd2 ♕a6

The queen gets to its desired diagonal.

18 ♗g5!? ♖fb8!?

Once again, offering the e7-pawn to accelerate the queenside attack.

19 ♕d2!

After 19 ♗xe7 I had planned to proceed with the standard knight infiltration: 19...c4!? (19...♖xb2 20 ♖xb2 ♗xc3 21 ♖b3 ♗e5+ 22 ♔g1 ♖e8 23 ♗g5 f6 24 ♗h6 c4 25 ♖b4 ♗xa1 26 ♕xa1 ♖xe4 27 ♕b1 ♖e8 is a wild and woolly continuation) 20 ♗g5 ♘c5 21 ♗e3 ♘d3 22 ♖b1 ♖b7 23 ♔g1 ♖ab8 24 b3 and amazingly this will most likely result in a draw by repetition after 24...♘b4 25 ♖cc1 ♘d3.

19...♘e5

Both sides start fighting for control of d3. White's job is to play around the eventual knight on d3 and chip away at its support, while Black's is to use the knight as a springboard to create tactical threats.

20 ♖d1

White does not fall for 20 ♗xe7 f6, temporarily entombing the bishop: 21 f4 ♘f7 22 e5 fxe5 23 ♘e4 ♖b4 24 ♖e1 ♕b7 25 ♗xd6 ♖d4 26 ♕e2 ♖xe4 27 ♕xe4 ♘xd6 28 ♕e2 exf4 with the better game for Black as the two minor pieces are stronger than the rook and pawn in this position.

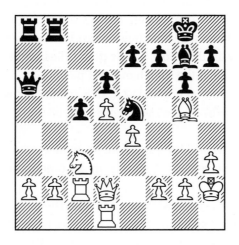

20...c4!?

A tactical solution.

Black can also play for the better minor piece ending, although White's pawn plus means that she retains good drawing chances. That said, over the board it is usually very tough to play White in positions like that which arises after 20...♘c4!? 21 ♕e2 ♗xc3!? 22 bxc3 f6 (a standard exchange followed by the blunting of the bishop; here the bishop doesn't have many chances to aid any kingside assault) 23 ♗c1 ♖b1 24 ♗h6 ♖xd1 25 ♕xd1 ♘e5 26 ♖b2 ♔f7 27 ♖d2 ♕a4. Now White must be careful not to trade queens or she would end up worse, even in an ending one pawn up. Thus after 28 ♕b1 the worst is over for White, but not 28 ♕xa4 ♖xa4 29 ♖e2 g5 30 f4 gxf4 31 ♗xf4 ♘d3 32 g3 e5 33 dxe6+ ♔xe6 34 ♔g1 ♖a3 35 ♖c2 h5 when she has to suffer a bit.

21 f4 ♘d3

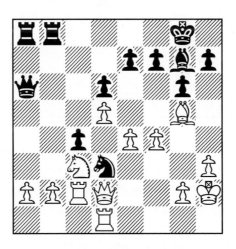

22 b3

After 22 ♗xe7 Black must be careful not to play too flashily with 22...♘xf4? because White can nonchalantly sacrifice her queen with 23 ♕xf4!! ♗e5 24 ♕xe5 dxe5 25 d6 and only White has winning chances, despite having just two minor pieces and a pawn for the queen. White can leisurely double rooks on the d- or f-files, while Black's heavy pieces are tied down to defending against the march of the d-pawn.

Thus after 22 ♗xe7 the correct choice is 22...♖e8 and only now 23 ♗h4 ♘xf4!? 24 ♖f1 ♘d3 25 ♗f6 ♗xf6 26 ♖xf6 ♕b7 27 ♕e3 ♕e7 28 ♕d4 ♖eb8 with the easier game for Black.

22...h6

Black seizes the chance to play for a small tactic on f4. Eleven years ago when this game was played, neither of the players saw that the whole combination is unfortunately flawed.

23 ♗xe7 cxb3??

Black must first control the e file with 23...♖e8! and then:

a) 24 bxc4 ♘xf4 25 ♕xf4 ♖xe7! (not 25...♗e5? 26 ♕xe5 dxe5 27 d6 when White has a large advantage) 26 ♕f1 ♖c8 27 ♘b5 ♖xe4 28 ♔h1 ♗e5 with a strong initiative for Black.

b) Only after 24 ♗h4 can Black play the pseudo-sacrifice: 24...♘xf4 25 ♗g3 cxb3 26 axb3 ♘h5 27 ♗f2 ♖ab8 28 ♗d4 ♖xb3 29 ♗xg7 ♔xg7 30 ♕d4+ ♔g8 31 ♖a2 ♕b6 32 ♕xb6 ♖xb6 with a likely draw.

24 axb3 ♘xf4 25 ♖a2?

Once again, White can simply sacrifice the queen with 25 ♕xf4!! ♗e5 26 ♕xe5 dxe5 27 d6.

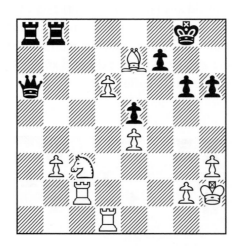

White has two minor pieces and a pawn for the queen, but all the winning chances because Black's pieces are tied down to defending against the d-pawn's march to d8: for example, 27...♖d8 28 ♖dd2 (or 28 ♖f2 ♕a7 29 ♖f3 ♖dc8 30 ♘d5 ♔g7 31 ♗f6+ ♔f8 32 ♖df1 and White is just too dominant) 28...♖ab8 29 b4 ♔h8 30 b5 ♕b6 31 ♘d5 ♕xb5 32 ♗f6+ and White is poised to win this.

25...♕b6 26 ♖xa8 ♖xa8 27 ♘a4 ♕xb3 28 ♗xd6 ♖xa4 ½-½

One possible continuation is 29 ♗xf4 ♖xe4 30 ♗g3 ♖d4 31 ♕xd4 ♗xd4 32 ♖xd4 when there is no chance for Black to play for a win due to the need to blockade White's strong passed d-pawn.

1 d4 ♘f6 2 c4 c5 3 d5 b5 4 cxb5 a6 5 bxa6 ♗xa6 6 ♘c3 d6 7 ♘f3 g6 8 e4 ♗xf1 9 ♔xf1 ♗g7 10 h3 0-0 11 ♔g1 ♘bd7 12 ♔h2 ♕a5

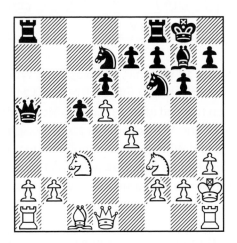

13 ♖e1 ♖fb8

A good alternative is 13...♘b6!? 14 ♖e2 ♘fd7 15 ♖c2 ♘c4 16 ♕e2 ♕a6 17 ♖b1 ♖fb8 18 b3 ♘ce5 19 ♕xa6 ♘xf3+ 20 gxf3 ♖xa6 with good compensation.

14 ♖e2

Commencing the standard rook manoeuvre.

14...♘e8 15 ♖c2 ♘c7

15...♖b4!? is a good alternative.

16 ♗d2

16 ♗g5 can be met by the stock pawn sacrifice 16...♕a6!?.

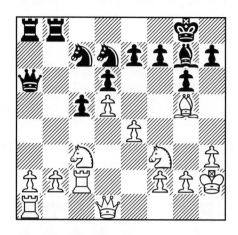

For example, 17 ♗xe7 (after 17 ♕c1 ♘b5 18 ♘xb5 ♖xb5 White erroneously hit on the idea of exchanging e-pawns with 19 ♗d2 ♘f6 20 ♗c3 ♘xe4 21 ♗xg7 ♔xg7 22 ♕e3 ♘f6 23 ♕xe7?? only to get his queen trapped after 23...♖e8 24 ♕c7 ♘xd5 25 ♕d7 ♘f6 26 ♕c7 ♖b7 and 0-1 in D.Stamenkovic-N.Ristic, Vrnjacka Banja 2009) 17...♘b5! 18 ♕e2 (or 18 ♘xb5 ♖xb5 19 ♕e2 ♖b7 20 ♖e1 f6 and White will have problems extricating that bishop on e7) 18...♘xc3 19 bxc3 ♖e8 20 ♕xa6 (if 20 ♗g5 ♕a4 with good compensation) 20...♖xa6 21 ♗g5 ♖xe4 and Black has a typical Benko endgame where White has to guard the a2, c3 and d5 weaknesses.

16...♕a6

Of course, the regular watering spot for the queen.

17 ♔g1

White readies himself for the endgame by putting the king closer to the centre. To be honest, it is quite difficult for him to find an active plan.

17...♖b4!

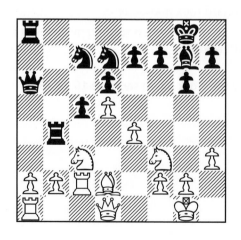

Encouraging White to kick the rook with a2-a3. This is an interesting psychological ploy as it gives White the opportunity to offer to return the pawn.

18 a3?!

Accepting the challenge.

Exercise: Can you find a stronger alternative for White to effect the ...♗xc3; bxc3 ♖xe4 exchange? Note that 18 ♕e1 runs into ♕d3.

Answer: White's strongest move is 18 ♕c1! as after 18...♗xc3?? 19 ♗xc3 ♖xe4 20 ♕h6 f6 21 ♘g5 it's all over. Although White can still hold on after the far superior 18...♘e5! 19 ♘xe5 ♗xe5 20 f3 ♕d3 21 ♔h1, under tournament conditions, it is highly likely that he would not be able to defend optimally against the sustained pressure.

18...♗xc3! 19 ♗xc3 ♖xe4

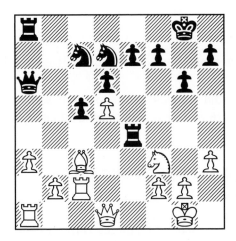

Georgiev's assessment is spot-on. Black has precisely calculated that White doesn't have enough time to launch a kingside attack with the help of the unopposed bishop. Black must calculate extremely accurately when trading his beloved dark-squared bishop for the c3 knight, as this leaves his kingside exposed on the dark squares. Thus, either he must have sufficient defensive cover or his queenside initiative has to be strong enough to prevent White from taking advantage of the bishop's absence.

20 ♕d2

Hoping to rush to h6. Instead, after 20 ♘g5 ♖f4! (a nice way to surround the d5-pawn) 21 ♕d2 ♖f5 22 ♖e1 ♖e8 23 ♘e4 ♖xd5 24 ♕h6 f6 White's initiative has fizzled out.

20...♘b5!

The dangerous bishop must be evicted from the board.

21 ♕h6 ♘xc3 22 ♘g5!

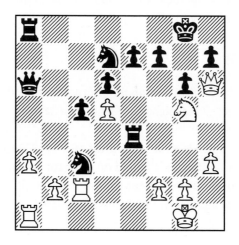

22...♘f8!

> ***Question:*** Why not the more active 22...♘f6?

Answer: Georgiev probably did not want White to obtain some counterplay after 23 ♖xc3 ♖e5 24 ♖f3 ♕b7 25 ♖xf6 exf6 26 ♕xh7+ ♔f8 27 ♕h6+ ♔e8 28 ♘h7 ♔e7 29 ♕h4 g5 30 ♕h6 ♕xd5 31 ♕xf6+.

23 bxc3

23 ♖xc3 is met by 23...♖e5 24 ♖f3 f6 25 ♘xh7 ♖h5! 26 ♘xf6+ exf6 27 ♕d2 ♔f7 with a clear advantage for Black.

23...♖e2!

Benko Gambit players love exchanging pieces as this accentuates the weaknesses of the white pawns.

24 ♖xe2 ♕xe2 25 ♘f3

Giving the queen a route back as Black was threatening to go pawn picking.

25...♕b2 26 ♖e1 ♖a7

Black is in no hurry.

27 ♖e3?

White attempts to defend laterally and perhaps hoped to use the rook for a last-ditch kingside assault. 27 c4 ♕xa3 was the lesser evil.

27...♕a2!

Once d5 drops, the rest is easy for Black as his central pawns start rolling.

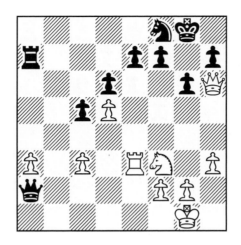

28 ♘g5 ♛xd5 29 ♖f3 e6

The end of the attack. Now the black central pawns take the limelight.

30 ♛h4 f5 31 ♖e3 e5 32 ♘f3 ♖xa3 33 ♛e7 ♖a1+ 34 ♔h2 e4 0-1

F) The Hockey Puck Punt 9 g4

Lastly, we examine the 'hockey puck punt' with g2-g4, which is an attempt by White to gain space on the kingside or to start a brazen kingside hack. Recent grandmaster games show that Black is holding his own here as we'll now see.

Game 13
S.Mamedyarov-O.Abdulov
Baku 2011

1 c4 ♘f6 2 d4 c5 3 d5 b5 4 cxb5 a6 5 bxa6 g6 6 ♘c3 ♗xa6 7 e4

White can also play in 'Four Pawns Attack style' with 7 f4: for example, 7...♗g7 8 ♘f3 ♛a5 9 ♗d2 0-0 10 e4 ♗xf1 11 ♖xf1 d6 12 e5 ♘e8 13 ♛e2 ♛a6 14 ♛e4 ♘c7 15 ♔f2 ♘d7 16 ♔g1. We've followed J.Murey-M.Hebden, London 1988, where Black could have seized the initiative with 16...f5! 17 exf6 (after 17 ♛e3 ♛b7 Black is calling the shots) 17...♘xf6 18 ♛xe7 ♖fe8 19 ♛xc7 ♖ac8 20 ♘b5 ♛xb5 21 ♛a5 ♛xa5 22 ♗xa5 ♘xd5 with an excellent game.

7...♗xf1 8 ♔xf1 d6 9 g4!?

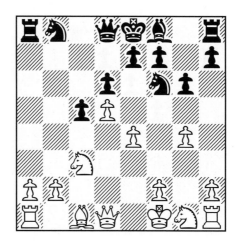

Question: What's this? Did White accidentally nudge his g-pawn a square too far?

Answer: Aside from proving the g2-square for the king to tuck itself into, 9 g4, if not stopped by Black, will lead to the space-gaining g4-g5 push and perhaps more aggression with h4-h5.

9...♗g7

Another option is to put the question to the g-pawn with 9...♕c8: for example, 10 g5 ♘h5 11 ♔g2 h6 12 h4 ♘d7 13 ♘ge2 ♘e5 14 ♘f4 (after 14 ♘g3 ♘xg3 15 fxg3 the e5-knight sits snugly on its unassailable outpost) 14...hxg5! 15 ♘xh5 ♖xh5 16 ♗xg5 ♗g7 17 ♖h3 c4! when Black already enjoyed a great space and developmental advantage in J.Clavijo-E.Real de Azua, Havana 2009.

10 ♔g2 ♘a6!?

Black develops the knight on a6 to give the f6-knight access to d7 if White goes for g4-g5. Also possible is 10...0-0 11 g5 ♘h5 when after 12 ♘ge2 e5 13 h4 f6 14 ♕d3 ♖a7 15 ♕h3 ♖af7 Black had a powerful attack looming on the kingside in M.Vlasenko-E.Solozhenkin, St Petersburg 2005.

11 g5 ♘d7 12 ♘f3 ♘b6

Black aims to play on the queenside with a future ...♘a4 or ...♘c4 foray.

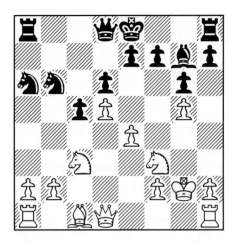

13 ♗f4 ♘c7

Giving the b6-knight even easier access to a4.

14 h4

Amazingly White is playing for mate.

14...0-0!?

Very brave, castling into the attack. Black trusts that White does not have enough fire-power to breakthrough on the kingside.

15 h5 ♛d7!

A dual-purpose move, contesting the g4- and a4-squares simultaneously.

16 ♖h4

Preventing ...♛g4+.

16...♘a4!

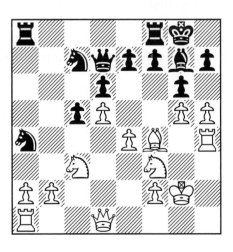

Forcing matters on the queenside.

17 e5!?

White goes for broke before he is positionally throttled.

17...♘xb2 18 ♕d2 ♘a4 19 ♘e2 ♘b6?!

After 19...♖fb8!, preparing an invasion on b2, White is in serious trouble.

20 ♘c3

White is allowed to restructure his set-up.

20...♘a4 21 ♘e4!

With this strong pawn sacrifice, White is able to lop Black's dangerous pieces off the board and pose some threats to the black king.

21...dxe5 22 ♗xe5 ♕xd5 23 ♗xg7 ♕xd2 24 ♘fxd2 ♔xg7 25 ♖ah1 gxh5 26 ♖xh5 ♖h8 27 ♘g3 ♘d5 28 ♖h6 ♘ac3 29 ♘f5+ ♔g8 ½-½

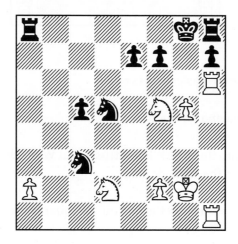

Here a truce was declared. Black is poised to win the a-pawn as well, but a draw against an opponent nearly 400 Elo points higher is not to be sneered at.

Chapter Two
Flummoxing the Fianchetto Variation

1 d4 ♘f6 2 c4 c5 3 d5 b5 4 cxb5 a6 5 bxa6 g6 6 ♘c3 ♗xa6 7 g3 d6

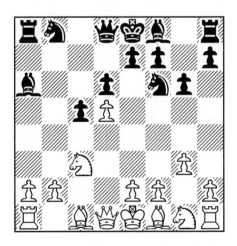

In the chapter, we'll examine White's second most popular line, the Fianchetto Variation. In this variation, White goes into a defensive huddle on the queenside and usually hopes to establish a solid barrier, often with b3 and ♗b2 (or ♗d2), and ♖ab1 (or ♖ac1). The central expansion e2-e4 is usually delayed so as not to give Black any targets on the f1-a6 diagonal, especially the d3-square, and White might be able to trade the light-squared bishops at a favourable moment.

The topical move in this line is 8 ♗g2 ♗g7 9 ♘f3 ♘bd7 10 ♖b1 (or 10 0-0 0-0 11 ♖b1), thanks mainly to the efforts of the Russian Grandmaster Vladimir Epishin. His concept of getting the rook out of the firing line of Black's dark-squared bishop followed by b2-b3 and, in time, a2-a4 and ♘b5, has made life really difficult for Benko Gambiteers.

Though GM Glenn Flear has pointed out on chesspublishing.com that "10 ♖b1 is now not considered quite as dangerous for Black as it was a few years back", it is still scoring heavily. In my database of Jan 2013-Jan 2014 games, White has scored 63% and my overall database showed 64% for White (10 0-0 0-0 11 ♖b1 also scores 64%). Of course, without specific variations, this is just plain statistics, but I'm not about to risk readers' chances by fighting the trend, especially when there's a viable and attractive alternative.

My preferred line is 8 ♗g2 ♗g7 9 ♘f3 ♘fd7!?, an idea introduced into mainstream practice by the Belorussian GM Sergey Kasparov.

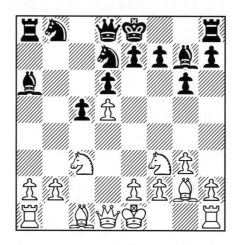

This move discourages White from setting up the Epishin structure of ♖b1, b2-b3 and ♗b2 without sufficient preparation as the knight on c3 would be left en prise. Black also has quite a few tricks to pull on a careless white player in lines where he plays b2-b3, based on ...♘xd5 or ...♗xe2. Indeed, I've lost count of the number of times I took these two pawns in online blitz play.

Also, one might argue that 9...♘fd7 is not denying the queen knight its natural square on d7, but merely exchanging places with it: the knight on d7 goes to b6 and the one on b8 then goes to d7. On the flip side, Black is denied the possibility of the manoeuvre ...♘g4-e5, but I don't think that's a big deal as sometimes this can be a tempo loser if White can avoid exchanging the knight, usually with ♘fd2, and then push away the knight with f2-f4.

My apologies for using statistics again, but in the 9...♘fd7 line, according to my database, White has been scoring a much more normal 54% in comparison (or 52% on my Jan 2013-Jan 2014 database).

A) 10 ♗d2 ♘b6 11 b3

In Sergey Kasparov's *The Dynamic Benko*, he explains how he first learnt about the line from GM Mikhail Ivanov who lost a game with 9...♘fd7 back in 2002. I was intrigued when the first published game in my database was none other than Epishin-Ivanov, where 'Mr. ♖b1' still managed to obtain his favourite set-up, although I believe Black can improve in the fight for light squares with 15...♕c8!.

White has also tried to play the Epishin system directly with 10 ♖b1, as in Wageih-Shoker, albeit without success.

Game 14
V.Epishin-M.Ivanov
Arco 2002

1 d4 ♞f6 2 c4 c5 3 d5 b5 4 cxb5 a6 5 bxa6 g6 6 ♞c3 ♝xa6 7 g3 ♝g7 8 ♝g2 d6 9 ♞f3 ♞fd7 10 ♝d2

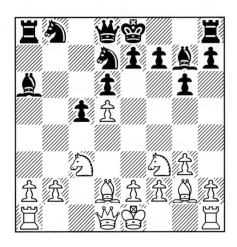

Epishin's plan is to secure the queenside pawn structure first and only then concern himself with kingside development.

Question: Hey! Isn't this similar to the Epishin Variation against 9...♞bd7?

Answer: Indeed, it is.
10...♞b6 11 b3
Cutting out ...♞c4 tricks.
11...♝b7
By hitting d5, Black forces White to decide if he wants to protect it with his e-pawn.
12 e4
Another possibility is 12 ♞h4!? ♕c8 13 0-0 g5!? 14 ♞f3 ♞xd5 15 ♞xd5 ♝xd5 16 ♝xg5?! (or 16 ♝c3! ♝xf3 17 ♝xf3 ♝xc3 18 ♝xa8 ♝xa1 19 ♕xa1 f6 when the bishop is a little stronger than in Adgestein-Djurhuus which we'll see in Game 19) 16...♕b7 17 e4 ♝xb3?! 18

🏜b1! ♝xd1 19 🏜xb7 and by now White had a clear advantage in Popilski-Haast, Cappelle la Grande 2013.

After 12 ♘h4, very interesting is 12...♘a6!?.

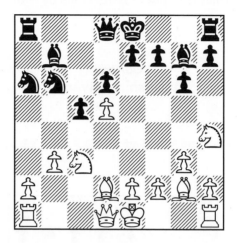

The idea is to pressure d5 with ...♘b4 or ...♘c7: for example, 13 0-0 (or 13 a3 ♘c7 14 e4 ♝a6) 13...♘b4 14 e4 ♝a6 with strong counterplay.

12...♝a6

Taking advantage of the diagonal which was further weakened by e2-e4.

13 🏜c1!

Moving the rook out of the range of Black's dark-squared bishop as well as protecting the knight on c3. I wonder how Epishin cooks up these ideas; he even has a variation in the Modern Benoni named after him (1 d4 ♘f6 2 c4 c5 3 d5 e6 4 ♘c3 exd5 5 cxd5 d6 6 ♘f3 g6 7 e4 a6 8 ♕e2!?).

Praxis has also seen 13 ♝f1 and then:

a) 13...0-0 14 ♝xa6 ♘xa6 15 0-0 c4 (extremely committal as Black is taking extreme risks in giving away the d4-square; instead, Sergey Kasparov recommended the ultra-sharp 15...f5!?) 16 🏜b1! ♘c5 17 ♕e2 cxb3 18 axb3 🏜a3 19 ♘b5 🏜xb3 20 ♘fd4 🏜xb1 21 🏜xb1 ♕d7 22 ♘c6. Even though White has obtained the c6 outpost, the fact that both sides have a similar pawn structure means that winning chances are limited, although the grandmaster handling the black pieces eventually managed to outplay his opponent in D.Housieaux-Y.Solodovnichenko, Condom 2005.

b) 13...♕c8 14 ♝xa6 (or 14 h4 ♝xf1 15 ♔xf1 h5 16 ♔g2 ♘8d7 17 a4 ♘f6 18 ♕c1 ♘bd7 19 🏜e1 ♘g4 and Black is well placed, as the h-pawn pushes have benefited him the most by giving his knight a fine square on g4, P.Bazant-S.Kasparov, Stare Mesto 2005) 14...♕xa6 15 a4 0-0 16 ♕e2 🏜c8 17 a5 ♕xe2+ 18 ♔xe2 ♘6d7 19 🏜hc1 ½-½ was the course of D.Nedic-R.Skytte, Bargteheide 2010.

13...♘8d7 14 a4

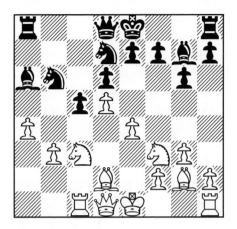

White annexes the b5-square and will attempt to gain full control of it by exchanging the light-squared bishops. It's not just one square at stake, but Black's entire queenside plan might be nipped in the bud if White succeeds in blockading b5 and, say, c4 with his knights.

14...0-0 15 ♗f1 ♗xf1?!

Losing control of the light squares. The other issue is that White actually gains a move after capturing on f1 as the king now move to g2 on the next move. 15...♕c8! was correct.

> *Exercise:* After 16 ♗xa6 ♕xa6 17 ♘b5 ♖fc8 18 0-0
> evaluate whether ...c5-c4 is possible.

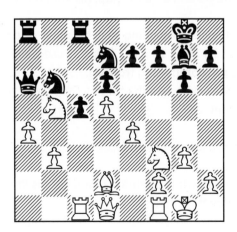

Answer: It is playable: 18...c4 19 ♘fd4 cxb3! 20 ♘c6 b2 21 ♘xe7+ ♔f8 22 ♖xc8+ ♘xc8 23 ♘c7 ♕xf1+ 24 ♔xf1 ♖xa4 25 ♘xg6+ hxg6 26 ♕xa4 b1♕+ 27 ♔g2 ♘f6 and Black can try for a win.

Instead, 16 ♘b5 (or 16 ♗b5 f5!) 16...f5! borrows Sergey Kasparov's idea. The key is that while White's kingside development is stunted, Black takes the opportunity to open up the f-file while chipping away at the white centre. The danger here is that the light-squared bishops remain which gives White lots of light-squared play on the kingside. However, the tactics (which the clever *Houdini* engine keeps on generating) seem to allow Black to keep the chances about level: for example, 17 ♘g5 (or 17 exf5 ♖xf5 18 ♗h3 ♖xf3 19 ♕xf3 ♘e5 20 ♕g2 ♘d3+ 21 ♔f1 ♕e8 22 ♕e4 ♗xb5 23 axb5 ♘xc1 24 ♗xc1 ♕xb5+ 25 ♔g2 ♕xb3) 17...fxe4 18 ♗h3 ♗xb5 19 ♗e6+ ♔h8 20 axb5 ♕b7 21 ♕e2 ♗d4 22 0-0 ♖a2 with counterplay.

16 ♔xf1 ♘f6?

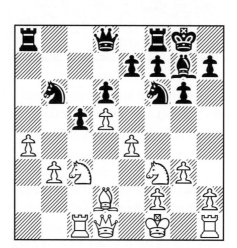

Even though Black's moves look sensible, he's already positionally lost. The problem for him is that after White's b2-b3 and a2-a4 set-up, his knights are already stepping on each other's toes.

Black had to take his chances in winning back his pawn and fighting against a superior minor piece with 16...c4 17 b4 ♗xc3 18 ♗xc3 ♘xa4 19 ♗d4, even if White has the better game with the strong bishop dominating from d4.

17 ♔g2

Completing development.

17...♕d7

Connecting the rooks and also preparing ...c5-c4.

18 ♖e1

White secures the e4-pawn while planning to anchor his knight on b5 to shield the b-pawn from any pressure down the file.

18...♖fb8 19 ♘b5

White is a shoe-in for a win after this. As the late Tay Cheong Ann (a former Singapore Zonal representative) would say: "Anchor for Anchor beer!"

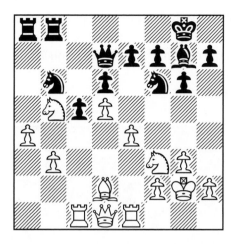

19...♕b7

Discouraging White from playing e4-e5.

> **Question:** What does White play if Black tries to undermine
> the queenside with 19...c4, with the idea of 20 bxc4 ♖xa4?

Answer: 20 ♘fd4 and once the knight reaches c6, the game practically plays itself as Black
is so suffocated.

20 ♖b1 ♘e8

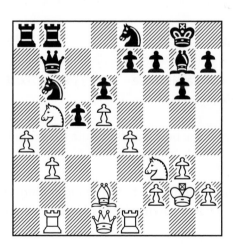

Now comes a series of moves which contest the c4-square.

21 ♕c2 ♖c8 22 ♘a3! ♕a6 23 ♗e3

To clear d2 for the knight which will head for the nice outpost on c4.

23...♘f6 24 h3 ♘fd7 25 ♖ec1 ♖ab8 26 ♘d2 ♘e5 27 ♘dc4 ♘exc4 28 ♘xc4 ♘xc4 29 ♕xc4

♕a5?!

After 29...♕xc4 30 ♖xc4 ♖a8 White has to work pretty hard to realize his advantage.

30 ♕c2 ♖a8

30...♕a8 at least allows the option of ...f7-f5, although White should have everything under control.

31 ♕d3 ♖cb8 32 ♖c4 ♕a6 33 ♕c2 h5

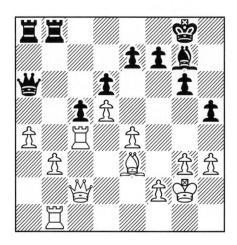

> *Exercise:* Now that White has arranged his pieces
> optimally, it's time to make a committal move, but what?

Answer: 34 b4!

The rest is a piece of cake.

34...cxb4

The alternative move 34...♕xa4 is futile – after 35 ♕xa4 ♖xa4 36 bxc5 White is winning.

35 ♖bxb4 ♖xb4 36 ♖xb4 ♖c8

> *Question:* What is the best way for White to realize his advantage?

37 ♖b6!

Answer: Always look for ways to liquidate to a winning ending. This move forces Black to either accept an ending one pawn down, which is virtually winning for White, or give up even more ground.

37...♕a8

Black cannot afford to play into the simplified ending: 37...♖xc2 38 ♖xa6 ♖c4 39 a5 ♗d4 40 ♖c6 ♖a4 41 ♗xd4 ♖xd4 42 a6 ♖a4.

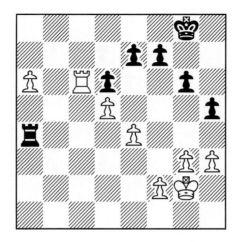

In this rook ending with the extra a-pawn, White is just winning. Three factors stand out:

1) White's rook is actively placed, as opposed to being stuck on the a-file on a7 or a8 in front of the pawn.

2) His king is well placed to roam up the board to help the a-pawn or to go after the weakened kingside pawns if Black's king moves towards the queenside.

3) Black's king is restricted thanks to the nature of the pawn chain.

Question: But how do those factors translate into a win?

Answer: White has two ways to win:

a) To play f2-f4, e4-e5 and force Black to weaken more of his pawns.

b) The king strolls to the queenside to help the a-pawn promote: 43 f4 (or 43 ♔f3 ♔f8 44 ♔e3 ♔e8 45 ♔d3 ♔d7 46 ♖b6 ♔c8 47 h4! – to prevent Black from playing ...h5-h4 and any ...♖a3+ tricks – 47...f6 48 ♔c2 ♖a3 49 ♔b2 ♖a4 50 f4 ♖a5 51 ♖b7 ♖xa6 52 ♖xe7+) 43...f6 (43...♖a2+ 44 ♔f3 ♖a3+ 45 ♔e2 ♔g7 46 e5! dxe5 47 fxe5 ♖a4 48 ♔d3 is all over too) 44 e5 fxe5 45 fxe5 dxe5 46 ♖xg6+ ♔f7 47 ♖h6 with a won game.

38 ♖c6 ♖b8 39 ♗b6

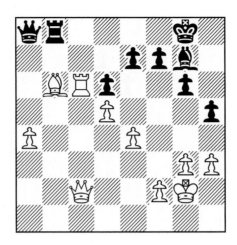

Reducing Black's heavy pieces to the back rank. The next part of the plan is to march the a-pawn all the way to a7.

39...♗f6 40 a5 ♔g7 41 ♕c4 g5 42 a6 h4 43 g4 ♗e5 44 ♗e3 ♔h6 45 a7 ♖e8

Finally the queen takes over the c6-square to effect a trade.

46 ♖c7 e6 47 ♕c6 exd5 48 ♕xa8 ♖xa8 49 exd5 1-0

> *Game 15*
> **K.Wageih-S.Shoker**
> Alexandria 2012

1 d4 ♘f6 2 c4 c5 3 d5 b5 4 cxb5 a6 5 bxa6 g6 6 ♘c3 ♗xa6 7 g3 d6 8 ♗g2 ♗g7 9 ♘f3 ♘fd7!?

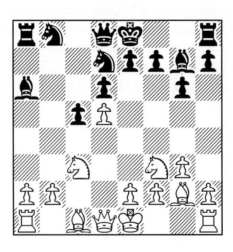

It would be appropriate to call this the Kasparov Variation since Sergey Kasparov has contributed so immensely to its theory, but there are two chess entities with this surname so perhaps the 'Sergey K' variation sounds more appropriate? The curse of a famous surname.

As mentioned earlier, 9...♘bd7 10 ♖b1! constitutes the Epishin Variation. Grandmasters Epishin, Malakhatko and Gustafsson have practically made a living from the white side of this position and at the very top level, Kramnik seems to win at will against 2700 types with it.

10 ♖b1

White tries to play for the Epishin set-up, but b2-b3 is not so easy to achieve with the g7-bishop making its presence felt.

10...♘b6

Toying around with move orders, perhaps possible too is 10...♕a5!?:

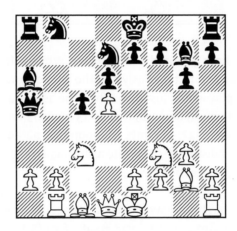

a) 11 ♕c2 ♘b6 12 a3 (12 0-0 ♘8d7 gives typical counterchances) 12...♗xc3+! 13 bxc3 (or 13 ♕xc3 ♕xc3+ 14 bxc3 ♘8d7) 13...♘8d7 with equality.

b) 11 0-0 0-0 is a typical type of position.

c) 11 ♗d2! looks quite critical: for example, 11...♘b6 12 ♕c1! ♘c4 (or 12...♘8d7 13 b3 ♘f6 when after 14 ♘d4 cxd4 15 b4 dxc3 16 bxa5 cxd2+ 17 ♕xd2 ♘c4 18 ♕b4 0-0 Black has sufficient compensation to cause trouble, but 14 0-0! ♘bd7 15 a4 0-0 16 ♖e1 ♖fb8 17 ♗f1 ♘g4 18 ♘b5 ♕b6 19 e3 results in a slight edge for White) 13 ♗h6 ♗xc3+ (if 13...0-0 14 h4! ♗xc3+ 15 bxc3 ♖e8 16 h5) 14 bxc3 f6 or here 14...♘a3 15 ♖b2 (15 ♖a1 f6 16 ♘d2 ♘d7 17 ♘b3 ♕a4 18 f4!? is possible too) 15...♘c4 16 ♖c2 ♘a3 17 ♖d2 ♘d7 18 0-0 f6 19 ♗h3 ♘b6 20 ♗e6 ♗c8 with a highly unclear state of affairs.

11 0-0

After 11 ♕c2 ♘8d7 12 a4 ♘f6 13 ♘d2 0-0 14 b3 ♗b7 15 e4 ♗a6 16 ♗f1 ♗xf1 17 ♔xf1 e6! Black is fighting back well.

11...♘8d7 12 ♕c2

To support the knight on c3 before White can play b2-b3 and ♗b2. However, Black gets to act first.

12...♗c4!

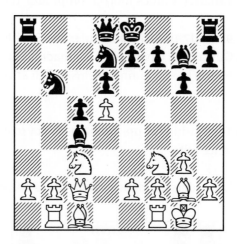

It's too late for White! Black gets in the first hit and White is forced to improvise. The cheeky bishop hits d5 and a2 simultaneously and the whole dynamics change.

However, stereotyped play would just give White the advantage: 12...0-0?! 13 b3! ♕c7 (if 13...c4 14 b4 or 13...♗xc3 14 ♕xc3 ♗xe2 15 ♖e1 ♗xf3 16 ♗xf3 and White is simply better as Black has no time to capture on a2, so White will soon play a2-a4 and consolidate) 14 ♗b2 ♖fb8 15 ♖fc1 with a stable advantage for White as he has arranged his queenside structure nicely without making any concessions.

13 ♘d2

If White chooses to defend his a-pawn instead, play could develop thus: 13 a3 ♘xd5! 14 ♘d2 ♘xc3 15 bxc3 ♗xe2 16 ♖e1 ♗a6 17 ♗xa8 ♕xa8 18 c4 f5 19 ♕a4 ♗b7 20 ♕b3 (after 20 ♕xa8+ ♗xa8 21 ♔f1 ♔f7 22 ♔e2 ♗c6 the position is much easier to play for Black) 20...♗c6 21 ♗b2 e5 when Black has excellent compensation for the exchange due to his strong centre and outstanding light-squared bishop.

13...♗xa2 14 ♘xa2 ♖xa2

The position is about equal. Although White has the bishop-pair, Black's knights can find good squares easily and his pawn structure is very compact and contains no weaknesses.

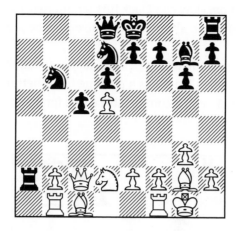

15 ♘e4 0-0

Of course, most definitely not 15...♘xd5? 16 ♘xd6+ exd6 17 ♗xd5 with a huge plus for White.

16 ♗d2

16 ♘c3 ♖a6 is equal.

16...♕a8!

Black is already calling the shots with his seamless development and White doesn't even have an extra pawn to compensate for the pressure. Don't be suicidal, though, and think of 16...♘xd5? 17 ♕b3 ♕a8 18 ♘c3 ♗xc3 19 ♗xd5 when Black is busted.

17 ♗c3

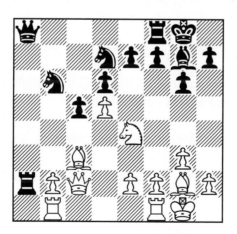

17...♘e5

The Egyptian International Master, who won a zonal to qualify for the 2013 World Cup, tempts White to weaken his position in order to trade bishops. This is a double-edged strategy, though, as White might use the space on offer to start a central advance.

> ***Question:*** How can Black further improve his piece
> placement as an alternative to Shoker's rope-a-dope idea?

Answer: By offering a queen trade with 17...♕a4! 18 ♕c1 (or 18 ♕xa4 ♘xa4 19 ♗xg7 ♔xg7 20 b4 cxb4 21 ♖xb4 ♘ab6 when Black has a pull due to his better minor pieces and active rooks) 18...♕b3 19 ♘d2 ♕b5, with a comfortable game for Black.

18 f4

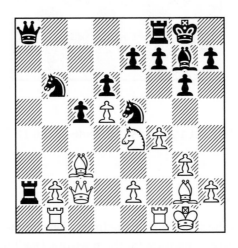

> ***Exercise:*** There are three decent squares for the knight, but what's the best choice?

Answer: **18...♘ec4!**

All three are okay, but Shoker's choice gets a slight nod because his knight is more active on c4 than d7 or f6.

After 18...♘ed7 19 ♗xg7 ♔xg7 20 ♘c3 ♖a5 Black has a slight pull and the same is true after 18...♘g4 19 ♗xg7 ♔xg7 20 ♗f3 ♘f6 21 ♘c3 ♖a5.

19 ♗xg7 ♔xg7

White, seeing that the black king is void of defenders, decides to go for broke.

20 ♕c3+ ♔g8

20...f6 gives White attacking chances after 21 ♘g5 when the knight gets to plonk itself on e6.

21 f5?!

Instead, 21 ♕c1 ♕a7 should hold for White.

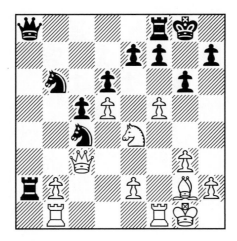

Exercise: Explain the pros and cons of this move.

Answer: It helps White to potentially open the f-file for his rooks and also threatens f5-f6 with chances of a strong kingside invasion. The bad news is that the move gives up the e5-square to the black knights and Black's kingside is shored up with:

21...f6! 22 ♕c1

Eyeing h6.

Exercise: Evaluate 22 ♘xc5. Is the knight sacrifice
sound and what's the best way to counter it?

Answer: It works and White can get a reasonable game after 22...dxc5 23 d6 ♕a7 24 dxe7 ♕xe7 25 ♗d5+ ♔g7 26 ♗xc4 ♘xc4 27 ♕xc4 ♖fa8 with mutual chances.

22...♔g7 23 ♔h1

The king sidesteps to prepare for an all-out pawn storm.

23...♘e5

Most definitely not 23...♕xd5?? 24 ♘c3, forking the queen and rook.

24 h4

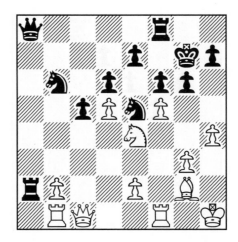

Question: What is the best way to meet White's kingside assault?

Answer: Shoker threatens to raid the White camp with a queen invasion.

24...♕a6! 25 ♘c3 ♖a5 26 ♕f4

Played to counter Black's ...♕c4 threat.

26...♘a4!

A standard Benko motif to increase the queenside pressure. The lynchpin knight is knocked off c3. Just look at the relative strengths of the knight on e5 and the g2-bishop and it is obvious that White cannot afford to exchange knights.

27 ♘e4

A desperate but well motivated pawn sacrifice. After 27 ♘xa4 ♖xa4 28 ♕d2 ♖b8 Black enjoys a superb knight and the more powerful major pieces as well.

27...♕xe2 28 fxg6 hxg6 29 ♖be1

The knight can be brought to the e6-square via 29 ♘g5!? ♖b8 30 ♘e6+ ♔h7 31 ♖fe1 ♕h5, but Black should still win this with a bit of care.

29...♕h5

Black is on top of things.

30 ♘g5 ♖b8 31 ♘e6+ ♔g8

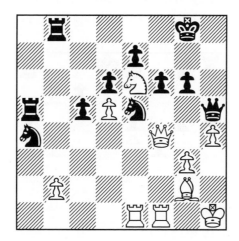

White's attack has been stopped cold. Now it's just a one-way street for Black.

32 ♖e4

After 32 b3 ♘b6 Black will still invade down the a-file.

32...♘xb2 33 ♕d2 ♘bc4 34 ♕c2 ♖b2 35 ♕c1 ♖aa2 36 ♘f4 ♕g4 37 ♘e2

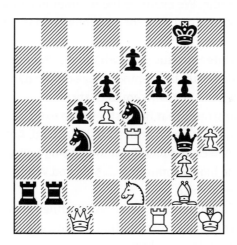

37...♖xe2!

Sac' like an Egyptian!

38 ♖xg4 ♖xg2 39 ♖ff4 ♖h2+ 40 ♔g1 ♖ag2+ 41 ♔f1 ♘d2+ 0-1

Black is denied a beautiful finish with symmetrical patterns: 42 ♔e1 ♘d3+.

B) 10 ♕c2 ♘b6

When Black shifts his knight away from kingside, it makes good sense for White to try to exploit its absence with an aggressive h2-h4 charge, with the idea of h4-h5 to weaken the black kingside. After Black got brutally hacked in early games after weakening his structure by stopping the kingside advance in its tracks with ...h7-h5, he has warmed to the idea of meeting h2-h4 with ...h7-h6, with the idea of meeting h4-h5 with ...g6-g5.

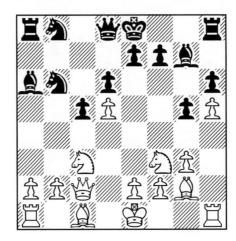

This gives Black a bit more space on the kingside at the expense of light-square weaknesses, especially the g4-square which the white king's knight usually find its way to after ♘h2-g4, as in Maiorov-Volodin. We examine the manner in which Black can develop his queenside initiative sans castling, due to the possibility of dangerous sacrifices on g5 as well as White's f2-f4 break.

In Schandorf-Skytte, White introduced 14 ♗h3 to disrupt Black's natural ...♘b6-c4, ...♕a5 and ...♖b8 queenside set-up by keeping an eye on the d7-knight. Perhaps Black does best to play 13...♗xc3 and 14...♗xe2 with equal chances.

Khenkin-Delfino demonstrates that Black still has to exercise caution after 'tricking' White into returning the gambit pawn after 11 b3!?. Instead, Antonsen-Skytte had White playing carefully with ♘d2, ♕c2 and ♖e1, intending b2-b3 and ♗b2. Black's response to the White manoeuvres was the highly committal ...c5-c4 and White tried to take advantage with an enterprising piece sacrifice.

Finally, in Nikolov-Cuenca Jimenez, White tried a refined version of the 11 h4 idea with ♗d2/♗f4 and ♕c1 to prevent Black from castling. In any case, it's early days for the 9...♘fd7 line with new ideas introduced constantly.

Game 16
N.Maiorov-A.Volodin
Tallinn (rapid) 2013

1 d4 ♘f6 2 c4 c5 3 d5 b5 4 cxb5 a6 5 bxa6 g6 6 ♘c3 ♗xa6 7 g3 d6 8 ♗g2 ♗g7 9 ♘f3 ♘fd7 10 ♕c2

White has also tried the accelerated h-pawn rush without ♕c2 recently, i.e. 10 h4:

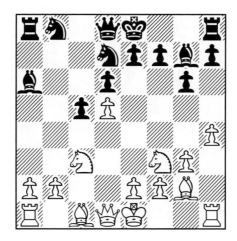

a) 10...h5?! 11 ♗d2 ♘b6 12 b3 ♘8d7 13 0-0 0-0 14 a4 ♘f6 15 ♘g5 ♗b7 16 e4 ♗a6 17 ♖e1 ♘bd7?! (Black should fight for d3 with 17...♘g4! 18 ♖c1 ♘e5 19 ♗f1 ♗xf1 20 ♖xf1 c4 and he has no problems here) 18 ♗f1! (White swiftly gains the upper hand with a series of solid, precise piece placements aimed at wresting control of the light squares) 18...♘g4 19 ♗xa6 ♖xa6 20 ♕e2! ♕c8 21 ♖ac1 c4? 22 ♘b5! ♘c5 23 ♖xc4 ♕b7 24 ♗c3 f6 25 ♘e6 ♘xe6 26 dxe6 f5 27 ♗xg7 1-0 was V.Neverov-I.Timmermans, Amsterdam 2013.

b) 10...h6 11 h5 (11 ♗d2 ♘b6 12 b3 ♘8d7 13 0-0 ♘f6 14 ♘h2 was K.Piorun-J.Westerberg, Pardubice 2013, when Black could try 14...g5!? with the idea of 15 hxg5 hxg5 16 ♗xg5?! ♖xh2! 17 ♔xh2 ♘g4+ 18 ♔g1 ♗xc3) 11...g5 12 ♗d2 ♘b6 13 b3 ♘8d7 14 ♕c2 ♘f6 (or 14...♘xd5 15 ♘xg5 ♘b4 16 ♕e4 hxg5 17 ♕xa8 ♘c2+ 18 ♔d1 ♕xa8 19 ♗xa8 ♘xa1 20 ♗c6 with mutual chances) 15 ♖d1 ♕c8 16 a4 ♘bxd5?! 17 ♘xd5 ♘xd5 18 ♘xg5 ♗b7 and here White overpressed with 19 ♘xf7?? (after 19 ♘f3! ♖b8 20 ♘h4 White probably has a slight edge due to Black's kingside light-square weaknesses) 19...♔xf7 20 ♕g6+ ♔f8 and Black is winning 'Quicker'-J.Tay, Internet (blitz) 2013.

When White plays his queen to the standard c2-square, it is not just concerned with touching base with b2 and c3, but the queen also keeps an eye on g6 because he intends to soften it up in a short while.

10...♘b6 11 h4!?

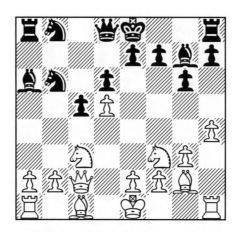

This brazen pawn lunge is actually well motivated from a positional perspective:

1) Black king's knight has left its base on f6 to foray on the queenside, so a kingside attack makes good sense.

2) Black has to make positional concessions with ...h7-h6 or ...h7-h5, or White will ram the pawn down to h6 and turn it into a real nuisance for the black king.

The 11-time champion of Belarus, GM Dydyshko, once outwitted Sergey Kasparov by setting up the queenside fianchetto in advance with the subtle 11 ♘d2.

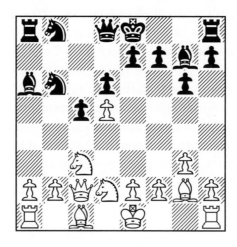

Once more, an innovative set-up to delay castling in favour of setting up the ideal queenside fianchetto structure. Sergey Kasparov did not try to stop him from establishing that and played 11...♘8d7, but after 12 b3! 0-0 13 ♗b2 White had a comfortable game in V.Dydyshko-S.Kasparov, Minsk 2006.

Question: Can Black take advantage of White's piece placement with ♕c2 and ♘fd2?

Answer: This set-up allows Black to try for ...♘a6-b4 instead of ...♘d7-f6. Since ...♘b6-c4 is not possible once White has attained b2-b3, it can help to press for ...c5-c4 instead. The knight on a6 might go to c7, c5 or b4 depending on the circumstances. In short, White will not find it easy to attain his ideal set-up and is in for a positional skirmish. After 11...0-0! 12 0-0 (12 b3 is well met by 12...♗b7, and if 13 e4 e6! or 13 ♗b2 ♘a6 14 a3 ♘c7) 12...♗c8! we have:

a) 13 ♖b1 ♘a6 14 a3 ♕c7 15 ♘d1 ♕a7 16 ♘c4 ♘xc4 17 ♕xc4 ♖b8 18 ♘c3 ♘c7 with good compensation.

b) 13 ♖d1 ♘a6 14 a3 is fairly well met by 14...♗f5 15 e4 ♗g4 16 f3 ♗d7 17 ♗f1 ♘c7 (or 17...f5!?).

c) 13 a3 ♘a6 14 ♖b1 ♕c7!? 15 ♘d1 (one pertinent idea behind ...♕c7 is 15 e4 ♘b4! 16 axb4 cxb4) 15...♕a7 16 ♖e1 ♘c7 with fluid play for Black.

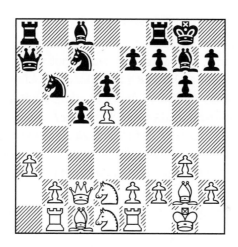

Practical tests are needed though.

Now we return to 11 h4:

11...h6

The safest way to meet White's aggressive idea. Black intends to bypass h4-h5 with ...g6-g5. Let's see the alternatives:

a) Black played creatively in a recent game with 11...♗b7!? 12 e4 ♘a6 13 ♗f1 0-0 14 h5 ♘b4 15 ♕d1 e6 16 dxe6 fxe6 17 ♗g5 (or 17 hxg6 ♗xc3+ 18 bxc3 ♗xe4 19 cxb4 ♗xf3 20 ♕b3 ♗d5 21 gxh7+ ♔f7 22 ♕d1 ♗xh1 23 ♗h6 ♗e4 24 ♕h5+ ♗g6 25 ♕f3+ ♕f6 26 ♕b7+ ♕e7 27 ♕f3+ with perpetual check) 17...♕d7 18 hxg6 hxg6 19 ♗f4 ♘a4! when Black's bishops were raking the board and White's development was abysmal in R.Gerber-S.Kuemin, Swiss League 2012.

b) Success came to the Indian GM Kidambi Sundararajan soon after he studied Boris Avrukh's h4 lines in his *GM Repertoire* work, as he reported in *New In Chess Yearbook 101*: 11...h5 12 ♘g5 ♘8d7?? (12...♗f6 13 ♘ce4)

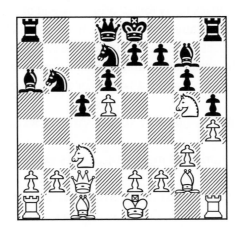

13 ♘e6! fxe6 14 dxe6 ♘e5 15 f4 ♘d3+ 16 exd3 ♕c8 17 0-0 with winning chances, K.Sundararajan-N.Situru, Mumbai 2010.

c) In one online blitz game, a Croatian GM nearly took my head off after my pre-moved 11...♘8d7? ran into 12 h5 ♘f6? 13 h6 ♗f8 14 ♘g5! ♗c4 15 ♗f4 (he could have dismantled my position after 15 b3! ♗xd5 16 ♘xd5 ♘bxd5 17 ♗xd5 ♘xd5 18 ♕c4 e6 19 ♗b2 when the end is nigh) 15...♘bxd5 16 ♘xd5 ♗xd5 17 e4 ♗xa2?! (17...♗c6) 18 0-0 e5 19 ♗e3 ♗e6 20 ♖xa8 ♕xa8 21 ♘xe6 fxe6 22 ♕c4 ♔f7 23 f4 ♗xh6 24 ♗xc5 exf4 25 ♗xd6 ♕a7+ 26 ♗c5 ♖c8 27 b4 ♕a3 28 gxf4 ♕g3 29 e5 ♘g4 30 ♖f3 ♕h2+ 31 ♔f1 ♖a8 32 ♕d4 ♗f8 33 b5 ♗xc5 34 ♕d7+ ♔f8 35 ♖d3 ♖a1+ 0-1, S.Matinovic-J.Tay, Internet (blitz) 2013.

12 h5

Black has to concede light-square weaknesses to keep the h-file closed.

12...g5 13 ♘h2

White starts to exploit the kingside light squares by discouraging castling.

13...♘8d7 14 ♘g4

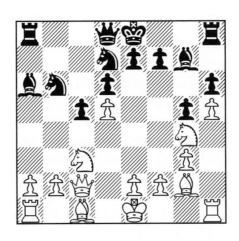

I like Sergey Kasparov's comment about this knight. He mused that the knight "looks great, but what next?" Indeed, if Black doesn't ask for trouble by castling too early, the knight doesn't seem to perform any major function if Black continues with queenside operations.

It's a matter of perspective, whether it's more important to stop the h8-rook from getting into action or to use the knight to trade one of Black's pesky knights. Note that White's rook is also still on the h-file. In some variations where he castles, he has to watch out for Black threatening to nab the h5-pawn.

14...♘c4

After 14...♘f6 15 ♘e3 ♗c8 16 ♘f5 ♗xf5 17 ♕xf5 ♕d7 18 ♕c2 0-0 White has a slight plus due to his light-square control, R.Eames-T.Chapman, British League 2012, and 14...0-0?? is for lemmings as 15 f4! denudes the black king's cover swiftly.

15 0-0

Black got an easy game when White opened the g-file prematurely: 15 f4 gxf4 16 gxf4 ♕a5 17 ♖h3 ♖b8 18 ♔f1 ♗d4 19 b3 ♘a3 20 ♕d2 and here Black should gain space and complete development with 20...f5! (20...♔d8 allowed White to hold on in V.Zakhartsov-J.Westerberg, Pardubice 2013) 21 ♘f2 ♔f7 when he is dominating the play.

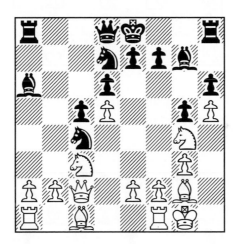

Now Volodin chose not to follow the standard 'garden path' idea, varying with:

15...♖b8

This makes perfect sense by doing the usual job of pressuring b2.

Practice has also seen 15...♕a5 16 a3 and then:

a) After 16...♘db6 17 ♘d1 White played a strong exchange sacrifice with 17...♕a4 18 b3!? ♕d7 19 bxc4 ♗xa1 and in this unclear position, a draw was agreed in L.Schandorff-R.Skytte, Borup 2010. With hindsight, the truce was a correct decision as after 20 ♗b2 ♗xb2 21 ♕xb2 f6 22 ♘xf6+ exf6 23 ♕xb6 ♗xc4 24 ♘e3 ♗a6 25 ♕b1 0-0 26 ♗h3 ♕e8 (Black can, of course, cop out with 26...♕xh3 27 ♕g6+ ♔h8 28 ♕xh6+ ♔g8 29 ♕g6+ with perpetual check) 27 ♗e6+ ♔h8 28 ♕c2 White has full compensation due to his strong knight and light-square control.

b) 16...♘de5 17 ♘xe5 ♗xe5 18 ♖a2 0-0 19 ♘d1 ♕b6 20 f4 gxf4 21 gxf4 ♗d4+ 22 ♔h1 ♔h8 23 e3 ♗f6 24 ♖g1 ♖fb8 25 ♕f5 ♗c8 26 ♕e4 ♕b3 27 ♖a1 (instead, 27 ♘c3! ♗xc3 28 bxc3 ♕xa2?? 29 ♕xe7 is crushing for White) 27...♗d7 28 ♗f3 ♖a4! with a winning attack, R.Diaz-J.Cuenca Jimenez, Havana 2013.

> *Question:* What is wrong with 15...0-0?

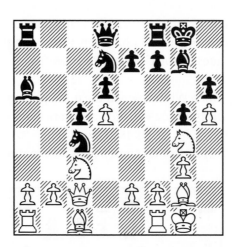

Answer: It's a sure way to get into hot soup after 16 ♕f5! ♘f6 17 ♘xf6+ exf6 18 ♗e4 and Black is left with the world's worst bishop.

16 a4!?

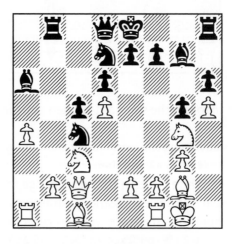

A tricky move.

Answer: The purpose of White's move is to meet 16...♕b6 with 17 ♘b5 ♗xb5 18 axb5 ♕xb5 19 ♖a7 when he has nice play on the light squares. And if Black is careless enough to put his king away, then 19...0-0?? 20 ♕f5 ♘f6 21 ♘xh6+!! ♗xh6 22 ♖xe7 ♗g7 23 h6 and it's all too easy for White.

16...♕a5 17 ♖b1?!

A novel way of contesting the a6-bishop is 17 ♗e4! with the idea of ♗d3.

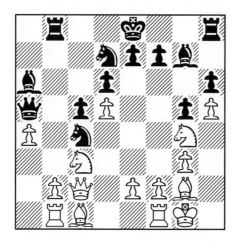

Instead, with the text, White offers the return of a pawn, aiming to exploit Black's lag in development.

***Answer:* 17...♕b4!**

This strong queen sally is very useful:

1) It introduces the threat to take on c3 and win a piece.

2) It lays claim to the b3-square.

3) It prepares ...♘a5-b3 or ...♘a3.

White was probably hoping for 17...♗xc3 18 bxc3 ♖xb1 19 ♕xb1 ♕xc3 20 ♕e4 ♔f8 21 ♘xh6 ♖xh6 22 ♗xg5 ♖xh5 23 ♕xe7+ ♔g7 24 ♗f3 ♖h8 25 ♗g4 ♘ce5 26 ♖c1 ♕b2 27 ♗xd7 ♘xd7 28 ♕xd7 ♖h5 29 ♕e7 ♗xe2 30 ♗f6+ ♕xf6 31 ♕xe2 with a draw in the bag.

18 ♘b5

This return of the pawn is probably White's best move to lessen the pressure on the b-file.

18...♗xb5 19 axb5 ♕xb5 20 b3 ♘de5 21 ♘xe5 ♘xe5 22 ♗b2 ♗f6

Also possible is 22...0-0 and if 23 ♕f5 ♕d7! when White must either trade queens or risk

Black playing ...♕g4xh5 (after 23...♕xe2 24 ♗e4 ♖fd8 25 ♔g2 White's light-square control helps him to hold the balance).

23 ♗c3

Protecting the b-pawn. Otherwise, 23 ♗h3!? ♖g8 (and not 23...♕xb3?? 24 ♗xe5) 24 ♗f5 g4 with the idea of ...♖g5 or, if White plays ♗c1, ...♗g5 is worth considering, while after 23 ♗a1 ♔f8 Black will complete his development after ...♔g7.

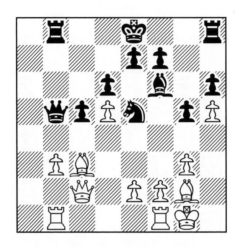

> **Exercise:** Taking into consideration the relative strength of the minor pieces on the board, what is a good continuation for Black to consider?

23...♕d7!?

Answer: Black should try to trade off the dark-squared bishops as his knight is stronger than the g2-bishop: 23...♘d7 24 b4 ♗xc3 25 bxc5 ♕xc5 26 ♖xb8+ ♘xb8 27 ♖c1 0-0 28 ♕xc3 ♕xc3 29 ♖xc3 ♘a6, although White should be able to draw this with careful play.

The text is an attempt to exploit the omission of ♗h3 to threaten ...♕g4xh5 and this provoked White to lash out.

24 b4?!

White attempts to liquidate one of his two weaknesses (the other being the lone ranger on h5). Instead, he might play on the light squares with 24 ♗e4! ♕h3 25 ♗xe5 ♗xe5 26 b4! c4 27 ♕xc4 0-0 with mutual chances.

24...cxb4 25 ♗xb4 ♖c8 26 ♕b3

26 ♕d1! is better.

26...♕g4 27 ♖fc1 0-0

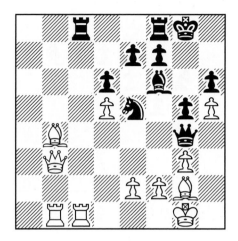

It is very difficult to contain Black's activity, especially in a rapid game.

28 ♖xc8 ♖xc8 29 ♗f3 ♘xf3+ 30 ♕xf3??

Better was 30 exf3 ♕xh5, although White is still suffering here.

30...♕xf3 31 exf3 ♖b8 0-1

White has no good way of extricating himself from the pin and so resigned.

Game 17
L.Schandorff-R.Skytte
Danish League 2011

1 d4 ♘f6 2 c4 c5 3 d5 b5 4 cxb5 a6 5 bxa6 g6 6 ♘c3 ♗xa6 7 g3 d6 8 ♗g2 ♗g7 9 ♘f3 ♘fd7 10 0-0 ♘b6 11 ♕c2 ♘8d7 12 ♖d1 0-0 13 ♖b1

Getting the rook off the long diagonal before making plans to secure the queenside pawns with a2-a4 and b2-b3.

13 ♗d2 to discourage a future ...♕a5 looks pretty artificial: 13...♘c4 14 ♗e1 ♕b6 15 b3 ♘a3 16 ♕c1 ♘b5 17 e3 ♖fb8 and Black has easy play, V.Malisauskas-S.Kasparov, Wroclaw 2012, and after 13 e4 ♘c4 14 ♘d2 ♕a5! 15 ♘xc4 ♗xc4 16 ♗d2 (if 16 ♗g5 ♖fe8) 16...♘e5 Black is again doing well.

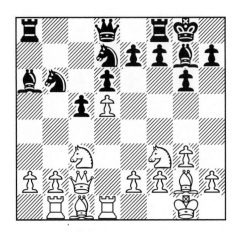

13...♘c4

Paving the way for ...♛a5.

> **Question:** Why not win a pawn with 13...♗xc3 14 ♛xc3 ♗xe2?

Answer: Perhaps this is actually the best way to play and after 15 ♗h6 ♘f6 16 ♖d2 (it is interesting that Topalov declined the win of the exchange with 16 ♖e1 ♘bxd5 17 ♛d2 ♗b5 18 ♗xf8 ♛xf8 19 a3 when Black has some compensation for the pawn; I quite like both White's material and Black's activity and central pawn mass, so it's a toss up) 16...♗xf3 17 ♗xf3 ♖e8 with equal play, V.Topalov-M.Leon Hoyos, Mexico City (rapid) 2010.

14 ♗h3!

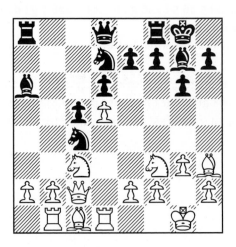

> **Question:** What is the point of wasting a move with the bishop?

Answer: The beauty of this subtle move is that Black's automatic and annoying ...♕a5 is immediately prevented. Hence White plans to push away the knight on c4 with b2-b3 without allowing it the chance to go to a3, blockading the a-pawn.

Instead, after 14 ♘d2 ♕a5 15 ♘xc4 ♗xc4 16 ♗d2 Black has two ways of winning his pawn back: 16...♗xa2 (or 16...♗xc3 17 ♗xc3 ♕xa2 18 ♕d2 ♘b6 which is okay for Black as the c3-bishop is only optically strong and he can defend with ...f7-f6 without problem, V.Neverov-N.Pedersen, Dieren 2010) 17 ♖a1 ♗xc3 18 ♗xc3 ♕b5 was fine for Black in F.Peralta-M.Leon Hoyos, Istanbul Olympiad 2012.

Note too 14 b3 ♕a5 15 ♘a4 (15 bxc4 ♕xc3 16 ♕xc3 ♗xc3 17 ♗g5 ♗f6 18 ♗xf6 ♘xf6 19 ♘d2 ♗c8 20 ♖b2 ♖a4 gives Black sufficient compensation) 15...♗b5 16 ♘d2 ♘cb6! 17 ♘xb6 ♘xb6 18 a4 ♗xe2 19 ♖e1 ♕a6 20 ♘c4 ♗xc4 21 bxc4 ♕xc4 22 ♕xc4 ♘xc4 23 ♖xe7 ♖xa4 with the upper hand for Black in A.Gallardo Garcia-D.Ortega Hermida,Mondariz 2007.

14...♗c8

To give the knight access to a3. The alternatives fail to equalize:

a) 14...♕c7 15 b3 ♘ce5 16 ♗b2 with a slight pull for White.

b) 14...♘ce5 15 ♘e1! leaves the black knights fighting for the same squares and, as Dvoretsky would say, the knight on e1 renders the e5-knight superfluous.

c) 14...♘de5 15 ♘xe5 ♘xe5 16 b3 ♕a5 17 ♗b2! (17 ♗d2 ♗d3! 18 exd3 ♘f3+ 19 ♔g2 ♘xd2 20 ♖xd2 ♗xc3 21 ♖e2 with equal play) 17...♗c8 18 ♗xc8 ♖fxc8 19 ♗a1 c4 20 b4 ♕a3 21 b5 ♖cb8 (not 21...♖ab8? 22 ♘a4! to place the bishop on d4 before playing ♘c3 again) 22 ♖dc1 and White's passed b-pawn gives him a slight edge.

15 b3 ♘a3?!

This merely gives White an extra tempo to solidify the queenside pawns, but even after 15...♘ce5 16 ♘xe5 ♘xe5 17 ♗xc8 ♕xc8 18 ♔g2! (if 18 a4 ♕h3 19 f3 ♖fb8 20 ♘b5 ♗f6 21 ♗d2 h5 with some attacking chances) 18...♕b7 19 a4 White has the better game after an eventual ♘b5.

16 ♗xa3 ♖xa3 17 ♘b5 ♖a8 18 a4! ♗a6

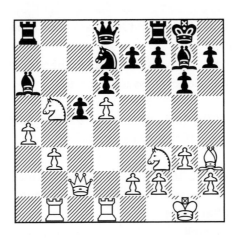

> **Question:** How does White make his pawn advantage count here?

Answer: 19 b4!

Schandorff does not waste time in making his extra pawn count. Aside from eradicating the backward pawn, White also tries to contest the d4-square for a knight.

19...♘b6

After 19...cxb4 20 ♘fd4 White is poised to plant a knight on c6.

20 bxc5 dxc5

Not 20...♗xb5 21 axb5 dxc5 22 ♕xc5 with winning chances for White.

21 e4 ♗c8

There's nothing else to do really, as shown by 21...♗xb5 22 ♖xb5 ♘xa4 23 e5.

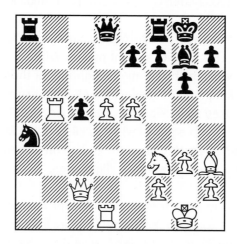

Despite the material parity, Black is almost lost. White just have to arrange the doubling of his rooks on the a-file and the c5-pawn will drop off.

For example, Black can try 23...♖a7 24 ♖b3 ♕a5 25 ♖a1 ♖fa8 26 ♖ba3 ♕b5 and White just plays ♗f1-e2-d1 when the black knight must abandon a4 and the defence of c5.

22 ♗xc8 ♕xc8 23 ♘a7 ♕a6

Better is 23...♖xa7 24 ♖xb6 which resembles an Exchange Grünfeld gone wrong for Black, but at least there's still a lot of chess to be played.

24 ♘c6 e6

If 24...♖fe8 25 a5 ♘c4 26 ♖b3 ♘xa5 27 ♖a3 ♕c4 28 ♕b1! ♘xc6 29 ♖xa8 ♖xa8 30 dxc6 and the passed c-pawn will win the game for White.

25 ♖b5

More clinical is 25 dxe6!? fxe6 26 ♘g5 ♘c4 27 ♘xe6 ♕xc6 28 ♕xc4 ♖xa4 29 ♕d5 and after the forced queen trade, the passed d-pawn will be unstoppable.

25...exd5 26 exd5 ♕xa4 27 ♖xc5 ♕g4

A desperate attempt to complicate.

28 ♕b3 ♘d7 29 ♖c4 ♕h5??

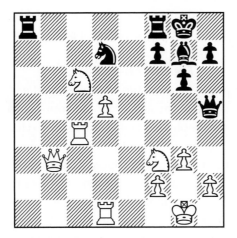

Whoops, the queen is now caught. The only move was 29...♖a3 when 30 ♕xa3 ♕xc4 31 ♔g2 just gives White a big advantage.

30 ♖h4 ♘c5 31 ♘e7+ ♔h8 32 ♕e3 1-0

Game 18
I.Khenkin-L.Delfino
Gallipoli 2012

1 d4 ♘f6 2 c4 c5 3 d5 b5 4 cxb5 a6 5 bxa6 g6 6 ♘c3 ♗xa6 7 ♘f3 d6 8 g3 ♗g7 9 ♗g2 ♘fd7 10 0-0 ♘b6 11 ♕c2 ♘8d7

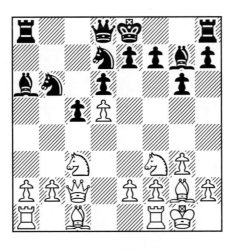

12 ♖d1

♕c2 and ♖d1 is a standard plan for White in the Classical and Fianchetto Benko lines. White does not allow Black to make use of the d3-square by delaying/or omitting e2-e4, and plans to secure his queenside first via b2-b3, ♖bc1 and ♗b2 or ♗d2. At the correct juncture, he might play a2-a4 and try to establish a piece on c4 or b5.

> **Exercise:** After 12 b3 do you:
> a) Hack off the e2-pawn, because White can't snag the bishop due to ...♗xa1?
> b) Clip the d5-pawn instead because it's more in-your-face and maybe White might just decide to go the whole hog and sacrifice the exchange with 13 ♘xd5?

Answer: Correct is 12...♗xe2!. I must admit though to taking the d5-pawn three times, twice in Internet blitz and once in a local blitz event. All three times I suffered massively having to defend for the rest of the game. At the Balestier blitz event, I recall CM Quek Suan Shiau, the former Welsh Champion, looking aghast as I lopped off the d5-pawn and then started looking more and more confident as the game progressed with one-way traffic. Perhaps the only reason he didn't finish me off eventually was because I was the organizer of the event.

It's no wonder Benko Gambit guru Sergey Kasparov plucked the e2-pawn against GM Rodshtein instead and ended up with a slight plus: 12...♗xe2 13 ♖e1 ♗a6 14 ♗g5 ♘f6 15 ♖ad1 0-0 16 ♘h4 ♖a7 17 ♕c1 ♖e8 18 ♗h6 ♗h8 and Black has a slight advantage as he can continue pressuring White's queenside.

Instead, after 12...♘xd5?! 13 ♘xd5 ♗xa1 14 ♗h6! ♗b7 (or 14...e6 15 ♖xa1 exd5 16 e4! d4 17 e5! dxe5 18 ♗g7 ♖g8 19 ♘xe5 ♘xe5 20 ♗xe5 ♖c8 21 b4! f6 22 ♗f4 g5 23 ♗d2 ♔f8 24 bxc5, again with fantastic compensation) 15 ♘g5 e6 16 ♖xa1 ♗xd5 17 ♗xd5 exd5 18 ♖d1 ♘b6 19 ♖d3 d4 20 ♘xf7! ♔xf7 21 ♖f3+ ♔e8 22 ♕e4+ ♕e7 23 ♕c6+ ♕d7 24 ♕xb6 White has very good compensation for the exchange.

Returning to Khenkin's 12 ♖d1:

12...0-0 13 b3!?

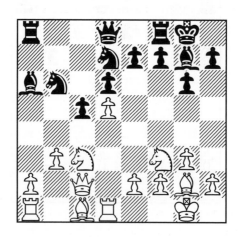

Annotators of this move tend to give it a question mark. However, the resulting positions are the sort of equality where Black must be very careful as White has opportunities to keep improving his position, especially by mobilizing his queenside pawns.

13...♗xe2 14 ♕xe2 ♗xc3 15 ♗b2

Both Sergey Kasparov and Igor Stohl (who annotated in *ChessBase Magazine*) felt that the resulting positions in this line are unclear. Likewise, 15 ♖b1 ♗g7 16 h4 ♘f6 17 ♘g5 ♕c7 18 ♗e3 ♖fb8 19 ♖bc1 ♕d8 20 ♖c2 ♖a7 21 ♗c1 ♖ba8 22 ♘h3 is deemed murky, M.Ezat-S.Kasparov, Abu Dhabi 2003.

15...♗xb2 16 ♕xb2 ♘f6

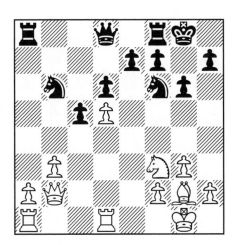

It would seem that Black has the better position with one solid pawn island, good pressure against d5 and the opportunity to exert heavy pressure down the a- and b-files. However, a strong knight manoeuvre puts White back in the mix. According to the *Houdini* engine, this position is equal, but during my online blitz games with it, I felt uncomfortable with Black, though I had mixed results: one win and one loss.

Actually, it's a matter of taste as to whether one prefers White or Black. I asked the current champions of Singapore and Malaysia, IM Goh Wei Ming Kevin and IM Lim Yee Weng respectively, which side they prefer in this position. Wei Ming unequivocally said he'll take Black anytime and Yee Weng preferred the white side. I suppose it's a matter of whether you prefer space (White) or latent chances (Black). IM Miodrag Perunovic also preferred Black, highlighting that the g2-bishop's job is just to hold d5 and that Black can pile up on the a-file at will.

17 ♘e1!

The knight is heading to e3 where it guards the d5-pawn, keeps an eye on c4 and, in good time, can help with the f2-f4-f5 advance.

Otherwise, 17 ♘g5?! ♕d7! with the idea of ...♕f5 adds further pressure on the d-pawn (in an online blitz game, I got slowly and surely outplayed after 17...h6 18 ♘e4 ♔g7?! 19 ♘xf6 exf6 20 a4 ♘d7 21 b4 cxb4 22 ♕xb4 ♘c5 23 a5 and White's passed pawn gives him good chances to win, D.Gicic-J.Tay, Internet (blitz) 2013), and after 18 ♖d2 (or 18 h4 ♖a7 19 ♕d2 ♖fa8 20 a4 c4! and White is in trouble as his queenside pawns are about to be dismantled, A.Goganov-S.Kasparov, Peterhof 2008) 18...♖fb8 19 ♕c3 ♕f5 20 h4 ♘fxd5 21 ♗xd5 ♘xd5 22 ♕c4 e6 23 ♖ad1 ♖b4 24 ♕c1 h6 Black won in B.Morchiashvili-S.Kasparov, Internet (blitz) 2007.

17...♕d7

After 17...♖a7 18 ♘c2 ♕a8 19 ♘e3 Miodrag Perunovic indicated that if Black wants he can simply take a draw after 19...♖a3 (or 19...♖b8 with a pleasant game) 20 ♘c2 ♖a7 21 ♘e3 ♖a3.

18 ♘c2

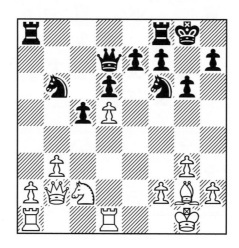

18...♖fc8

This was played with the intention of pushing ...c5-c4 under favourable situations.

Even Sergey Kasparov himself relaxed too soon and a crucial pawn was swiped off after 18...♖fb8 19 ♘e3 ♕a7 20 ♖d2 ♕a3 21 ♕c2 ♘bd7 22 ♖e1 ♖a7?? 23 ♘c4 ♕a6 24 ♖xe7, with winning chances as Black's pieces were too badly placed to fend off White's central breakthrough in M.Rodshtein-S.Kasparov, Internet (blitz) 2006.

With hindsight, I think Black can try 18...♕b7! to tie the white bishop and knight down to defending the d5-pawn while still putting pressure on the a- and b-files, and if 19 ♘e3 ♖fb8 20 ♖d2 ♖a7 with the idea of ...♖ba8.

19 ♘e3 ♕a7

Aiming to put the queen on a3 to blockade the a-pawn. The funny thing is that if Black 'blunders' a pawn with 19...c4!? 20 ♕d4 ♕b7 21 bxc4 ♘a4 22 ♖ab1 ♕a7 23 ♕d2 ♘c5 then his position is suddenly easier to play. The difference is that he can put pressure on the a-pawn more easily and White will end up with the inferior position if the pawn drops.

20 ♗f1 ♕a3 21 ♕d2!

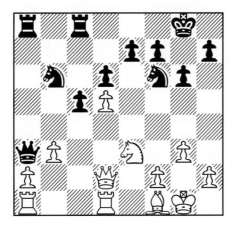

White must keep the queens to retain winning chances. In order to do that, he must:

1) Evict the queen from a3.

2) Push the a-pawn to a4 under favourable conditions.

3) Stick the bishop on b5 when the queenside should be secure.

21...♖c7 22 ♗b5

A clever little move, eyeing the c6 outpost and tempting Black.

22...♕b4

Delfino aims to switch pieces on a3 and perhaps double rooks on a3 and a7, but this allows Khenkin to improve his position and, suddenly, White's winning chances have improved significantly.

22...♖ac8 with the idea of ...♖ca7 gives Black equal chances, since 23 ♗c6 will be met by 23...e6 and now Black really has something to play for, or 23 ♘c2 ♕b2 with the idea of ...♕e5, attempting to pluck the d5-pawn.

23 a4!

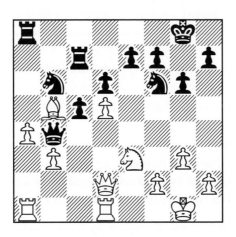

> ***Question:*** What's the difference between having the pawn on a2 and a4?

Answer: On a4, it has become a strong protected passed pawn supported by the bishop and b3-pawn. Also, Black has far less space to play with on the queenside. Lastly, the b3-pawn is poisoned.

23...♞e4??

Black misjudges the queenless ending and it's all over. After 23...♛xb3? 24 ♜db1! ♞e4 25 ♛d3 ♛xd3 26 ♝xd3 one of the knights must go, but he should have chosen 23...♛xd2 24 ♜xd2 ♜b8 25 f3, although even here Black must manoeuvre carefully on the back three ranks while White first tries to gain space on the kingside.

24 ♛xb4! cxb4 25 ♝c6

Surrounding the b-pawn. Black was already having trouble dealing with the passed a-pawn and now it's nigh on impossible to deal with two passed queenside pawns.

25...♜a5

It would make no difference to play 25...♞c3 26 ♝xa8 ♞xd1 27 ♜xd1 ♞xa8 28 ♜d4 ♜b7 29 ♞c2 and once the b-pawn falls, it's two connected pawns too many.

26 ♜d4 ♞c3 27 ♜xb4 ♞cxd5 28 ♝xd5 ♞xd5

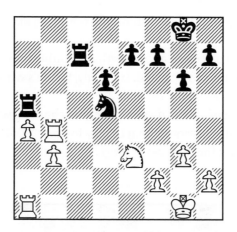

Black gets a pawn back, but the writing is already on the wall.

29 ♜b8+

Even simpler is 29 ♞xd5 ♜xd5 30 a5 ♜a7 31 a6 ♚g7 32 ♜b8 and the b-pawn marches to glory.

29...♚g7 30 b4 ♞xe3 31 bxa5

Not 31 fxe3? ♜d5 with drawing chances.

31...♞c4 32 a6 ♜a7 33 ♜b7 ♜xa6 34 ♜xe7 ♚f6 35 ♜e4 d5 36 ♜f4+ ♚e6 37 ♜e1+ ♞e5 38 ♚g2 f5 39 ♜h4 ♚d6 40 ♜xh7 ♜xa4 41 ♜h8 ♜e4 42 ♜d1 ♞d7 43 h4 ♞f6 44 ♜h6 1-0

That was pretty scary. Black only made one positional error and Khenkin adroitly took him to the cleaners.

Game 19
M.Nikolov-J.Cuenca Jimenez
Roquetas de Mar 2013

1 d4 ♘f6 2 c4 c5 3 d5 b5 4 cxb5 a6 5 bxa6 g6 6 ♘c3 ♗xa6 7 ♘f3 d6 8 g3 ♗g7 9 ♗g2 ♘fd7 10 ♗d2

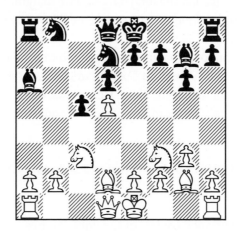

This move, in conjunction with Black's next, intends to meet ...0-0 with the standard ♗h6, h2-h4-h5 attack more commonly associated with the King's Indian Sämisch, the Closed Sicilian and the Sicilian Dragon.

Instead, after the 10 ♗f4 ♘b6 11 ♕c1 h6 12 0-0 (or 12 h4!? ♘8d7 13 a4 ♘c4 and thanks to the weakening h2-h4, Black can happily put one knight on e5) 12...♘8d7 13 ♖d1 ♘c4 14 b3 of Y.Yakovich-S.Kasparov, Sochi 2004, the black player pointed out that the ultra-sharp 14...g5! gives Black good play in his *The Dynamic Benko Gambit*.

10...♘b6 11 ♕c1 h6!

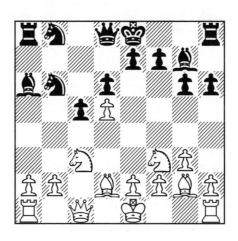

Preventing the d2-bishop's access to h6. This also means that the black king must remain in the centre for quite a while, but it sure beats getting swiftly plucked on the kingside: 11...0-0? 12 ♗h6 ♘8d7 13 h4 ♘f6 14 h5! and White is having a jolly good time.

12 b3

White prevents ...♘c4.

12...♗b7

Now that White has weakened the long dark-square diagonal, Black reroutes his bishop temporarily to hit d5 as the c3-knight has been pinned down by the bishop on g7.

13 e4

White decides to hold on to his pawn. In an earlier game, he returned the pawn to trade a couple of minor pieces: 13 0-0 ♘xd5 14 ♘xd5 ♗xd5 15 ♗c3 0-0 16 ♗xg7 ♔xg7 17 ♕c3+ ♔h7 18 ♘g5+ hxg5 19 ♗xd5 ♖a7. Here Glenn Flear remarked that Black's centre pawn phalanx counterbalanced White's better minor piece in S.Agdestein-R.Djurhuus, Sandefjord 2012.

13...♗a6

Mission accomplished. Black's bishop returns to a6 to take control of the light squares once again.

14 ♗f1

Opposing the aforementioned control of the light squares.

14...♕c8

A tricky little queen shift which threatens to allow the lady access to h3 if allowed.

Instead, 14...e6!? 15 a4 ♕f6, exacting strong pressure on the long dark-square diagonal, is an interesting suggestion of Glenn Flear's on chesspublishing.com.

15 h3

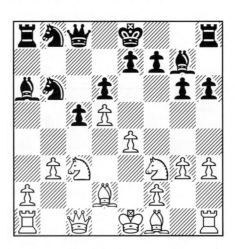

To deny the queen access to h3 after ...♗xf1.

15...♘8d7?!

A trifle careless as now White gets in his ideal queenside advance.

Taking a leaf from Sergey Kasparov's analysis of his game against Yakovich, Black should consider the sharp 15...g5 16 a4 f5! when he has a nice aggressive game.

16 a4!

Creating an outpost on b5 for White. This b2-b3 and a2-a4 set-up together with a knight on b5 is usually the bane of Benko Gambiteers, who in certain variations go to extreme lengths to prevent it from happening.

16...♞f6

The b6-knight must have somewhere to go to after a4-a5.

17 ♝xa6?!

White returns the favour in his attempt to set up the standard queenside blockade plan with ♞b5. This allows Black to regain his gambitted pawn with a reasonable game. White should continue 17 a5! ♞bd7 18 ♝c4 with little chance for Black to do anything active.

17...♛xa6 18 ♞b5?! 0-0 19 0-0 ♞xe4 20 ♝xh6 ♞xd5

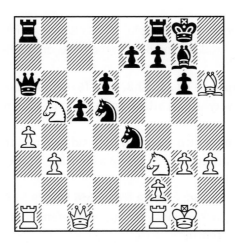

Black has equalized. Though White has attained the desired queenside blockade, Black has a nice centre and a compact V-formation pawn structure.

21 ♖e1 ♞ef6 22 ♛g5 ♛b7 23 ♝xg7 ♚xg7 24 ♞h4

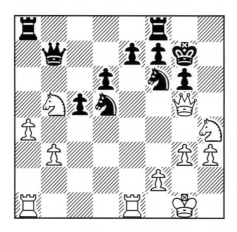

Exercise: Can Black play 24...♖h8 here, intending
to play ...♖h5 and double the rooks on the h-file?

Answer: Black would be stunned by 24...♖h8? 25 ♘f5+ ♔f8 26 ♖xe7! ♘xe7 27 ♕xf6 ♖h7 28
♘fxd6 when White has a very strong attack and still retains the material balance.
24...♘h7 25 ♕d2 ♘df6

Now some jostling in the centre occurs by both sides; White tries to restrain Black's central advance and Black, in attempting to set up a kingside attack, makes use of the light
squares around the white king.
26 ♕e3 ♖fe8 27 ♖ac1 ♕d7 28 ♔g2 ♘d5 29 ♕d2 ♘hf6 30 ♘f3 ♖h8 31 h4 e5!

Black threatens ...e5-e4, kicking away the natural defender of the white king and gaining even more space in the centre.
32 ♖c4!

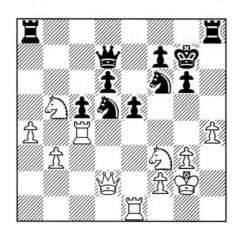

Rooks operate not only on files, but also on ranks. This is a fine defensive idea by the Bulgarian Grandmaster. In response, the Spanish IM, who has already obtained his three GM norms, decided to up the ante.

32...♘f4+!?

> **Question:** How does White respond against 32...e4?

Answer: He must not hesitate to sacrifice the exchange and trust his extra pawns to hold the balance: 33 ♖cxe4! (after 33 ♘g5 Black can prise open the kingside with 33...♖xh4!) 33...♘xe4 34 ♕xd5 ♘f6 35 ♕xd6 ♕xd6 36 ♘xd6 ♖ad8 37 ♘b7 ♖d5 38 ♖e5 ♖xe5 39 ♘xe5 ♘e4 40 a5 ♖a8 41 ♘c4 ♖a7 42 ♔f3 f5 43 ♘d8 ♖a6 44 ♘b7 ♔f6 45 ♔e3 ♖a7 46 ♘d8 and White should be able to hold.

33 ♖xf4?!

Also 33 gxf4 ♕g4+ 34 ♔f1 ♕xf3 is bad for White, but he can coolly play 33 ♔g1! ♕h3 34 ♖xf4 exf4 35 ♖e7 and now the threat of ♖xf7 or ♘g5 is so great that Black is forced to go on the defensive: 35...♖af8? (after 35...♖hf8 36 ♘g5 ♕g4 37 ♕c3 fxg3 38 fxg3 ♔g8 39 ♕xf6 ♕xg3+ 40 ♔h1 ♕xh4+ 41 ♔g2 ♕g4+ 42 ♔f2 ♕h4+ White cannot avoid the checks, or 35...♖h5 36 ♘xd6 ♖f8 37 ♕xf4 ♖d5 38 a5 ♖d1+ 39 ♘e1 ♖d4 40 ♕e5 ♖d5 41 ♕f4 ♖d4 42 ♕e5 ♖d5, perpetually checking the queen) 36 ♘g5 ♕g4 37 ♕xf4! ♕xf4 38 ♘e6+ ♔g8 39 ♘xf4 d5 40 ♖c7 with the advantage to White. Of course, *Houdini* spit out these variations which are probably beyond human calculation, especially with a punishing time control.

33...exf4 34 ♕xf4 ♖ae8 35 ♖d1 d5

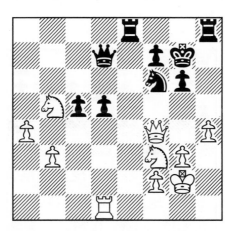

Black has the advantage thanks to his strong centre and his rooks can be mobilized easily on the e-file. White is, however, very solid with his well-placed knights and those fixed deposits (the a- and b-pawns) on the queenside. At this point, both sides started swapping blunders, with the 90 minutes plus 30 seconds increment time control most likely a contributing factor. Hence, the final drawn result after 41 moves was a fair result of this interesting fight.

36 b4 cxb4 37 ♕xb4 ♕g4 38 ♖d4 ♘e4 39 ♘c3 ♕f5 40 ♘xe4 dxe4 41 ♖xe4 ♖b8 ½-½

C) Fianchetto Sidelines

White can deviate from the standard fianchetto set-up with g3, ♘f3 and ♗g2 by placing the knight or bishop on h3 or even interpolate an early h2-h4. Indeed, in Kordts-Tay, White employs the set-up h2-h4 and ♘h3-f4, with the idea of a kingside attack with f2-f3 and g3-g4. In this system, Black should counter h2-h4 with ...h7-h5 and plant a knight on e5 to help watch over the kingside.

Alternatively, White can play for ♘h3-f4 positionally without the h4 lunge, as in Bukal-Brkic, but Black nevertheless develops smoothly on the queenside. White can also play 9 ♗h3 to give the bishop a more active role compared to the sleeping g2 slot, as in Nenciulescu-Evans, but the pressure on d5 exerted by Black makes the bishop superfluous there.

Last but not least, I would like to introduce you to FIDE and ICCF GM Vasily Borisovich Malinin, a hyper-aggressive attacking player, who, according to my database, has scored seven wins and no losses with 9 h4. From a theoretical viewpoint, perhaps the Malinin games are not critical as Black can transpose back into the 9...♘fd7 lines with 9...h6 before playing ...♘fd7. So just sit back and enjoy his attempts at hacking Benko Gambiteers.

> *Game 20*
> **W.Kordts-J.Tay**
> Correspondence 2000

1 d4 ♘f6 2 c4 c5 3 d5 b5 4 cxb5 a6 5 bxa6 ♗xa6 6 ♘c3 d6 7 g3 g6 8 ♘h3 ♗g7 9 ♘f4 ♘bd7 10 h4

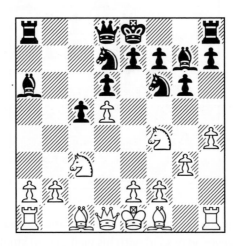

After the game, my opponent told me that this plan has scored 70+% in his databases. The idea is to attack Black on the kingside while keeping the queenside as compact as possible. GM Aleksandrov has been successful with this idea.

10...h5!

This is indicated as Black has virtually no chance of playing the ...e7-e6 break and thus has to operate entirely on the queenside. Moreover, allowing the pawn to advance to h5 would be a positional disaster. Why would anyone want to chance opening the h-file when Black is virtually operating only on the queenside?

In an earlier game, Black had unsuspectingly castled into a full-blooded attack by Aleksandrov and was promptly dispatched: 10...0-0?! 11 h5 ♞e5 12 hxg6 hxg6 13 ♕c2 ♕a5 14 ♗g2 ♗c8 15 ♗h3 ♗xh3 16 ♖xh3 ♖fb8 17 ♔f1 ♕b4 18 ♔g2 ♕b7 19 f3 ♖a6 20 g4 c4 21 ♕d1 ♕a8 22 ♕e1 ♞ed7 23 ♗e3 ♖xb2 24 ♗d4 g5 25 ♖d1 gxf4 26 g5 ♞g4 27 ♗xg7 ♔xg7 28 ♕h4 ♕g8 29 ♕xg4 ♞e5 30 ♕xf4 ♖a8 31 ♖dh1 ♞g6 32 ♕d4+ 1-0, A.Aleksandrov-G.Kochetkov, Minsk 1996.

11 ♕c2

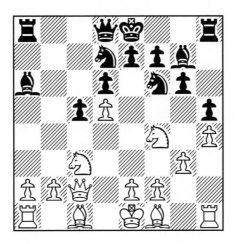

Keeping an eye on b2, c3 and especially g6 where a potential knight sacrifice looms.

11...♞e5

Question: Why 11...♞e5 instead of 11...♞b6?

Answer: On b6 the knight attacks d5, but in this line that point is firmly secured thanks to the f4-knight. On the other hand, e5 is a great outpost as the knight cannot be dislodged from that square easily as a future f2-f4 will allow an outpost even closer to the white king on g4. Also, it's good to have a knight to cover the g6-square in the event of any sacrifice by White on e6 or g6.

12 ♗h3

Aside from taking control of the h3-c8 diagonal, this move also supports g3-g4 and sets up potential ♗e6 and ♞e6 sacrificial ideas.

12...0-0 13 0-0

My opponent was contemplating too 13 f3 ♕b6 14 g4 hxg4 15 fxg4 ♞fxg4 (15...♕b4 might be a better move) 16 h5 g5 17 ♘g2 with a complex position as both kings are exposed.

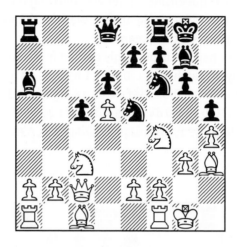

13...♕b6

Question: Is 13...♕b6 a better choice than 13...♕a5?

Answer: In this instance, the dark-squared bishop's diagonal is blocked by both knights and tactics based on ...♕a5 are less likely to succeed. Having said that, ...♕a5 is still a good move and there's nothing really wrong with it.

14 f3?!

White aims for g2-g4 with gxh5, ♘xh5, ♘xg6 and ♘e6 threats, but due to Black's pressure on the centre it never gets started.

14...♖fb8 15 ♔h2

White needs the rook on g1 before he can play g3-g4. The aggressive 15 g4 does not work though Black has to be careful: 15...hxg4 16 fxg4 ♘fxg4! (best: after 16...c4+ 17 ♔g2 ♘exg4 18 h5 gxh5 19 ♘xh5 ♕d4 20 ♘xg7 ♔xg7 21 ♖f4 ♘e3+ 22 ♗xe3 ♕xe3 23 ♖f3 White has activated all his pieces, 16...♕b4 17 g5 ♘fg4 18 ♘e6! fxe6 19 ♖f4 ♗c4 20 ♗xg4 ♘xg4 21 ♕xg6 ♘e5 22 ♕xe6+ ♔h8 23 h5 gives him attacking chances, or 16...♘exg4 17 h5 gxh5 18 ♘xh5 ♘xh5 19 ♗xg4 ♘f6 20 ♖f4 with counterchances) 17 h5 gxh5 18 ♘xh5 c4+ 19 ♔g2 ♘e3+ 20 ♗xe3 ♕xe3 21 ♘xg7 ♔xg7 22 ♖h1. Both of us reached this position in our analysis and concluded that Black stands better.

15...♗c4

Adding pressure to d5.

16 ♖g1 ♕a6!

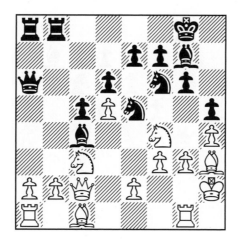

Question: What's the big deal about this move? What does it achieve?

Answer: It prevents the g3-g4 break: 17 g4?! ♗xe2! 18 ♕xe2 (after 18 ♘cxe2 ♘xf3+ 19 ♔g3 ♘xg1 20 ♘xg1 Black has the dominant position) 18...♕xe2+ 19 ♘fxe2 ♘xf3+ 20 ♔g3 ♘xg1 21 ♘xg1 ♘xg4 22 ♗xg4 ♗e5+ 23 ♔f3 hxg4+ 24 ♔xg4 ♖b4+ 25 ♔h3 ♖c4 26 ♘ge2 (if 26 ♗d2? ♖b8!) 26...♔g7 with the idea of ...♖h8 when Black's pieces are swarming all over the board.

17 ♖g2

17...♕b7

Question: What is Black doing, seemingly wasting moves with the queen?

Answer: The idea is to exert pressure on d5 to force the white queen away from the c2-square to the less dangerous d1-square.

18 ♕d1 ♗b3

Winning a tempo and forcing White to block his dark-squared bishop in. The a2-pawn is also pinned so the bishop is immune.

19 ♕d2 ♕b4

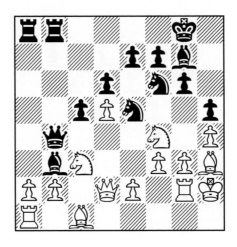

Question: Not again! How about this queen move – what does it do?

Answer: It is aimed primarily at 20 g4 hxg4 21 fxg4 ♘e4 22 ♘xe4 ♛xe4 when the queen obtains a great central square to direct operations from.

20 ♛e3

Now there is a way for Black to stop White's kingside threats in one fell swoop.

20...♘fg4+!

Thanks to the position of the white queen, this blow is possible. Black wins back his pawn with the better position.

21 ♗xg4 hxg4 22 h5

Hoping to create some weaknesses around the black king.

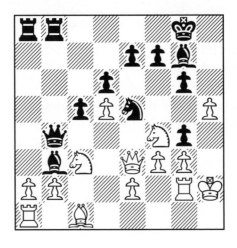

22...gxf3?!

Answer: 22...♕d4! 23 hxg6 (or 23 ♕f2 gxf3 24 exf3 g5 25 ♗e3 ♕b4) 23...♕xe3 24 gxf7+ ♔xf7 25 ♗xe3 ♗c4! with chances for Black to win due to his superb queenside pressure supported by the bishop-pair.

23 exf3 gxh5 24 ♘xh5 ♕d4

Now Black merely has the better game.

25 ♖f2 ♗h6

Taking advantage of the unfortunate position of the rook on f2 to angle for a favourable queen trade.

Instead, after 25...♕xe3 26 ♗xe3 ♘d3 27 ♖d2 (if 27 ♘xg7 ♘xf2 28 ♘f5 ♘d3 29 ♘xe7+ ♔f8 30 ♘c6 ♖b6 31 a3 ♗xd5 32 ♘xd5 ♖xc6) 27...♘e5 28 ♔g2 ♘c4 29 ♖e2 ♗xc3 30 bxc3 ♘xe3+ 31 ♖xe3 ♔f8 Black has an edge, while 25...♗h8 26 ♕g5+ ♘g6 27 ♗e3 ♕e5 sees him forcing a trade of queens with the advantage.

26 ♘f4

A forced move and one which avoids 26 ♕xd4?! cxd4 27 ♗xh6 dxc3 28 bxc3 ♗xd5 29 ♗f4 ♘xf3+ 30 ♔h3 ♖b5 31 g4 ♖a3 with the advantage for Black

26...♗c4

Sooner or later the bishop needs to retreat to this square and now a ...♗xf4 and ...♘d3 mechanism is looking dangerous.

27 ♕e1!

Threatening to trap the black queen with ♗e3.

27...♗xf4 28 gxf4

Of course, not 28 ♗xf4?? ♘d3.

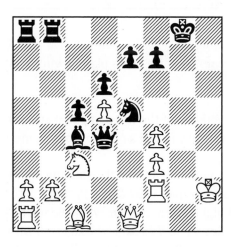

28...♘g6!

> **_Question:_** Why not 28...♘d3, putting more pressure on b2 and f4?

Answer: White gets counterplay after 29 ♖g2+ ♔f8 30 ♕h4 ♔e8.

29 ♖g2 ♔f8!

Removing the only source of counterplay from White by bringing the king to safety in the centre.

30 ♕f2 ♔e8

Possible too were 30...♘xf4!? 31 ♕xd4 cxd4 32 ♗xf4 dxc3 33 bxc3 ♗xd5 34 ♔g3 ♖c8 with a clear advantage for Black, as pointed out by Kordts, and 30...♕f6!? 31 ♔g1 ♔e8 32 ♗e3 ♔d7 when Black has access for his rooks to the kingside while the pressure on the queenside and in the centre continues.

31 ♕xd4 cxd4 32 ♘e2 ♗xe2 33 ♖xe2

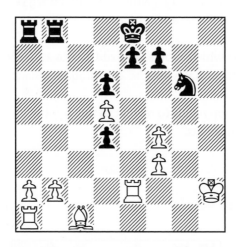

> **_Exercise:_** What is Black's plan to win from here?

33...d3?

A terrible move. I only worked out the win of a pawn and didn't look further. From here onwards, my opponent practically forced a draw by forcing me to liquidate into a rook ending.

Answer: Black can play for a win with 33...♔d7!, using the might of the two rooks against the exposed white king: for example, 34 a4 ♖h8+ 35 ♔g1 ♘h4 36 ♔f2 ♘f5 37 ♔e1 d3 38 ♖f2 ♘d4 and the superb knight dominates the whole board, or 34 ♔g1 ♖g8 35 ♖d2 (if 35 ♖e4 ♘h4+ 36 ♔f1 ♘f5 37 ♖e1 d3 38 ♖d1 ♖g3 39 ♖xd3 ♖h8 with a winning attack for Black) 35...♖ac8 36 ♔f1 ♖h8 37 f5 ♘e5 38 f4 ♘g4 39 ♔e2 ♖h1 and White is doomed.

34 ♖d2! ♘xf4 35 ♔g3! ♘e2+ 36 ♔f2 ♖c8 37 ♖d1 ♘xc1 38 ♖dxc1 ♖xc1 39 ♖xc1 ♖xa2 40 ♔e3 ♖xb2 41 ♔xd3 e6 42 dxe6 fxe6 43 f4 ♔e7 44 ♖c8 ♖b3+ 45 ♔e2 d5 46 ♖a8 ♖b4 47 ♔f3 ♖e4

48 ♖a6 ♖c4 49 ♖a8 ♔d6 50 ♖a6+ ♖c6 51 ♖a5 ♔c7 52 ♖a8 ♔b6 53 ♖e8 ♔c5 54 ♔e3 ♔d6 55 ♖d8+ ♔e7 ½-½

1 d4 g6 2 c4 ♘f6 3 g3 c5 4 d5 b5 5 cxb5 a6 6 bxa6 d6 7 ♘c3 ♗g7 8 ♗g2 0-0 9 ♘h3

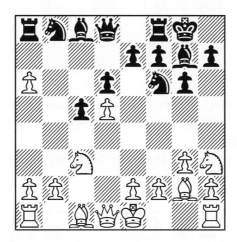

White doesn't want his knight impeding the fianchettoed bishop's access to d5 and plans to place the knight on f4 to further support that pawn. However, this manoeuvre is too slow and the knight will soon merely perform a defensive duty.

9...♗xa6 10 0-0 ♘bd7 11 ♘f4

The knight supports the d-pawn, but has too little influence on defending against Black's queenside play.

In *Play the Benko Gambit*, Nicolai Pedersen indicated that Black has good compensation after 11 ♕c2 ♖a7!? 12 b3 ♕a8 13 ♖b1 ♖b8 with equal chances, while top GM Alexander Grischuk demonstrated a model way of handling the ♖b1, b2-b3, a2-a4 and ♘b5 plan: 11 ♗d2 ♕b6 12 ♕c2 ♖fb8 13 ♖ab1 ♘e5 14 b3 ♗c8 15 ♘g5 (or 15 a4 ♗f5 16 e4 ♗d7) 15...♗f5 16 e4 ♗d7! (White's plan has been scuttled; Grischuk now plays to undermine the white centre) 17 ♘f3 ♘fg4 18 ♘e1 f5!. Objectively the position is equal, but White had been diverted from his typical play in E.Alekseev-A.Grischuk, Elista 2008.

11...♕a5 12 ♕c2

12 h4 is met by 12...h5, securing the g4-square.

12...♘b6 13 ♖b1 ♘fd7

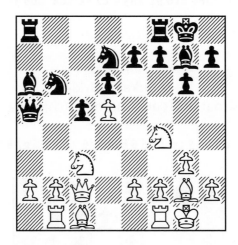

It's smooth sailing for Black, especially when White can't even use the king's knight to contest the c4-square unlike in the ♘f3 variations where White has ♘fd2.

14 ♗d2 ♘c4 15 ♗e1 ♖fb8

Yes, Black is risking a discovered attack, but there isn't a good one.

16 ♕c1 ♗c8!

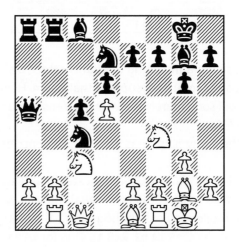

Great anticipation.

Question: What is the point of this retreat? Why retreat the bishop unnecessarily?

Answer: Black's plan is to answer 17 b3 with 17...♘a3 and after 18 ♘a4, uncovering an attack on the queen, Black can play 18...♕b5 19 ♕xa3 ♖xa4! 20 bxa4 ♕xb1 with the better game and pawn structure.

17 ♗e4

Perhaps to play ♗c2 to support a future a2-a4 and b2-b3 set-up.

17...♛b6

The pressure on b2 is just too excruciating for White.

18 ♘d3

Adding another defender to b2, but Black can put even more pressure on that spot.

18...♘de5!

Exchanging one of the pawn's defenders. White is forced to trade to prevent Black from playing ...♗h3.

19 ♘xe5 ♗xe5

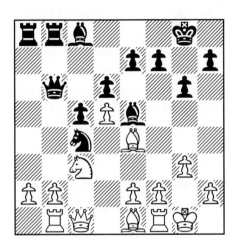

Exercise: Work out how can Black press ahead after 20 b3.

Answer: Black meets 20 b3 with 20...♘a3 21 ♖a1 c4! 22 bxc4 ♗h3 23 ♗g2 ♗xg2 24 ♔xg2 ♛c5 when White is in serious trouble.

20 ♔g2

Preventing ...♗h3. This might be the reason why White played ♗e4 earlier.

Question: Is 20...♘xb2 walking into a self-pin playable?

Answer: Yes, but it's pretty risky as Black will need a few moves to get the queen out of the pin.

20...♘xb2

Black must have worked out that he can get away with this.

21 h4?

Now the initiative goes back to Black and this time there's no coming back. Instead, 21 f4! ♗g7 22 f5 ♗d7 23 ♛f4 gives White some chances on the kingside.

21...♛b4!

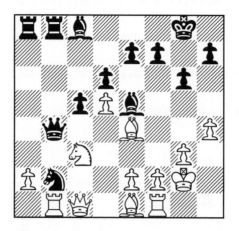

Preventing the knight on c3 from moving such as to d1. White must now do something about the potentially loose bishop on e4.

22 ♕c2 ♕c4

Getting out of the pin at last.

23 f3??

This attempt to protect the bishop doesn't work. White had to accept a worse position after 23 f4 ♗xc3 24 ♗xc3 f5 25 ♗f3 ♘a4 26 ♖xb8 ♖xb8 26 ♗c1 when he has the inferior pawn structure.

23...f5

The rest is like that proverbial piece of cake.

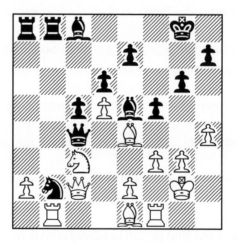

24 ♖xb2

Exercise: Work out the ramifications of 24 ♗d3.

Answer: 24...♘xd3 25 exd3 ♖xa2!! is a beautiful shot.

24...♖xb2 25 ♕xb2 fxe4 26 ♕b3 ♕xb3 27 axb3 e3

Jamming in the white king, rook and bishop which is sufficient to win in a while.

28 f4 ♗d4 29 ♔f3 h5 30 ♘b5 ♗g4+ 0-1

1 d4 ♘f6 2 c4 c5 3 d5 b5 4 cxb5 a6 5 bxa6 g6 6 ♘c3 ♗xa6 7 ♘f3 d6 8 g3 ♗g7 9 ♗h3!?

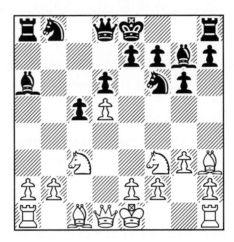

Question: What is the bishop doing here? Isn't it just hitting air and shouldn't it be on g2 instead?

Answer: Well, firstly, it prevents the ...♘g4-e5 manoeuvre and, secondly, it is arguably more active than on g2. However, the placement of the bishop means that there is less protection of the e4-square (for the e2-e4 push), and the d5-pawn.

9...♘bd7

There is no rush to castle here.

10 0-0 ♘b6!

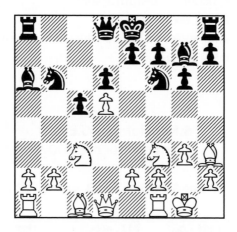

> **Question:** What if anything is the difference between
> ...♘b6 here and 10...0-0 followed by 11...♘b6?

Answer: After 10...0-0, the d5-pawn is hit only once. Thus White can switch pieces to defend it with 11 ♕c2! ♘b6 12 ♖d1 when he can plan for a solidifying e2-e4, a2-a4, ♖b1 and b2-b3 set-up. The early ...♘b6 idea also works well in lines where White plays 9 ♗g2 ♗g7 10 0-0, as we have seen.

11 ♖e1

Removing the rook from the bishop's gaze and preparing e2-e4.

Instead, 11 ♗f4 0-0 12 ♖e1 ♘c4 13 b3 (or 13 ♕c1 ♕a5 14 ♖b1 ♖fb8 with a comfortable game for Black) 13...♘h5 14 ♖c1 ♘xf4 15 gxf4 was P.Kiriakov-Y.Solodovnichenko, Internet (blitz) 2006, when Black can continue 15...♕a5 16 ♕c2 ♘a3 with an easy game.

11...0-0

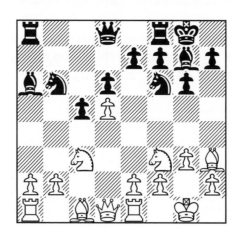

Answer: After 12 ♖b1?!, Black can reply 12...♗c4! 13 e4 (if 13 b3 ♘bxd5) 13...♗xa2 14 ♘xa2 ♖xa2 with equal chances. Black has the better structure and White has the bishop-pair to compensate for it.

12 e4 ♘fd7!

Restraining the e4-e5 advance. I just don't see the need to give White what he wants. That said, after 12...♘c4!? 13 e5 dxe5 14 ♘xe5 ♘xd5!? 15 ♕xd5 ♕xd5 16 ♘xd5 ♘xe5 17 ♘xe7+ ♔h8 18 ♗g2 ♖a7 19 ♘c6 ♘d3 20 ♘xa7 ♘xe1 Black is at least equal with his hyper-active minor pieces.

13 ♕c2!

Preparing b2-b3 by protecting the knight and also still keeping in touch with the d3-square. Alternatively:

a) 13 a4 ♘c4 14 ♖a2 ♖a7! 15 ♗f1 ♕a5 and Black developed smoothly in J.Murey-B.Avrukh, Israeli League 2009.

b) 13 ♗f4 ♘c4 14 ♕c2 h6! has the idea of ...g6-g5 to boot the bishop off f4 where it seeks exchanges. It's also a subtle finesse as with the bishop on h3, White cannot play h2-h4 to prevent ...g7-g5. Moreover, Igor Stohl demonstrated that Black even has sufficient counter-play after 14...♘de5 15 ♘xe5 ♘xe5 16 ♗xe5 ♗xe5 17 ♖ac1 ♕a5 18 b3 ♖fb8 19 ♗d7 ♖a7 20 ♗a4 c4!.

13...♘c4 14 ♗xd7

Since the bishop has no scope, White decides to trade it and hopes after his eventual b2-b3 and ♗b2 to exchange the strong bishop on g7. The late, great GM Tony Miles demonstrated how to meet 14 ♗f1: 14...♕a5 15 ♗xc4 ♗xc4 16 ♗d2 ♕a6! and White was already struggling in M.Gerusel-A.Miles, Bad Lauterberg 1977.

14...♕xd7 15 b3 ♘e5 16 ♘xe5 ♗xe5 17 ♗b2

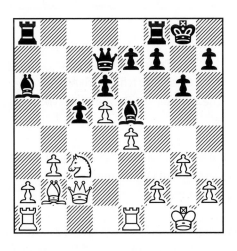

> **Question:** What would you recommend for Black here?

Answer: 17...f5!

Black should exploit the weak light squares around the white king by opening up the f-file.

If you had decided on the standard 17...♖fb8, let GM Beliavsky demonstrate how to snuff out any counterplay for Black: 18 ♘d1! ♗xb2 19 ♘xb2 ♕b7 20 ♖e3! ♗b5 21 ♘d1 ♗d7 22 ♖c3! (to overprotect the c4-square so there won't be any ...c5-c4 breaks in the near future; the rook also helps to protect b3 when White eventually evicts the a3-rook after ♘e3-c2, which is the deep point of ♖e3) 22...♖a3 23 ♘e3 with a solid edge for White in A.Beliavsky-S.Palatnik, Kiev 1978. White has a pleasant advantage here as Black cannot improve his position anymore to make up for his pawn deficit, whereas White can still continue to make pawn advances on both flanks and in his own time.

18 ♘d1 ♗xb2 19 ♘xb2

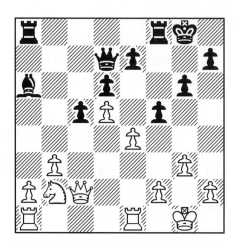

> **Exercise:** Does Black:
> a) Open the f-file with 19...fxe4?
> b) Go for the king with ...f5-f4 and maybe ...fxg3 or ...f3?

Answer: 19...f4

Give up the Benko, as well as the Dutch Defence, if you chose 19...fxe4? 20 ♕xe4 ♖f7 21 f4. This looks like a very sad Leningrad Dutch where White has successfully carried out the e2-e4 break and Black is just hemmed in.

20 ♘c4 ♕h3

Also good is 20...♖f7 21 ♕e2 (correct is 21 e5! ♕h3 22 exd6 exd6 23 ♕e4 and after 23...f3 24 ♘e3 there is no mating attack on g2, while 23...♖f5 24 ♕g2 ♕xg2+ 25 ♔xg2 fxg3 26 hxg3 ♖af8 f4 ♖xd5 28 ♖ad1 ♗xc4 29 bxc4 ♖xd1 30 ♖xd1 ♖a8 31 ♖xd6 ♖xa2+ 32 ♔f3 ♖c2 33 ♔g4 ♖xc4 34 ♔g5 ♖d4 35 ♖c6 ♖d5+ 36 ♔f6 ♖f5+ 37 ♔e6 h5 38 ♖c7 h4 39 gxh4 ♖xf4 40 h5 gxh5 41 ♖xc5 results in a draw) 21...♖af8 22 ♖ac1 ♕h3 23 ♖c2 ♗c8 when Black had an irresistable attack in A.Alekseev-G.Sagalchik, Minsk 1986.

21 ♕d3!

To give the queen access to f1.

21...f3 22 ♕f1

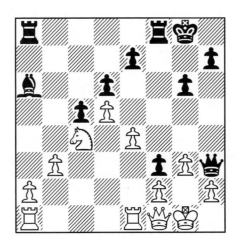

14 years ago, I had this position and simply couldn't find a way for Black to win. To my surprise, this more recent correspondence game saw Dr Gordon Evans winning with a direct attack.

22...♕h5?!

A tremendous gamble by Evans. When one takes such a chance in correspondence chess, if it backfires the suffering goes on for weeks or months, not mere minutes as during a normal game.

I preferred to simplify to a drawn ending with 22...♕xf1+ 23 ♔xf1 ♗xc4+ 24 bxc4 ♖a4 25 ♖e3 ♖fa8 26 ♖c1 ♖a3 27 ♖b3 ♔g7 28 ♔e1 ♔f6 29 ♖cc3 ♖xa2 30 ♖xf3+ ♔e5 31 ♖f7 ♖c2 32 ♖d3 ♖a1+ 33 ♖d1 ♖a7 34 ♖xh7 ♖xc4 35 f3 ♖c2 36 ♖h6 ♖aa2 ½-½, W.Utesch-J.Tay, correspondence 1999.

23 ♖e3 g5

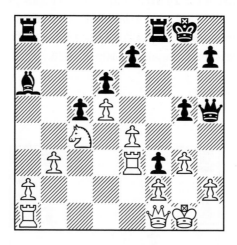

Exercise: Complete this sentence: A flank attack
is usually best met by counterattack in the...?

24 h3?

This seemingly useful defensive move weakens the white kingside and allows Black to add another piece into the attack.

Answer: Centre! After 24 e5! I think Black is worse. White has a nice space advantage and Black's pieces are pretty stuck on the flank: 24...♖f5 (or 24...♗c8 25 exd6 ♗h3 26 ♕c1) 25 exd6 exd6 26 ♖e7! ♖xd5 27 ♖d1! ♖xd1 28 ♕xd1 with a huge position for White. This was why I did not play 22...♕h5 back then. Moreover, when I rechecked my notes, *Houdini 3* verified my assessments.

24...♗c8!

Immediately Black zones in on the kingside.

25 ♔h2 ♖f6! 26 e5

Now the central break is too late.

26...♖h6 27 e6 ♕g4!

The queen is making its way to f5 where it still has an eye on h3 and targets d5.

28 a3 ♗a6

Multipurpose, pinning the knight and giving the other rook access to the kingside.

29 ♖c1 ♖f8 30 ♖ce1 ♖ff6!

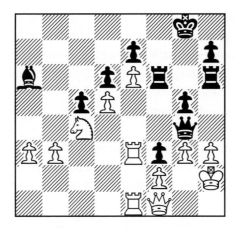

Preparing ...♖hh5 and ...♖fh6. White is in virtual zugzwang and has to cough up the d-pawn for starters.

31 ♖e4 ♕f5 32 ♖1e3 ♕xd5 33 ♖g4 ♕f5 34 ♔g1 ♗xc4 35 bxc4 ♖xe6 36 ♕d1 ♖xe3 37 fxe3 ♔h8 38 e4 ♕e5 39 h4 ♕b2 40 ♕f1 ♕d4+ 41 ♔h2 ♕e3 42 a4 gxh4 43 ♖xh4 ♖g6 44 g4 ♖f6 0-1

Game 23
V.Malinin-O.Vozovic
Sudak 2002

---

1 d4 ♘f6 2 c4 c5 3 d5 b5 4 cxb5 a6 5 bxa6 ♗xa6 6 ♘c3 d6 7 ♘f3 g6 8 g3 ♗g7 9 h4!?

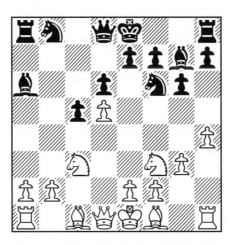

Question: What's this? A space-gaining move or an attacking lunge?

Answer: To Vasily Malinin, it is the start of a hackfest. The Russian GM is so successful in this line, I think we should refer to it as the Malinin Massacre line. My databases show him winning seven of his encounters and with no draws or losses. Just imagine four of these wins are from correspondence events. With months to analyse against such blatant aggression, as well as access to resources, Malinin's opponents nevertheless succumbed. Hence, I think we should look at this variation carefully to avoid getting blown off the board like those seven hardly shabby opponents.

9...♘bd7

A recent online blitz game showed how dangerous White's attack can be if Black ignores h2-h4 and simply plays 9...0-0 10 h5 ♘xh5 11 ♖xh5!? gxh5 12 ♕c2 ♘d7 13 ♘g5 ♗xc3+?! 14 bxc3 ♘f6 15 c4 ♖b8 16 ♗d2 ♖e8 17 ♖c1 h6

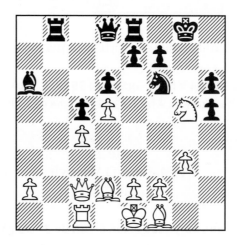

18 ♘e6! ♕b6 19 ♕f5 fxe6? 20 ♕g6+ ♔h8 21 ♕xh6+ ♔g8 22 ♗h3! ♗c8 23 dxe6 ♖d8 24 ♗c3 d5 25 ♕g6+ ♔h8 26 cxd5 ♗b7 27 ♗f5 ♗xd5 28 ♕h7#, O.Urcan-K.Jarriah, Internet (blitz) 2013.

Safest is 9...h6 which usually transposes to positions previously seen in the 9...♘fd7 lines, such as after 10 ♗g2 ♘fd7.

10 ♗h3

Developing this bishop to the more active h3-square gives White more kingside attacking options. It also prevents Black from playing ...♘g4 so there is method to Malinin's 'madness'.

10...♘b6

Continuing with the standard ...♘b6, ...c4 and ...♕a5 plan if left uninterrupted.

11 ♗g5

Not just a developing move. White aims to provoke Black into kicking the bishop with ...h7-h6 to induce a weakness in the kingside pawn chain.

11...h6

Putting the question to White: keep the bishop-pair or opt for speedy development?

A Ukrainian IM was on the receiving end of yet another 9 h4 Benko disaster against Malinin even with the stronger move 11...♗c4!. Play continued 12 e4 h5! 13 ♕c2 0-0 14 0-0-0?! ♗xa2 15 b3.

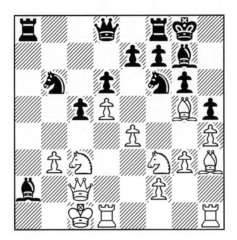

Exercise: It's Black to play and blast open the white queenside.

Answer: Black should prise open the queenside with a temporary piece sacrifice with 15...c4!. After 16 ♘xa2 cxb3 17 ♕xb3 ♘xe4 18 ♘d4 ♕c7+ 19 ♘c6 e6 the c6-knight has to be returned and Black's attack on the a-, b- and c-files aided by the superb bishop on g7 should prevail. What makes it so hard for Black to find this line is that the piece can only be claimed back six moves later as well as the precise calculation required.

Instead, after 15...♗xb3?? 16 ♕xb3 ♕c7 17 ♔d2?? ♖fb8 (17...♖a3! with the idea of 18 ♕xa3?? ♘c4+) 18 ♔e2, confused by the irrational position, Black blundered horribly with 18...♘bxd5?? 19 ♘xd5 and there was no coming back in V.Malinin-O.Gladischev, St Petersburg 1998.

12 ♗xf6 ♗xf6 13 ♕c2

The natural square for the white queen as it eyes g6 in connection with h4-h5 and ♗e6 ideas.

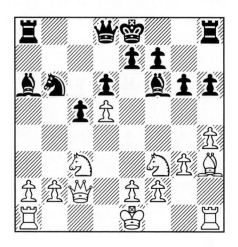

13...♞c4!

Giving the queen access to a5, clearing the b-file for a rook and setting up ...♞xb2 and ...♞a3 ideas.

14 ♞d2

Trying to bait Black into castling first so that he can weaken the black kingside with h4-h5. Indeed, White might be angling for a position like 14...0-0 15 h5 g5 16 ♞xc4 ♝xc4 17 0-0 ♛a5 18 ♞e4 ♛a6 19 ♞xf6+ exf6.

14...♛a5!

There is no hurry to castle yet. Moreover, the black queen belongs on a5, especially with the c4-knight and f6-bishop exerting pressure on c3 and b2.

15 ♜c1 ♜b8

Natural development by the Ukrainian WGM and kickboxer/karate champion. The veteran Russian Grandmaster has been outplayed in the first third of the game, but now he demonstrates that chess is also about psychology as he gives Vozovic a test in decision making.

16 0-0!?

Leaving b2 en prise. Malinin obviously did not want to grovel with 16 ♞b3 ♛b4 17 ♚f1 h5! 18 ♚g2 0-0 when Black is having a dandy time on the queenside.

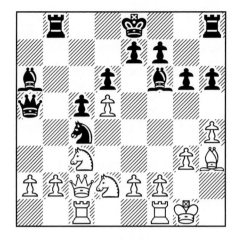

16...♖xb2?!

Unfortunately for Vozovic, this natural capture, which seemingly gains a tempo, actually allows the wily Russian to slip away. Now comes a series of forced exchanges.

Answer: Correct was 16...♘xb2! 17 ♘b3 ♕xc3 18 ♕xc3 ♗xc3 19 ♖xc3 ♘c4! when Black still has her wonderful Benko pawn structure intact and without the pawn deficit (both 19...♗xe2 20 ♖e1 and 19...♘a4 20 ♖e3 give White chances to complicate).

17 ♘xc4 ♖xc2 18 ♘xa5 ♖xc3 19 ♖xc3 ♗xc3 20 ♘c6

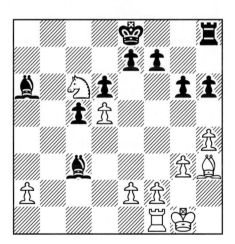

Although Black has the bishop-pair, White's lead in development cannot be underestimated.

> ***Question:*** How does Black complete development
> while protecting e7 at the same time?

Answer: 20...f5!? allows Black to put her king on f7, thereby guarding e7 while freeing the rook.

20...♔f8!?

A strange decision. Black might as well play 20...0-0 to get on with business after 21 ♘xe7+ ♔g7.

The greedy 20...♗xe2 isn't too bad, but White begins play with 21 ♖b1 0-0 22 a4! ♗f6 (if 22...♖a8 23 a5!) 23 a5. Although *Houdini* indicates that the position is a sterile equality, in practical play the chances belong to White.

21 ♖b1 ♔g7

21...♗xe2 22 a4 ♔g7 23 a5 ♖a8 24 ♗f1 ♗f3 25 ♗c4 at first looks dangerous for Black.

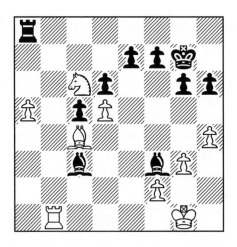

> ***Exercise:*** In reality Black has a way to neutralize White's pressure. What is it?

Answer: Black can sacrifice a piece by allowing a self pin: 25...♗xa5! 26 ♖a1 e6! 27 ♖xa5 ♖xa5 28 ♘xa5 exd5 29 ♗d3 c4 30 ♗c2 ♔f6 31 ♔f1 c3 32 ♘c6 ♗e4 33 ♘d4 ♔e5 34 ♘c6+ ♔f6 35 ♘d4 with a likely draw.

22 ♘xe7?

Something of a bluff. Instead, 22 ♗f1!? and 22 e4 both give equal chances.

22...♖e8

Black takes over the initiative and gets to activate her rook with tempo. With the white rook on b1, there wasn't any open file for Black to play on. Thus ...♔e8-f8-g7 was a clever little ploy indeed.

23 ♖b6

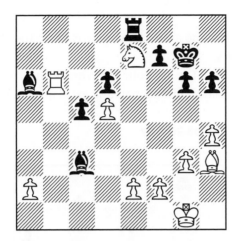

From this move and Malinin's 16th, we can see the GM's style. When he is in trouble, instead of passively defending, he randomizes the position by forcing his opponent to make concrete calculational decisions.

After 23 ♖c1 ♖xe7 24 ♖xc3 ♖xe2 White must suffer as in typical Benko endings where the a2- and d5-pawns require pieces to defend them.

23...♗xe2?!

Too hasty a move. The uber-cool 23...♗c4! leads to a won position after 24 ♘c8 (or 24 ♖b7 ♔f8 25 ♘c6 ♖xe2 when both White's a- and d-pawns will drop) 24...♖xe2 25 ♘xd6 ♗xd5 26 ♗g2 ♗e6! 27 a4 ♗d4 with winning chances for Black.

24 ♖b7!?

Malinin is not playing for a draw, but rather keeping his attacking chances alive.

24...♗c4

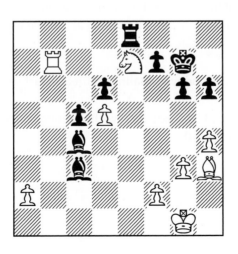

Black must be winning here, but this doesn't stop the Russian GM from lobbing the rest of his grenades into the enemy camp.

25 ♗f1

This, in essence, gains a tempo as Black needs to capture the a-pawn to try for a win.

25...♗xa2 26 ♗b5 ♖a8 27 h5

Softening up the black king. The key point for White is that he has nothing to lose by going for an all-out attack as Black's bishop-pair and extra material mean that he must burn all his bridges.

27...gxh5 28 ♗c6 ♔f6 29 ♖d7 ♖b8 30 ♗b7

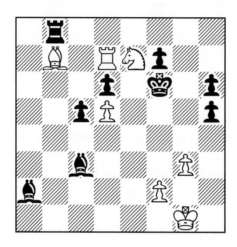

> ***Exercise:*** What is the best way for Black to nurse her advantage home?

30...♖e8?

Answer: The age old adage that "passed pawns must be pushed" is relevant here: 30...c4! 31 ♘c6 ♖e8 32 ♖xd6+ ♔g7 and White can do nothing about the pawn's march to glory, short of sacrificing a piece for it.

31 ♘c8

Now things become really dodgy as Malinin's threats start to look quite concrete.

31...♗b1?!

Black could still play 31...c4 32 ♘xd6 ♖e7! with winning chances.

32 ♘xd6 ♖e1+ 33 ♔g2 ♗g6 34 f4!

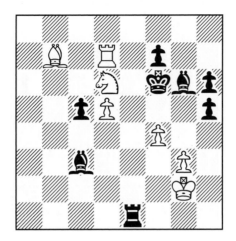

Cutting off the king's access to e5. White is still keeping Black on her toes.

34...h4

Very risky play by Black.

35 g4

Now it begins to look a bit scary for Vozovic, with her king denied access to the fourth rank.

35...♖e3!

A strong and precise move, aiming to nurse the front h-pawn down the file while also cutting off the white king's forwards access.

36 ♗c8 h3+ 37 ♔h2 ♗e1! 38 ♘f5!?

Again Malinin finds the sharpest option for Black to work out, even if he risks losing.

38 f5 ♗g3+ 39 ♔xh3 ♗xd6+ 40 ♔g2 ♔e5 41 fxg6 fxg6 42 ♖g7 g5 43 ♖g6 ♔xd5 44 ♖xh6 is objectively White's best chance to survive, but Malinin isn't thinking of wimping out so.

38...♗xf5 39 gxf5 c4?

Unfortunately, this is probably the only seemingly sensible move that allows White to draw. Sometimes, chess is really not fair. Just when it looks safe to push the passed pawn, the tables are turned and, more often than not, such an upheaval of events happens just before time control.

Instead, following, say, 39...♖c3 40 ♖d6+ ♔g7 41 f6+ ♔g6 White will be in dire straits after ...♗d2xf4.

40 ♖d6+ ♔e7 41 ♖c6 ♗g3+ 42 ♔xh3 ♗xf4+ 43 ♔g4 ♗e5 44 d6+ ♗xd6 45 f6+

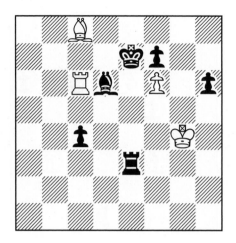

I have no clue how White won from here as the score ends here, albeit in a '1-0'. The position is just equal. What we cannot deny, however, is the extreme resourcefulness of Malinin in worse positions. 45...♔xf6 46 ♖xd6+ ♔e5 47 ♖xh6 c3 48 ♖c6 is drawish and 45...♔d8 46 ♗f5 ♗c7 47 ♖xc4 should be easily drawn.

Chapter Three
Benko Schmenko

1 d4 ♘f6 2 c4 c5 3 d5 b5 4 cxb5 a6 5 b6

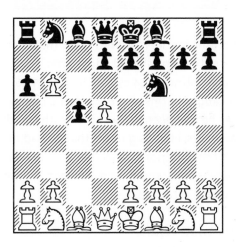

White in essence tells Black that he's not remotely interested in the Benko Gambit pawn and returns it immediately. His aim is to beat Black at his own game by trying to cramp him on the queenside with a4-a5 and ♘d2-c4. One notes that Garry Kasparov has made frequent use of 5 b6 in his simultaneous exhibitions, beating the likes of future GMs Stuart Conquest and Miguel Illescas.

My proposed repertoire option is to reply with the Blumenfeld-like 5...e6!?.

I like the counterattacking and tense central fight in this line as compared to the 5...d6 and 5...♕xb6 lines where both sides spend a lot of time manoeuvring knights and light-squared bishops to obtain ideal queenside squares for their pieces.

With 5...e6, Black would like to undermine White's centre having already deflected away the c-pawn. However, because White has control of d5 and can continue to dominate that square, Black's counterplay is often concentrated more with the b- and e-files. There is often tension on the a2-g8 and a1-h8 diagonals with bishops opposing each other. White usually exerts pressure on the d-file, aiming to force through e4-e5, and a knight typically finds its way to c4 to aid that push.

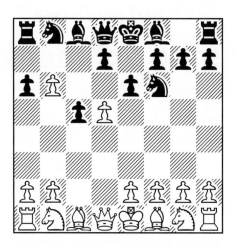

Note too that it is important for the reader to know that if one plays 5...e6 exclusively, then the opening move order that one should adopt after 1 d4 ♘f6 2 ♘f3 should be 2...c5. If Black plays 2...g6, White can continue 3 c4 c5 4 d5 b5 5 cxb5 a6 6 b6! when 6...e6 looks pretty lame. I actually got caught in this sequence by the Filipino IM Enrique Paciencia at the 2012 Cairnhill Open. As he had been preoccupied with training the National Junior Squad for the previous few years, I took a gamble that he had not been following opening developments by pulling off the inferior 6...a5?! (see the next game, Petrukhina-Bukhteeva, to learn why the ...a6-a5 idea is bad), and it paid off when he later fluffed a pawn.

Our repertoire, as discussed, continues:

5...e6

Trying to undermine the white centre.

6 ♘c3

White defends the pawn.

6...♘xd5 7 ♘xd5 exd5 8 ♕xd5

This exchange leaves White's queen on d5, seemingly a dubious decision as Black's backward d-pawn is suppressed and White obtains a nice space advantage. However, it transpires that Black can in time boot away the queen, either with ...♘b4 or ...♗e6 after preparation, and the queen usually moves to safer pastures, such as h5 or d2.

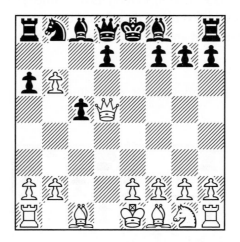

8...♘c6

Developing a piece and, of course, defending the loose rook on a8.

A) White plays for a draw with 9 ♗g5

White used to be able to attain a quick draw after 9 ♗g5 ♛b6 10 ♘e5 ♘xe5 11 ♛a8 ♛b2 12 ♖d1 ♛c3+ with perpetual check. However, our next game demonstrates that Black can instead simply sacrifice the exchange for a nice centre and a swift counterattack.

> *Game 24*
> **I.Petrukhina-V.Bukhteeva**
> Dagomys 2009

1 d4 ♘f6 2 c4 c5 3 d5 b5 4 cxb5 a6 5 b6 e6

Black undermines White's centre at the first opportunity.

It is important to know that the attempt to place the bishop on a6 is flawed. The most comprehensive way of refuting 5...a5?! is 6 ♘c3 ♗a6 7 ♘f3 g6 8 e4 ♗xf1 9 ♚xf1 d6 10 ♛a4+! ♘fd7 (or 10...♛d7 11 ♘d2 ♗g7 12 f3 0-0 13 ♘c4 with a huge position for White) 11 e5 dxe5 12 b7! ♖a7 13 ♘xe5 ♖xb7 14 ♘c6! ♛b6 15 ♗f4! ♗g7 16 ♗xb8 ♛xb2 17 ♖b1 ♛xb1+ 18 ♘xb1 ♖xb1+ 19 ♚e2 ♖xh1 20 ♘e5 ♗xe5 21 ♗xe5 f6 22 ♗g3 ♖a1 23 ♛c6! and the d7-knight is a goner. This was mostly forced play in C.Blanco Gramajo-M.Wang, correspondence 2000, so the whole line is unplayable.

What's ironic from my experience is that I have played 5...a5?! in quite a few blitz games against grandmasters and IMs, but none of them have replied with the 10 ♛a4+ idea and I tend to obtain an easy game.

6 ♘c3

6 dxe6?! just relinquishes control of the centre. In the Blumenfeld Gambit (1 d4 ♘f6 2 c4

e6 3 ♘f3 c5 4 d5 b5 5 dxe6 fxe6 6 cxb5), Black gets the same type of structure, but with one pawn less. After 6...fxe6 7 ♘f3 ♕xb6 8 g3 d5 9 ♗g2 ♗b7 10 0-0 ♘bd7 11 ♘c3 ♗e7 12 b3 0-0 Black has a space advantage and an f-file to play with, J.Hebert-J.Degraeve, Montreal 2002. **6...♘xd5**

> **Question:** How about putting pressure on d5 with 6...♗b7?

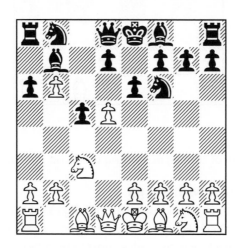

Answer: I tried for many hours to make this work, but just could not find anything to overcome the Russian GM Alexey Dreev's concept: 7 e4 exd5 8 exd5 d6 (this looks visually attractive as Black can summon many pieces to hit d5, but there doesn't seem to have enough time for him to carry out his aim) 9 a4! (to play a4-a5 to restrict Black further) 9...a5 10 ♗b5+ ♘bd7 11 ♘ge2 ♗e7 12 0-0 0-0 13 ♖e1 ♘xb6 14 ♘f4 ♖c8 (to support ...c5-c4 and ...♖c5 in hitting d5) 15 ♕f3! ♘fd7 16 ♗d2 ♘e5 17 ♕e4! (an excellent plan, rerouting the queen to c2, setting up ♖ad1 and ♗c1 to hold d5 and, finally, centralizing the knight with ♘e4) 17...♗g5 18 ♖ad1 g6 19 ♕c2 ♗e7 20 ♘e4 ♖a8 21 ♗c3! and Black is really suffering from congestion, A.Dreev-B.Kutuzovic, Sibenik 2006.
7 ♘xd5 exd5 8 ♕xd5 ♘c6 9 ♗g5?!

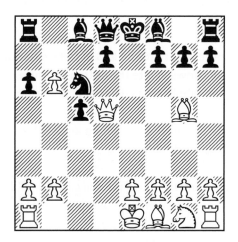

An attempt to draw quickly.

9...♛xb6

9...f6 is not bad either, but the text move is more incisive. After 10 ♗d2 ♛xb6 11 ♗c3 (or 11 0-0-0 ♜b8 12 ♗c3 ♞b4 13 ♛e4+ ♗e7 14 ♗xb4 cxb4 15 e3 ♗b7 16 ♛g4 0-0! When Black has fantastic play for the pawn) 11...♗b7 12 ♛h5+ g6 13 ♛h4 ♗e7 14 e3 ♞b4! 15 ♗xb4 cxb4 16 b3 f5 17 ♛d4 ♛xd4 18 exd4 ♗f6 Black already had a decisive advantage in E.Gavin Roche-Wong Zi Jing, Amsterdam 2005.

10 ♛e4+ ♗e7 11 ♗xe7 ♞xe7 12 ♛xa8

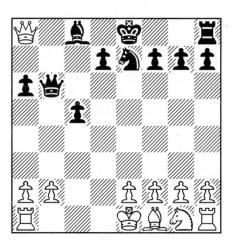

Question: Isn't Black just an exchange down? She only has a slight lead in development for it, right?

Answer: Wrong! Black can now play for more than just a draw because her initiative will soon increase exponentially as the white rooks and minors can hardly get into the thick of action when the game unfolds.

12...d5!!

An incredibly nonchalant response to the loss of the exchange. This variation, which is also advocated by Aveskulov, allows White the option of 'winning' two rooks for the queen or to stay a pawn up with her whole kingside asleep. Both options give Black a very strong attack.

If Black so wishes, she can accept the truce here and both sides can take an early shower after 12...♕xb2 13 ♖d1 ♕c3+ 14 ♖d2 ♕a1+.

13 ♘f3

If White prefers to keep queens on the board, she can play 13 0-0-0 0-0 14 ♖xd5 ♗e6 (or 14...♗f5 15 ♕xf8+ ♔xf8 16 ♖d1 ♘c6 with huge developmental problems for White to solve) 15 ♖d6 ♕xd6 16 ♕f3 ♗xa2, which was K.Gorbatenko-V.Golubenko, Kharkov 2006. Black has already created threats against the white king and White is yet to even mobilize her kingside.

Alternatively, 13 ♖d1 0-0 14 ♖xd5 ♗e6 15 ♕xf8+ ♔xf8 with a strong attack for Black.

13...0-0 14 e3 ♗b7 15 ♕xf8+ ♔xf8 16 0-0-0 ♘c6

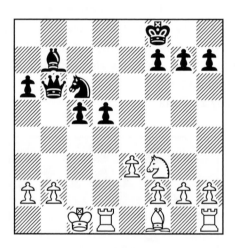

Question: White has won two rooks for the queen. Isn't that good?

Answer: Nominally White has a material advantage, but in this case Black has a very strong and mobile centre. Moreover, Black's pieces can be activated very quickly to create threats on the queenside, giving her a large advantage.

17 ♗e2

Prudent development by White, but Black's initiative is still too strong. Also insufficient is 17 ♗d3 c4 18 ♗b1 ♕c5 19 ♘d4 ♘e5 20 ♖d2 a5 21 f4 c3 and Black is close to winning already.

17...♘b4

Black commits the knight to the 'trapped' a2-square, but her concept is backed by the fact that she can create such insurmountable queenside weaknesses that the knight will become a strong piece there.

18 a3 ♘a2+!

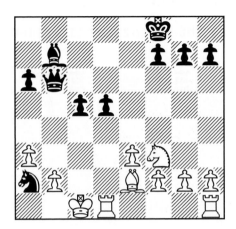

Sending the knight into a dead zone, but it is surprisingly difficult to nab.

19 ♔c2 ♗c6

Threatening the dangerous ...♗a4+ and thereby forcing White to further weaken her king's pawn shield.

20 b3

20 ♖d2 c4 with the idea of ...c4-c3 is devastating.

20...♕a5 21 ♔b2 ♘c3 22 ♖de1 f6

Black can even pause to deny White the e5-square for the knight and 22...♗b5 is also very strong.

23 ♖hf1 ♗b5 24 ♗xb5

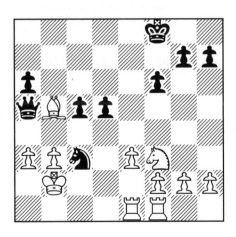

This is forced, but now White can no longer defend the hapless king.

24...♘xb5

24...axb5?! would allow White back into the game after 25 ♖c1 ♘e4 26 ♖fd1.

25 ♔b1 0-1

White resigned before 25...♕c3 arrived.

B) Georgiev's Line: 9 ♘f3 ♖b8 10 ♗d2 ♗e7 11 ♗c3 0-0 12 e4

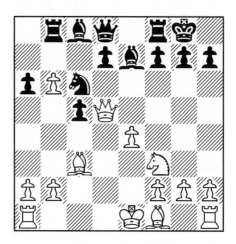

This is Kiril Georgiev's proposed move order in his *Squeezing the Gambits* book as it cuts out various secondary variations for Black. Galojan-Pogonina illustrates how Black can take advantage of the fact that White has yet to castle with 12...♖xb6 13 ♗c4 ♘b4, gaining a tempo on the queen and planning to put the light-squared bishop on b7.

Game 25
L.Galojan-N.Pogonina
Istanbul 2003

---

1 d4 ♘f6 2 c4 c5 3 d5 b5 4 cxb5 a6 5 b6 e6 6 ♘c3 exd5 7 ♘xd5 ♘xd5 8 ♕xd5 ♘c6 9 ♘f3

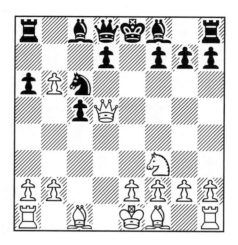

9...♖b8!

An idea patented by Alterman.

> ***Question:*** Why not complete kingside development first with 9...♗e7 and then decide if the rook has to go b8, since Black might want to play ...♕xb6 instead?

Answer: The problem with this is that White is better after 10 ♘e5 0-0 11 ♘xc6 dxc6 12 ♕xd8 (and not 12 ♕xc6? ♖b8 13 ♕c7 ♖xb6 14 ♕xd8 ♖xd8 when Black's big developmental lead far outweighs the pawn deficit and he can put even more pressure on the queenside with ...♗f6 and ...♗e6) 12...♗xd8 (also, 13...♗xb6 14 ♗c4 gives White a slight but enduring pull: 14...♗e6 15 ♗xe6 fxe6 16 ♗d2 ♖ad8 17 ♗c3 ♖d3 18 ♔e2 c4 19 ♖hc1 and Black's weaknesses are telling, H.Ness-D.Willenberg, German League 2003) 13 e3 ♗f6 14 ♗d2 ♖b8 15 ♗a5 ♗e6 16 ♖c1! ♗xa2 17 ♖xc5 ♗d5 18 ♗xa6 ♗xg2 19 ♖g1 ♗d5 20 b7 and by now the extra b7-pawn gives White a decisive advantage, S.Lputian-O.Annageldyev, Azov 1991.

9...♕xb6 commits Black to an unsound exchange sacrifice, although the late mercurial Spanish GM David Garcia Ilundain once defeated Van Wely with it: 10 ♘e5 ♘xe5 11 ♕xa8 ♕c7 12 ♗f4?! (the variation is unsound: 12 e3 ♗d6 13 f4! ♘g4 14 ♕f3 ♘f6 15 ♗c4 ♗b7 16 ♕e2 0-0 17 0-0 ♖e8 18 ♗xa6 and Black doesn't have enough for his material deficit) 12...♗d6 13 0-0-0 ♘d3+ (13...0-0 14 ♕d5 ♘d3+ 15 ♖xd3 ♗xf4+ 16 e3 ♗e5 gives Black excellent compensation in the form of a superb dark-squared bishop) 14 ♖xd3 ♗xf4+ 15 e3 0-0! 16 ♕d5 ♗e5 17 ♖d2 d6 18 ♗c4 ♗e6 19 ♕e4 ♗d7 20 ♖hd1 ♗c6 21 ♕c2 ♖b8 22 b3 ♖d8 23 f4 ♗f6 24 g4 g6 25 g5 ♗g7 26 f5 gxf5 27 ♕xf5 ♕a5 28 ♕xf7+ ♔h8 29 ♖c2? ♗e4! 30 ♕f2 ♕a3+ 31 ♖b2 ♖f8 32 ♕d2 d5! 33 ♖f1 ♖b8! 34 ♗e2

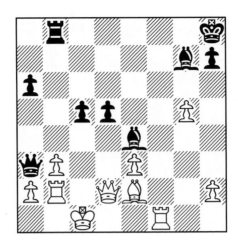

34...♖xb3! 35 ♖f6 ♕xa2 0-1, L.Van Wely-D.Garcia Ilundain, Las Palmas 1993. The last four moves really are visually stunning.

Returning to 9...♖b8:

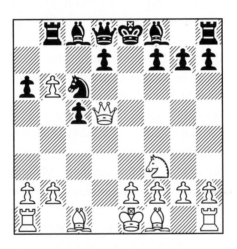

10 ♗d2

Planning to reroute the bishop to c3 where it guards b2 and controls the long dark-square diagonal. Note that there are plenty of other ways to reach the position at move 13, such as 9 ♘f3 and 10 ♗d2, 9 e4 and 10 ♗d2, 9 ♗d2 and 10 ♗c3, or 9 ♘f3 and 10 e4. Georgiev prefers the text move, though, as according to him, it limits Black's options. However, it does give Black the option of delaying/doing away with ...d6 in favour of ...♘b4.

White also has the option of saddling Black with ugly queenside pawns after 10 ♘e5 ♕f6 11 ♘xc6 dxc6 12 ♕e4+ ♗e7, but Flear showed that Black has full compensation with active play by citing the following: 13 g3! ♖xb6 14 ♗g2 ♗e6 15 ♕a4 0-0 16 0-0 c4 17 ♕a5 ♗d8 18 ♕c5 ♕f5 "with a double-edged position" in N.Templier-A.Vaisser, French League 2005.

10...♗e7 11 ♗c3 0-0 12 e4

The insipid 12 e3 merely gives Black the upper hand after 12...♖xb6 13 ♗e2 (or 13 ♗c4 ♘b4 14 ♕d1 d5, as in E.Romero Perera-A.Picanol Alamany, Barcelona 1996, where Black already had an imposing position with the active b6-rook and strong centre) 13...♘b4 14 ♕d2 ♖d6 15 ♕c1 ♘d3+ 16 ♗xd3 ♖xd3 with the bishop-pair and a nice centre for Black, Z.Kamadadze-B.Shovunov, Batumi 2001.

12...♖xb6 13 ♗c4 ♘b4!

Black immediately starts active play before White can castle.

Instead, 13...d6 transposes to positions similar to the next game.

14 ♕d2 ♗b7

White is practically forced to castle long to win back the d7-pawn as the e4-pawn has been compromised.

14...♖d6!? is an interesting suggestion of Aveskulov's, but I think White can obtain the better position after 15 ♕e2 ♖g6 (after 15...♗b7 16 0-0 White is very solid) 16 0-0 d6 17 ♔h1 ♕b6 18 a3 ♘c6 19 ♖ad1 ♖e8 20 h3 a5 21 ♖fe1 with a spatial advantage.

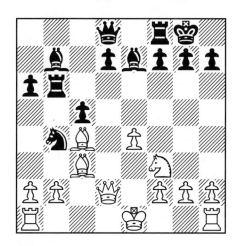

15 0-0-0

Question: Why not 15 a3, booting the knight away from its active square?

Answer: This is met by the counterattacking 15...d5! 16 exd5 ♘xd5 17 ♗e5, as in E.Vladimirov-V.Mikhalevski, Kolkata 2001, and here Tyomkin pointed out that Black should play 17...f6 18 ♗g3 ♖e6+ 19 ♔f1 ♕d7 with a slight advantage.

15...♗xe4 16 ♕xd7 ♗g5+ 17 ♘xg5 ♕xg5+ 18 ♕d2

Flear pointed out that 18 ♖d2 should be met by the prosaic retreat 18...♖bb8! (the razor-sharp nature of this line can be seen when Black takes a time-out to guard f7 and White simply pounds home the advantage: 18...♗g6?! 19 ♖e1 ♖bb8 20 g3 ♕h5 21 a3 ♖bc8 22 f4 ♕f3 23 ♕d6 ♖ce8 24 ♖xe8 ♖xe8 25 axb4 cxb4 26 ♕e5 ♕h1+ 27 ♖d1 ♖xe5 28 ♗xe5 1-0,

A.Rakhmanov-I.Nepomniachtchi, Moscow 2010) 19 ♖e1 and now *Houdini* unveils the stunning 19...♗d3! 20 ♗xd3 ♖bd8 21 ♗xh7+ ♔xh7 22 ♕h3+ ♔g8 23 ♗xb4 cxb4 24 ♕e3 ♕xg2 with a slight edge for Black.

18...♕g6

18...♕h4 with the idea of ...♗c2 is also playable: 19 ♕e2 ♗g6 20 ♕e5?! ♖f6! and just like that, White is in serious trouble. G.Tallaksen-G.Michelakis, Copenhagen 2003, concluded 21 ♕xc5?? ♖xf2 22 ♗d2 ♕e4 23 ♕xf8+ ♔xf8 24 ♗xb4+ ♔e8 25 ♖he1 ♖c2+ 26 ♔b1 ♖xc4+ 0-1.

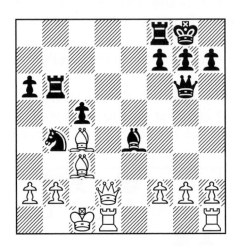

19 a3

White hopes to drive the knight away.

Pogonina has also faced 19 ♖he1 ♗b1 20 ♗xb4 and here in E.Ubiennykh-N.Pogonina, Voronezh 2004, Black could have considered 20...cxb4 21 ♗xf7+ ♕xf7 22 ♔xb1 ♕g6+ 23 ♕c2 ♕xg2!? 24 ♕c4+ ♔h8 25 ♖g1 ♕f3 with a small edge due to White's isolated kingside pawns, although White has very strong drawing chances due to the fact that only the heavy pieces are left.

Instead, the kingside advance 19 h4 can be parried, as *Houdini* demonstrated, by 19...♗c2! 20 ♖de1 ♗b3! 21 ♗xb4 ♗xc4 22 h5 ♕f5 23 g4 ♕d5 24 ♗c3 ♗xa2 25 ♕xd5 ♗xd5 with a slight pull for Black.

19...♘c2!

Right into the frying pan.

20 ♗d3

Trying to blot out the dangerous light-square diagonal, but this won't save White.

If 20 ♕f4 ♘d4 21 ♖he1 (or 21 ♗xd4 ♗b1 22 ♖d2 cxd4 23 ♕xd4 ♖c6 24 b3 ♕xg2 25 ♖e1 ♗g6 when Black has the better chances due to White's split pawns and more exposed king) 21...♗c2 22 ♖d2 ♗b3 23 ♗d3 ♕xg2 24 ♗xd4 cxd4 25 f3 ♕h3 26 ♕xd4 with the better game for Black.

20...♘d4!

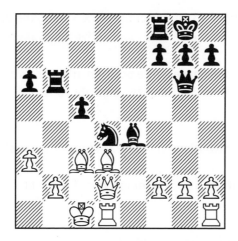

The pesky knight keeps on harassing White and now threatens a fork on b3.

21 ♔b1

If White removes the knight, Black still keeps the advantage after 21 ♗xd4 cxd4 22 ♖he1 ♕c6+ 23 ♔b1 ♗xg2.

21...♕xg2

Question: Isn't it dangerous for Black to take the g-pawn, as White now might use the open g-file to generate a strong kingside attack?

Answer: Black plans to meet 22 ♖hg1 with the sneaky 22...♘f3!, winning an exchange.

22 ♗xe4 ♕xe4 23 ♕d3

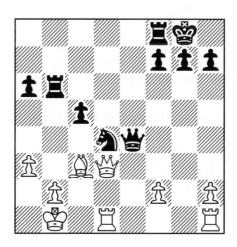

23...♕xd3+

> ***Question:*** Isn't it better for Black to keep the queens
> on as she has the more active heavy pieces?

Answer: That's true. Black does have a nice position after 23...♕b7 24 ♗xd4 ♖d6!, but it will still be another double rook ending after 25 ♖hg1 g6! 26 ♕c3 ♕e4+ 27 ♕d3 ♖xd4 28 ♕xe4 ♖xe4.

24 ♖xd3 ♖f6

Now Black focuses her attention on the weak kingside pawns.

25 ♖f1 ♖f4 26 ♖e3 h6

Not merely creating luft, but also opening a door for the black king to advance in the endgame.

27 ♖e7 ♖c8 28 ♖d7 ♘e6

A multipurpose move, guarding c5 and g7.

29 ♖d5 ♔h7 30 h3 0-1

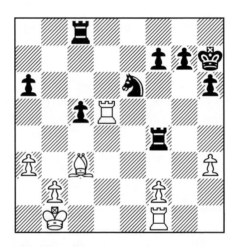

Black is a pawn up and has the more active rooks and better minor piece, but it's a mystery why the game ended here as White can still put up much resistance. When I asked Natalia Pogonina about this game, she replied that she could only remember that she won the game, but not how.

C) 13 ♗d2 intending ♗c3 and ♕d2

After 9 e4 ♗e7 10 ♗c4 0-0 11 ♘f3 ♖b8 12 0-0 ♖xb6 White can still play 13 ♗d2, angling to follow up with ♗c3.

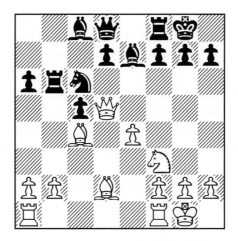

Often in this line, White is content to trade off both bishops, with the idea of playing against Black's weak d6-pawn with his heavy pieces. Khurtsidze-Pogonina shows the importance of playing actively on the b- and e-files so as not to get tied down to total defence of d6.

Game 26
N.Khurtsidze-N.Pogonina
Batumi (blitz) 2012

1 d4 ♘f6 2 c4 c5 3 d5 b5 4 cxb5 a6 5 b6 e6 6 ♘c3 exd5 7 ♘xd5 ♘xd5 8 ♕xd5 ♘c6 9 e4

9 ♘f3 ♖b8 10 e4 ♗e7 11 ♗c4 0-0 12 ♗d2 is another move order.

9...♗e7 10 ♗c4 0-0 11 ♘f3 ♖b8 12 0-0 ♖xb6 13 ♗d2

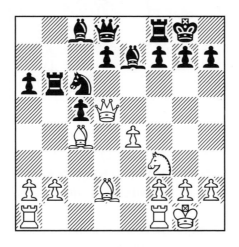

13...d6

Answer: Although White does not have anything forcing, she can build up an attacking
formation as well as generate central pressure after 14 ♗c3 ♖b6 15 ♖ad1 d6 16 ♕h5 ♗f6
(or 16...♗d7 when White simply increases the pressure with 17 ♖d2! a5 18 ♖fd1 and enjoys
very strong pressure for her pawn; the build-up on the c- and d-files is certainly impressive)
17 e5! g6 18 ♕h6 ♗g7 19 ♕e3 with a marvellous position where White is poised to win
back the pawn with a large advantage, Br.Thorfinnsson-B.Zueger, Ohrid 2001.

Note that if Black plays 13...♘b4 in the spirit of Galojan-Poganina, she runs into 14 ♕h5
♗b7 (or 14...d6 15 ♗c3 ♗e6 16 ♗xe6 fxe6 17 ♕g4 e5 18 ♘d2 ♕c8 19 ♕xc8 ♖xc8 20 ♘c4
♖bb8 21 ♗xb4 ♖xb4 22 ♖ac1 when White has a slight but enduring edge, thanks to the
better pawn structure and stronger minor piece, or here 18...d5 19 exd5 ♕xd5 20 ♕c4 with
a slight but enduring edge for White) 15 ♗c3 with a easy game for White. If 15...♗xe4 16
♕e5 ♖g6 17 ♕xe4 d5 18 ♕e2 dxc4 19 ♘e5 ♖e6 20 ♕xc4 and White has an edge due to
Black's weak queenside pawns. The placing of the knight on b4 instead of d4 doesn't help
matters at all.

14 ♗c3 ♗f6

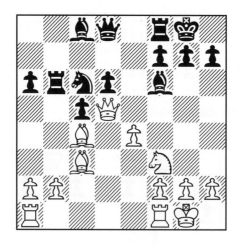

15 ♖ad1

15 ♕d3 is parried by 15...♗g4! 16 h3 ♗xf3 17 ♕xf3 ♘e5 18 ♕e2 ♘xc4 19 ♕xc4 ♗xc3 20
♕xc3 ♖b4 21 f3 ♕b6 22 ♖f2 ♖b8 23 ♖d1 h6 24 b3 c4! 25 bxc4 ♕c5 26 ♕d4 ♖b1 27 ♖fd2
♖xd1+ 28 ♖xd1 ♖b1! 29 ♔h2 ♖xd1 30 ♕xd1 ♕xc4 with staid equality.

15...♗xc3

Alternatively, 15...♗e6 16 ♕d3 ♘b4 17 ♗xb4 (after 17 ♕e2 ♘xa2! 18 ♗xa2 ♗xa2 19
♗a5 ♖xb2 20 ♕xb2 ♗xb2?! 21 ♗xd8 ♖xd8 22 ♖d2 ♖b8 23 ♖xd6 h6 24 ♖fd1 White has a

slight edge, but 20...♕xa5! 21 ♕d2 ♗c3! 22 ♕xd6 ♗b3 23 ♖c1 c4 24 ♘d4 ♗xd4 25 ♕xd4 ♕d8 26 ♕c5 a5 equalizes, as shown by Georgiev) 17...♗xc4 18 ♕xc4 ♖xb4 19 ♕xa6 ♖xb2 and the position is about even, V.Iotov-G.Szamoskozi, Albena 2009.

16 bxc3 ♗e6 17 ♕d3 ♗xc4 18 ♕xc4 ♕f6

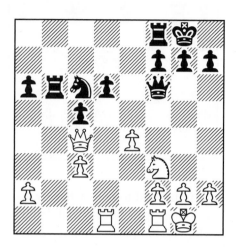

White has the better pawn structure, but Black is very active especially on the b-file. It is imperative that Black continues playing very actively so that White cannot consolidate and start hitting on the d6 weakie.

19 ♖d5?!

Ditching a tempo as now Black regroups her knight to g6, a good square where it still covers e5 and can help generate kingside threats with ...♘f4. White does better with:

a) 19 ♖d3 ♖e8 (Black should just mobilize rapidly with 19...♖fb8! 20 ♖fd1 ♖b1 21 h3 ♖8b6, and if 22 ♕d5 h6 23 ♕xd6 ♖xd1+ 24 ♖xd1 ♖b1! 25 ♔h2 ♖xd1 26 ♕xd1 ♕xc3 when the position is equal, but Black has a passed c-pawn to play with) 20 ♕a4 (better than 20 ♖fd1 ♘e5 21 ♘xe5 ♖xe5 22 f3 and ½-½, K.Landa-P.Tregubov, French Team Championship 2011) 20...♔f8 21 ♖fd1 ♘e5?! 22 ♘xe5 ♕xe5 was D.Kuljasevic-T.Andrews, Internet 2007, and was a typical slight plus position where White can play for two results.

b) 19 ♖d2 ♖fb8 20 ♖fd1 ♘a5! 21 ♕e2 (otherwise, 21 ♕a4 ♕xc3 22 ♖d3 ♕b4 23 ♕xb4 cxb4 24 ♖xd6 ♖xd6 25 ♖xd6 b3 26 axb3 ♘xb3 27 ♖xa6 ♘c5 28 ♖a1 ♘xe4 draws or 21 ♕d3 h6 with equal chances) 21...h6.

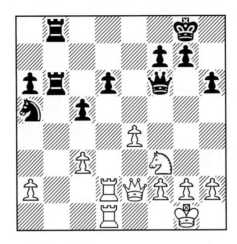

As already emphasised, it is important to keep active by doubling on the b-file and targeting the c3-pawn. If, instead, one gets tied down to defending d6, it'll become a long and arduous defence for Black with only chances to eke out a draw.

19...♘e7! 20 ♖d2 ♘g6 21 ♖fd1 h6

It's always a good idea to create some luft when the position does not call for an immediate critical decision.

22 h3

Ditto for White, although the black queen and knight tandem might make her regret this weakening.

22...♖e8 23 ♕a4

White is aiming to tie the black rooks down to the queenside.

23...♖e7 24 ♕a5 ♖eb7 25 ♖d5?

Planning to play e4-e5.

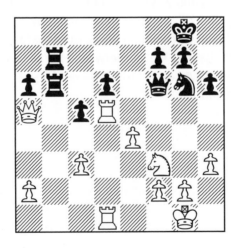

25...♘e7?!

Answer: Black can put White on the defensive after 25...♘f4! 26 ♖f5 (26 e5 is not possible because of 26...♕g6) 26...♘e2+ 27 ♔h2 ♕e6! when she is poised to invade with ...♖b2.

26 e5!

Black's slight slip has allowed White to get back into the game.

26...dxe5

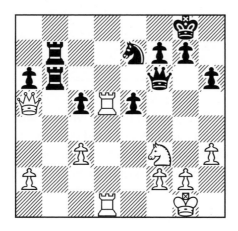

27 ♖d8+?

With the choice of two captures and a check, White elects to go for the latter and Black now happily pockets the extra pawn.

Answer: 27 ♖xc5? allows Black to seize a decisive advantage with 27...e4! 28 ♘d4 ♖b2.

On the other hand, 27 ♖xe5 ♖b1 28 ♖ee1 ♖xd1 29 ♖xd1 ♖b2 30 ♕xc5 ♖xa2 gives equal chances.

27...♔h7 28 ♕xc5

The white queen now protects f2, but after Black's next move White remains on the defensive. Moreover, in blitz the initiative is everything.

28...e4 29 ♘d4 ♖b2 30 ♘b3 ♖xa2 31 ♖8d6?

31 ♘d2 was forced.

31...♕f4! 32 ♘d2 ♖bb2 33 ♖d7?

A further mistake, but even after 33 g3 ♕f5 Black is winning whether or not White trades the queens.

33...♘g6 34 ♕d4 ♘e5 35 ♖d8 ♘c6 36 ♕xe4+ ♕xe4 37 ♘xe4 ♘xd8 38 ♖xd8 f5 39 ♘c5 ♖xf2

0-1

D) 13 ♕h5

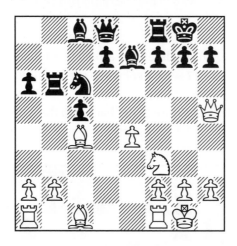

In this variation Black has the option of playing with a fixed centre after 13...d6 14 b3 ♗e6 15 ♗xe6 fxe6 16 ♕g4 ♕c8 17 ♗b2 e5 or a fluid one after 16...♖f6 or 16...♕d7. One has to be exceedingly careful playing with the fixed centre (pawns on c5, d6 and e5), as can be seen from Shabalov-Bartholomew. Various grandmasters like to keep the pawns fluid; perhaps this has something to do with their strong positional sense, not wanting to play something too positionally committal unless necessary.

Game 27
A.Shabalov-J.Bartholomew
Philadelphia 2007

---

1 d4 ♘f6 2 c4 c5 3 d5 b5 4 cxb5 a6 5 b6 e6 6 ♘c3 ♘xd5 7 ♘xd5 exd5 8 ♕xd5 ♘c6 9 e4 ♗e7 10 ♗c4 0-0 11 ♘f3 ♖b8 12 0-0 ♖xb6 13 ♕h5

The most common move and one that makes good sense. White threatens to win the bishop-pair by ♘g5 and clears the d-file for a rook.

Before we continue, note that Stohl maintained that Black can hold the balance after 13 b3 with the energetic 13...♘a5! 14 ♗f4 ♗b7 15 ♕d3 ♘xc4 16 bxc4 ♖e6 17 ♘d2 ♗c6 18 f3 ♗g5 19 ♗d6 ♗e7, with equality.

13...d6

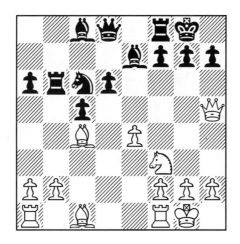

14 b3

This move is more subtle than it seems. On the surface, it gives protection to the c4-bishop and the b-pawn, as well as setting up a nice diagonal for the dark-squared bishop, but it also restrains the c5-pawn from jamming White's queenside with a later ...c5-c4.

Instead, after 14 ♖d1 ♗e6 15 ♗xe6 (the position can rebound very quickly on White if he is careless in exchanging: 15 ♘g5?! ♗xg5 16 ♗xg5 ♕d7! 17 ♗xe6 ♕xe6 18 ♗f4? ♘d4! and White cannot avoid the loss of at least a pawn, V.Huang-J.Tay, Singapore 2010) 15...fxe6 16 ♕g4 ♕c8 17 ♗d2 e5 18 ♕xc8 ♖xc8 19 ♗c3 ♘d4 20 ♘d2 c4! the position is equal, while 14 ♘g5 ♗xg5 15 ♗xg5 ♕e8 16 ♗f4 ♘d4 gave Black no problems in M.Arnold-M.Molner, Los Angeles 2012.

14...♗e6 15 ♗xe6

Some other possibilities:

a) 15 ♗d5 ♕c8 16 h3 ♗f6 17 ♖b1 ♘b4 and Black's pieces are considerably the more active, D.Rajkovic-A.Vaisser, Arco 2010.

b) 15 ♘g5 ♗xg5 16 ♗xg5 ♕e8 17 ♗d3 ♘b4 18 ♗b1 was L.Van Wely-A.Vaisser, Cap d'Agde 1996, and in this relatively sedate position, *Houdini* demonstrates some impressive tactics: 18...♗xb3! 19 ♕h4! (or 19 axb3 ♕e5 20 ♖a4 f6 21 f4 ♕d4+ 22 ♔h1 fxg5 23 ♕xg5 with the slightly better position for Black) 19...♕e5 20 axb3 h6! (not 20...♕xa1?? 21 e5!) 21 ♗xh6 ♕xa1 22 e5 ♕d4 23 ♕h3 gxh6 24 ♕xh6 f5 25 ♕g6+ ♔h8 26 ♕h6+ and Black cannot avoid a draw by perpetual check.

15...fxe6 16 ♕g4

White tries to force Black's centre pawns to become fixed.

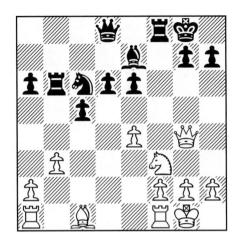

Answer: 16...♕d7 does not allow Black the option of playing ...e6-e5 with the idea of ...♘d4.
On the other hand, it allows the queen easier access to the kingside.

Black can also keep the centre fluid with 16...♖f6 17 ♗e3 ♖g6 18 ♕h3. This was S.Drazic-
B.Vuckovic, Vrnjacka Banja 2010, and here I think Black can maintain his structure and
keep plugging on the queenside with 18...a5! 19 ♖ad1 ♕c7 20 ♘d2 a4 21 f4 ♖h6 22 ♕f3 (if
22 ♕g3 d5!) 22...axb3 23 axb3 ♖f6 when the black rooks are applying strong pressure.
16...♕c8 17 ♗b2 e5

Black has fixed his central pawns in order to play ...♘d4. If White takes on d4 with the
bishop, he will give Black a protected passed pawn.

After 17...♗f6 White can trade off all the minor pieces with 18 e5 ♘xe5 (if 18...dxe5?! 19
♘d2 ♖b4 20 ♘c4 and White is already better) 19 ♘xe5 ♗xe5 (19...dxe5 20 ♖ac1 is easier for
White to play despite the pawn minus) 20 ♗xe5 dxe5 21 ♖ac1 ♖d6 22 ♕e2 ♖d5 23 b4 ♖fd8
24 ♖xc5 ♖xc5 25 bxc5 ♖d5 26 ♖c1 ♖xc5 27 ♖xc5 ♕xc5 28 ♕xa6, with equality, A.Sharevich-
N.Pogonina, Vladimir 2005.
18 ♕xc8 ♖xc8 19 ♘d2 ♘d4 20 ♘c4

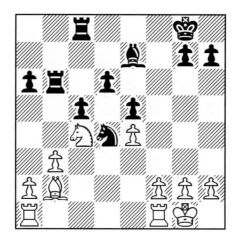

I think this position supplies good study material for the Benko Gambit player.

Question: Who is better in this position, and why?

Answer: We examine:

1) The pawn structure. White has two solid pawn islands which are quite mobile, whereas Black has three, of which the V-formation central pawns are pretty hard to advance, given that White has blockaded on c4 and ...d6-d5 will isolate the e5-pawn. Black, however, has the option of playing ...a5-a4 to put pressure on White's queenside duo. White, for his part, can prepare to mobilize the central pawns with g2-g3 and f2-f4, which can be quite troublesome for Black as the c4-knight helps any subsequent e4-e5 break.

2) The minor pieces. White has the better-placed minors as the c4-knight is a good blockader and the b2-bishop can become useful if he can get in f2-f4. Black's knight is sitting pretty on d4 and he is not worried about White exchanging it, as previously mentioned. However, Black's bishop is quite a sorry piece unless it can be moved to g5, but this will require constant defence of d6.

Hence, it is easier for White to play this position than Black. However, Black's position is very solid and compact. His king also has easy access to e6. I think we can conclude that White has a slight advantage in this position, so Black has to play exactly, which is what Bartholomew impressively did (the main reason for me including this game).

20...♖b5!

An excellent move from Bartholomew. Black supports ...a6-a5 with the idea of ...a5-a4, softening up the white queenside pawns. In prior games, Black went on the defensive with 20...♖bc6 21 g3 ♗f6 22 ♔g2 ♔f7 23 f4 and, in both cases, White opened the f-file for his rooks and switched the knight via e3 to d5 when Black had to give up the exchange to remove the strong knight.

21 ♖ae1 a5

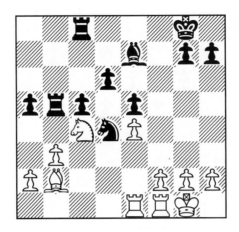

22 ♗c3!

Preventing ...a5-a4.

> *Question:* How should Black deal with 22 f4?

Answer: He can ignore it with 22...a4! 23 fxe5 (after 23 ♗xd4 cxd4 24 fxe5 dxe5 25 bxa4 ♖b4 26 ♘xe5 ♖xa4 27 ♖e2 ♗g5 Black is slightly better) 23...dxe5 24 ♖e3 axb3 25 axb3 ♖d8 26 ♗xd4 exd4 27 ♖d3 ♖db8 28 ♖ff3 ♗d8!, with the idea of ...♗c7.

22...♖a8 23 ♘b2

Lots of tai-chi is going on. Both sides are not giving an inch.

23...♗g5

Putting the bishop on its most active diagonal, which also helps to restrain f2-f4.

24 ♔h1

It's good to get the king out of the way before planning f2-f4.

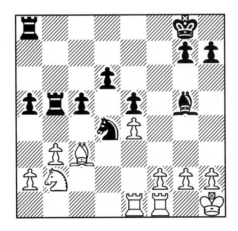

Exercise: White seems to have stopped Black's queenside
offensive cold and will gradually prepare f2-f3, g2-g3 and finally
f3-f4. Can Black take immediate action to distract White here?

24...♖b7!?

Black clears the b5-square for the knight.

Answer: However, he missed the marvellous move 24...a4! when 25 ♘xa4 (after 25 bxa4?!
♖b7! Black threatens to invade with ...♗d2) 25...c4 26 bxc4 ♖b7 27 ♘b2 ♖xa2 sees Black's
activity compensate for the pawn deficit.

25 ♖d1 ♘b5

Timing is everything as the knight attacks the bishop and holds d6 simultaneously.

26 ♗e1 ♔f7

Heading for e6.

27 f4!?

If 27 ♘c4 ♔e6 28 ♗xa5 ♘d4 Black will win back the pawn after ...♖ba7.

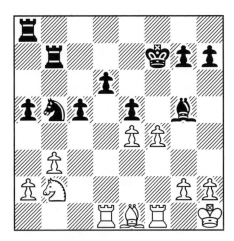

Over the past moves, Shabalov has been manoeuvring carefully, not allowing Black to
get his foot in the door at all. This is kind of un-Shabalov as he is famed for his tactical
prowess. However, now, all of a sudden, he gets in a tactical shot.

27...exf4 28 ♖d5 ♗f6 29 ♘c4!

Not 29 ♖xf4 ♔g8 when White's knight is forced to vacate b2 and allow ...a5-a4.

29...a4

Tit for tat. Black counterattacks immediately.

30 b4

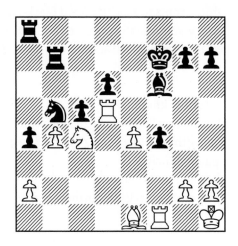

30...罝c8

> *Exercise:* What strong move did Black miss in the heat of the battle?

Answer: After 30...罝e8! the initiative swings back to Black: 31 罝xf4 含g8 and White is suffering, no thanks to his weak back rank. For example, 32 bxc5 runs into 32...匂c3!.

Houdini also demonstrated the incredible 30...cxb4 31 罝xb5 罝xb5 32 匂xd6+ 含e6 33 匂xb5 皿e5 when White's extra knight is doomed and thus Black equalizes nicely.

31 bxc5 dxc5 32 皿d2 含e6 33 皿xf4 罝d8!

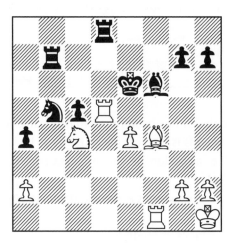

It is important to stay active, even at the expense of the c5-pawn. If Black is prepared to donate a pawn on move 3, why not on move 33 for the sake of the wresting the initiative?

34 罝xc5 罝d4 35 匂a5

Tempting White to play 35 e5 皿e7 36 罝c6+ 含d5 37 罝b6 罝xb6 38 匂xb6+ 含e6 when

Black has the upper hand due to the bad position of the white king.

35...♖b6 36 e5

Similarly, White cannot retain his extra pawn without making concessions.

36...♗e7 37 ♖cc1

Now Black decides to trade down to a draw.

37...♖xf4 38 ♖xf4 ♗g5 39 g3 ♗xf4 40 gxf4 ♘d4 41 ♖c4 ♔d5 42 ♖xa4 ♖a6

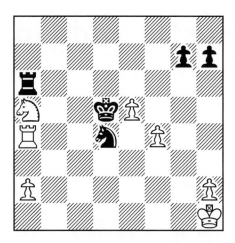

A permanent pin? Of course, both sides had worked out this position quite a few moves in advance.

43 ♘c4 ½-½

If the opponents had continued, they might have reeled off the moves 43...♖xa4 44 ♘b6+ ♔e4 45 ♘xa4 ♔xf4 46 ♔g2 ♔xe5 with a drawish position.

What an excellent fighting game and a draw was a fair result indeed.

Chapter Four
Hustle and Flow

1 d4 ♘f6 2 c4 c5 3 d5 b5 4 cxb5 a6 5 f3

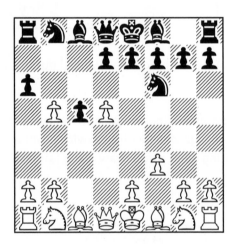

White accepts the gambit pawn, but immediately returns it to build a Sämisch-like centre. He aims to use his control of the f1-a6 diagonal (after e2-e4) to establish a light-square grip, especially on the key c4- and b5-squares. Once he has achieved that, he will gradually concentrate on his ideal central advance with e4-e5.

The American GM Max Dlugy has racked up a superb plus score (in my database, 10 wins, 3 draws and 2 losses) with this line and today it often bears his name. My recommendation for countering the Dlugy variation is to wrest control of the dark squares, beginning with 5...e6 6 e4 c4!?. This requires the sacrifice of two pawns instead of the usual one and the resulting positions are razor-sharp, with one misstep often fatal to either side.

Usually in the Benko Gambit, the game follows positional considerations with a gradual build-up by both sides in terms of piece placement. In this line, however, Black eschews structural and positional niceties to try and blow White to bits before he gets to castle. So if this line is not to your taste, I have also included some coverage of the more positional line 5 f3 axb5 6 e4 ♛a5+ as an alternative.

A) White goes the whole hog and grabs two pawns: 7 ♗xc4 axb5 8 ♗xb5

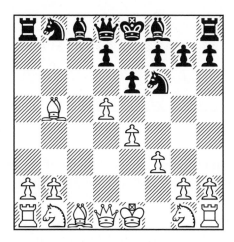

The fight for the d5-square is of the utmost importance. If White wins control over it and sinks a piece permanently on it, Black can kiss his game and sacrificed pawns goodbye. If White loses control of it, though, then usually Black can make use of the long light-square diagonal to create havoc, especially when White still has not found a safe abode for his king.

In Müller-Tay, White barely managed to retain control of the d5-square before becoming too complacent and allowing Black to break with ...d6-d5 with a irresistible attack.

Game 28
Kl.Müller-J.Tay
Correspondence 2002

1 d4 ♘f6 2 c4 c5 3 d5 b5 4 cxb5 a6 5 f3 e6
    Just like in the line recommended against 5 b6, Black tries to undermine White's centre without delay.
6 e4 c4!?

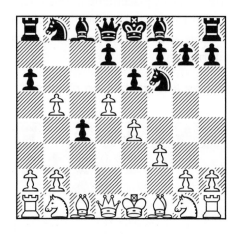

> **Question:** Isn't this ridiculous? Black sacrifices a pawn with a move that even helps White to develop his king's bishop.

Answer: This square-clearance sacrifice has the following logic:

1) White has weakened his structure with f2-f3, creating dark-square weaknesses around his king.

2) Black is going to seize control of the g1-a7 diagonal with his queen and dark-squared bishop.

3) The white king is unable to castle kingside and as Black has opened files on the queenside, it would be extremely dangerous for him to put his king there as well.

4) White's king rook will be hemmed in for a long time.

5) If Black can mobilize all his pieces before White completes development or gets his king to safety, the chances are White will get mated.

However, the cost is two pawns, so it's hustle and flow.

7 ♗xc4

A continuation where White gives up the centre can go 7 dxe6 fxe6 8 ♗xc4, but after 8...♗c5 9 ♘c3 axb5 10 ♗xb5 0-0 11 ♘ge2 ♕b6 12 ♗f4 ♘c6 13 ♕d2 ♗f2+ 14 ♔d1 d5 Black has attacking chances.

One game in which White played prudently, eschewing the proffered b5-pawn at every juncture went 7 ♘c3 axb5 8 ♗e3 ♗b4 9 ♔f2 0-0 10 ♘ge2 d6 11 a3 ♗a5 12 b4 cxb3 13 ♕xb3 ♘a6 14 ♖d1 ♗b6 15 ♘d4 e5 16 ♘c2 ♘c5 17 ♕b2 ♘h5 18 ♗xb5 f5. However, as GM Gawain Jones opined in *Dangerous Weapons: The Benoni and Benko*, "Black has a powerful attack which more than compensates for the rather meaningless extra pawn on a3", with reference to M.Notkin-L.Nisipeanu, Bucharest 1997.

7...axb5 8 ♗xb5 ♗c5 9 ♘c3

As pointed out too by Jones, after the howler 9 ♗g5?, 9...♕b6 wins a piece on either b5 or g1.

9...♗b7

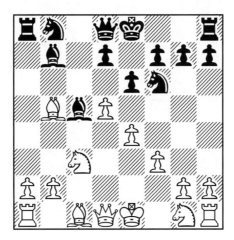

An idea borrowed from Indian GM Harikrishna who used the move in an exciting draw only 9 days before I had to make my 9th move. Black wants to detonate the white centre to get at the king. I had the opportunity to ask about that game and his ...♗b7 idea, and he described it as "very risky, but interesting and fun".

10 ♗g5

This is also Schandorff's recommendation in *Playing 1.d4: The Indian Defences*. By pinning the knight, White is fighting for control of d5.

Instead, after 10 ♘h3 exd5 11 e5 ♘h5 12 ♘xd5 0-0 13 ♘g5?? (necessary was 13 a4 ♖e8 14 f4 ♘f6! 15 ♘xf6+ ♕xf6 16 ♕e2 ♕h4+ 17 ♔f1 ♘c6 18 ♗e3 ♗xe3 19 ♕xe3 ♖ec8 with a difficult defensive task for White) 13...♗xd5 the bishop on b5 hangs after ...♕a5+, J.Hawkins-G.Jones, British Championship, Torquay 2009.

The mind-boggling game which Harikrishna played went 10 ♘ge2 0-0 11 ♔f1 exd5 12 exd5 ♗a7!? 13 g3 ♕b6 14 ♔g2 ♕f2+ 15 ♔h3 ♕xf3 16 ♘f4 ♕f2 17 ♖f1 ♕c5 18 ♖e1 ♕d6 19 ♘h5 ♘xh5 20 ♕xh5 ♗d4 21 a4 ♗xc3 22 bxc3 ♗xd5 23 ♗a3 ♗e6+ 24 ♔g2 ♗d5+ 25 ♔h3 ♗e6+ 26 ♔g2 ♗d5+ 27 ♔h3 ½-½, R.Wojtaszek-P.Harikrishna, Goa 2002.

10...♕b6 11 ♘ge2 0-0!

Schandorff pointed out that 11...exd5 is met by 12 ♗xf6 ♕xf6 13 ♘xd5 ♕d6 14 ♕d2 0-0 15 b4 ♗a7 16 ♕f4 with a huge advantage. The important thing to glean from this is that Black must never stop fighting for control of d5 as once White manages to safely maintain a piece there, he can deal with Black's threats easily.

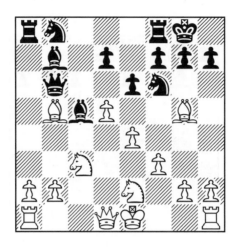

12 ♕b3!

Citing my notes in *New in Chess Yearbook 71*: "A good square for the queen, from which it oversees the b5-bishop, the d5 -quare and with a future ...♗c4, can threaten to exchange queens or maybe even castle queenside."

Otherwise, 12 ♕d2 exd5 13 e5 ♘e8 14 a4 ♘c7 15 ♖d1 (or 15 b4 ♗xb4 16 ♗e3 ♕a5 17 0-0 ♘c6 with a strong initiative for Black) 15...♖e8 (after 15...♘c6! 16 ♘xd5 ♘xd5 17 ♕xd5 ♖ae8 18 ♔f1 ♖xe5 19 ♕d2 ♖fe8 Black's initiative should prevail) 16 b4 ♗xb4 17 ♗e3 ♕a5 18 0-0 ♘c6 19 ♕b2 d4 20 ♖xd4 ♘xd4 21 ♗xd4 ♘e6 22 ♗f2 ♗c6 23 ♖b1 ♗c5 24 ♗xc5 ♘xc5 25 f4 ♗xb5 26 axb5 ♘d3 27 ♕c2 ♕b6+ 28 ♔h1 ♘f2+ 29 ♔g1 ♖ac8 0-1 was V.Seifert-A.Vajda, Austrian League 2004.

12...exd5

Of course, Black must try to open lines for the assault on the white king.

13 e5

Alternatively, 13 ♗xf6 ♕xf6 14 exd5 ♕g5 15 ♘e4 ♗xd5 16 ♘xg5 ♗xb3 reaches a level ending. However, if White tries to keep his extra pawn with 17 a3?! ♗e3!, suddenly the position seems dangerous for him.

13...h6!?

13...♖a5 14 exf6 d4 15 0-0-0 dxc3 16 ♘xc3 ♗d4 was Z.Csiszar-A.Szieberth, Hungarian League 2007, which Black won in short order, but 17 a4! securing the bishop and hence solidifying White's queenside defence would have given him a big advantage.

Also interesting is 13...♘e8!? 14 ♘a4 (and not 14 ♘xd5?? ♗xd5 15 ♕xd5 ♘c7) 14...♗f2+ 15 ♔f1 ♕a7 16 ♗e7 ♘c7 17 ♗xf8 ♔xf8 18 ♘ac3 ♔g8, keeping the queens on the board. My feeling is that Black should have sufficient compensation for the material deficit.

14 ♘a4!

Disrupting Black's queen and bishop battery by forcing those pieces to go to more awkward squares.

White can also focus on development with 14 ♗d2!? ♘e8 15 ♖c1! ♖a5 16 a4! (or 16 ♗a4

♕a6 17 ♘b5 ♗b6 18 ♗xa5 ♕xa5+ 19 ♘ec3 d4 20 ♘xd4 ♕xe5+ 21 ♘de2 ♕c5 with a strong attack and good compensation for Black) 16...♘c7 17 ♘a2 ♖a8 18 ♖xc5 ♕xc5 19 ♗b4 ♕b6 20 ♗xf8 ♔xf8 with the dark squares and developmental compensation for the exchange, while after 14 ♗h4 ♘e8 15 ♖d1 ♘c7 16 ♗d3 ♕a7 Black maintains the pressure with White struggling to complete development.

14...♗f2+ 15 ♔f1 ♕a7 16 exf6

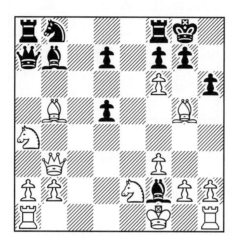

Wrecking Black's pawn structure. By this juncture, though, Black is past caring about positional considerations as he rushes to mobilize his pieces pronto before the white king gets to safety.

16...hxg5 17 fxg7 ♖e8

There's no time for a snack on g7.

18 ♘ac3 ♕e3

Bringing the queen as close as possible to the enemy king. Black's idea is to deny White the possibility of g2-g3 after ♗h4 as the f3-pawn would be en prise.

19 ♖d1

The only reasonable developing move for White and one which has the added incentives of covering the d4-square and hitting d5.

19...♗h4

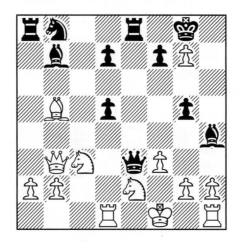

We can't get more obvious than threatening mate in one, can we?

20 ♘g3 g4

Trying to prise open the kingside.

21 ♗d3

Uncovering an attack on b7 as made possible by 20 ♖d1.

21...♗c6 22 ♘xd5

Cashing in on the second pawn with tempo.

22...♕e5

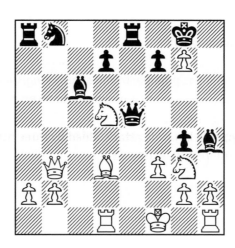

This is the critical stage for White: to liquidate into an endgame with a slight plus, if excellent drawing chances for Black, or to play for more.

23 ♗e4?!

White decides to forgo the endgame, trusting that his spatial advantage will give him the advantage. Unfortunately for him, this is a temporal advantage as once Black's remaining two pieces come into the picture, the unsafe white king and the undeveloped rook on h1 will become significant factors.

White missed the chance to go into an ending two doubled pawns up with 23 f4! ♗xd5 24 fxe5 ♗xb3 25 axb3 ♗xg3 26 hxg3 ♘c6! (after 26...♔xg7 27 ♖h7+ ♔g8 28 ♖h4 ♘c6 29 ♖xg4+ ♔f8 30 ♖h4 ♘xe5 31 ♗e2 ♔e7 32 b4 White has better winning chances by keeping the passed pawns active) 27 ♗e4 ♔xg7 28 ♖h7+ (or 28 ♗xc6 dxc6 29 ♖h4 ♖xe5 30 ♖xg4+ ♔f8 with good drawing chances) 28...♔g8 29 ♖h5 ♖a2 30 ♖xd7 ♘xe5 31 ♖d2 ♖a1+ 32 ♔f2 ♖a5 33 ♖f5 ♔f8 34 ♗d5 ♖e7 35 ♗e4 ♖b5 36 ♗c2 ♔g7 37 ♖f4 ♖c7 38 ♗d1 ♖cb7, although it is by now extremely difficult for White to make any headway.

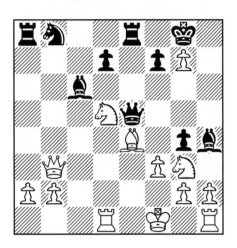

23...♖a5

Not merely to put pressure on d5, but also to prepare ...♖b5, hitting b2.

> ***Question:*** What is wrong with 23...♗a4, winning the exchange?

Answer: Black would be in for a shock after 24 ♕e3! ♗xd1 25 ♕h6! when it is he who has to defend against an unstoppable kingside attack, aided by three huge minor pieces: 25...♕xg7 26 ♕xh4 ♖a6 27 ♘h5 and Black is toast.

24 ♘c3

Playing for trades, which makes sense when one is defending.

24...d5! 25 ♘xd5?

White has effectively lost an important tempo and now Black can accelerate his attack to insurmountable proportions.

White had to settle for a draw here with 25 ♗xd5! ♗xd5 26 ♘xd5 ♗xg3 27 hxg3 ♖xd5 28 ♕xd5 (or 28 ♖h8+ ♔xg7 29 ♖xe8 ♖xd1+ 30 ♕xd1 ♕xe8 31 ♕d4+ ♔h7 32 a4 gxf3 33 gxf3 ♘c6 with a likely draw) 28...♕e2+ 29 ♔g1 ♕e3+ 30 ♔h2 ♕h6+, perpetually checking the white king.

25...♖b5! 26 ♕d3

Another try is 26 f4 ♕d6 (after 26...♕xg7 27 ♕c3 ♖xb2 28 ♕xg7+ ♔xg7 29 ♘c3! ♗xg3 30 ♗xc6 ♘xc6 31 hxg3 ♖c2 32 ♘d5 ♖ee2 33 ♖h2 ♖xa2 34 ♘c3 ♖f2+ 35 ♔g1 ♖ac2 36 ♘d5 White manages to stave off the attack, despite the weird placement of his king's rook) 27 ♕a3 ♕xa3 28 bxa3 ♖xe4 29 ♘xe4 ♗xd5 when Black's minor pieces call the shots and White still has problems developing the h1-rook.

26...♖xb2

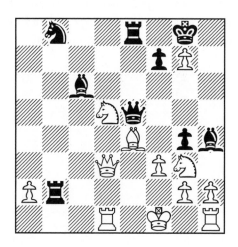

27 f4

Booting the queen off the strong e5-square, but as long as it maintains access to the dark squares, the writing is on the wall for White.

> *Exercise:* Calculate the forced win after 27 ♔g1.

Answer: 27...♗xd5!! 28 ♗xd5 (or 28 ♕xd5 ♖d8 29 ♕xd8+ ♗xd8 30 ♖xd8+ ♔xg7 31 ♘f5+ ♔h7! when there's no good way to make use of the discovered check: 32 ♘g3+ f5 and White is defenceless against ...♕c5+) 28...♕e1+ 29 ♖xe1 (if 29 ♕f1 ♕e3+ 30 ♕f2 ♕xf2# or 29 ♘f1 ♗f2#) 29...♖xe1+ 30 ♕f1 ♖xf1+ 31 ♔xf1 ♗xg3 and White can't save his rook on h1.

27...♕xg7 28 ♘c3

Also insufficient is 28 ♘f5 ♕h8 29 ♘d6 ♖xe4! 30 ♕xe4 ♖f2+ 31 ♔g1 ♖d2 32 ♖b1 ♘a6 33 ♘f5 ♖xd5 34 ♘xh4 ♖b5! 35 ♕d3 ♖xb1+ 36 ♕xb1 ♕d4+ 37 ♔f1 ♗e4 38 ♕c1 ♘c5 when White has no defence.

28...♕h6

Forcing White to trade bishops in order to defend f4 with a knight.

29 ♗xc6

29 ♘ge2 is met by 29...♖xe4! 30 ♘xe4 ♗b5.

29...♘xc6 30 ♘ge2 ♕e6

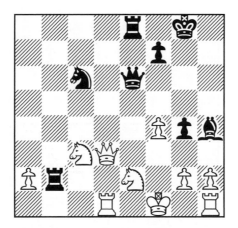

Played with the idea of kicking the white queen off d3 with ...♘b4 so that the black queen can go to e3 with mating threats.

31 g3

After 31 a4 ♘b4 32 ♕b5 ♕e3 the end is near.

31...♗f6 32 f5

Alternatively, 32 ♖g1 ♗xc3 33 ♘xc3 ♘b4 and it's over.

32...♕c8

Citing *New in Chess Yearbook 71* again: "Black's plan is simple. Knock White's queen off the f1-a6 diagonal with ...♘e5, seize control of the diagonal and mate will soon follow."

32...♕e5 was winning too, but I preferred to introduce my knight into the final attack.

33 ♘d5 ♗g7 34 ♘ef4 ♘e5 35 ♕e4 ♘f3 36 ♘e7+ ♖xe7! 0-1

37 ♕xe7 ♗d4 would have been a fitting finish for this variation which focuses on dark-square control at all costs.

B) White keeps only one pawn: 7 ♗xc4 axb5 8 ♗b3

White can choose not to pilfer the second pawn and so offer Black many targets (the half-open b-file, the potentially hanging bishop on b5, a tempo for bringing the queen to b6, ...♘a6-c7 hitting the bishop on b5, etc). This is a prudent concept as Black will need to play ...b5-b4 to open up the a6-f1 diagonal, but White's ♘a4, hitting a bishop on c5 and/or queen on b6, will likely result in trades.

In Rapport-Tate, the Scottish FIDE Master Alan Tate contested d5 with nifty piece play and was rewarded with a GM scalp when the Hungarian teenage wonder spurned a draw.

> *Game 29*
> **R.Rapport-A.Tate**
> Gibraltar 2011

1 d4 ♘f6 2 c4 c5 3 d5 b5 4 cxb5 a6 5 f3 e6 6 e4 c4 7 ♗xc4 axb5 8 ♗b3

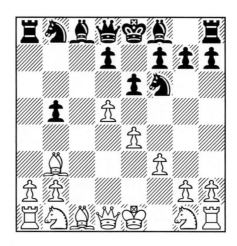

Answer: White would rather not let Black open all three queenside files and keeps a grip on d5 with the bishop. Also, he is satisfied with just one extra pawn. Psychologically, it is often easier to play one pawn up rather than two. With two extra pawns, it is easier to lose objectivity and think that the win is in the bag, but with one extra pawn, one somehow retains the sense of danger that one's opponent has some compensation.

8...♗c5 9 ♘e2 ♛b6 10 ♘bc3 0-0 11 ♗g5 ♘a6

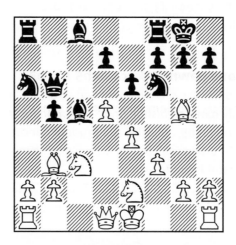

A very logical move as the knight can go to c7, pressuring d5 and protecting the c5-bishop, which will come in handy if White plays ♛c2 or ♖c1.

Instead, after 11...♗b7 12 ♛d2 ♘e8?! (12...♘a6!) 13 ♘c1! f6 14 ♗h4 ♔h8 15 ♗f2 Black does not even have the dark squares to compensate for the pawn deficit, R.Sheldon-

A.Rodriguez, Menorca 1996.

12 g3

White prepares an abode on g2 for the king.

12...♗f2+!

Black played this not so much to scuttle White's chances of castling, but more to indirectly contest d5 with his next move.

13 ♔f1 ♘c5

Enterprising play by Tate, removing or deflecting some defenders of d5.

14 e5!?

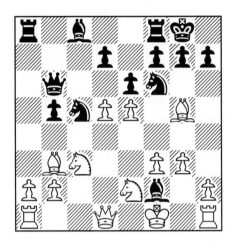

The young grandmaster attempts to engage the Scottish FIDE master in a tactical melee as justified by his 200+ point rating difference.

The planned 14 ♔g2 would have given Black sufficient counterplay after 14...b4 15 ♘a4 ♘xa4 16 ♗xa4 exd5. One interesting follow-up is 17 ♗xf6 dxe4! when White cannot keep the extra piece safely: for example, 18 fxe4 ♕xf6 19 ♖f1 ♕a6 with a decent game for Black.

14...♘xb3!

Removing a defender of d5 and gaining the bishop-pair in the process.

15 exf6

Inflicting structural damage on Black's kingside.

15 ♕xb3?! ♘xd5 16 ♘xd5 exd5 just gifts Black the bishop-pair with the slightly better game.

15...♘xa1 16 fxg7 ♔xg7 17 ♕c1!

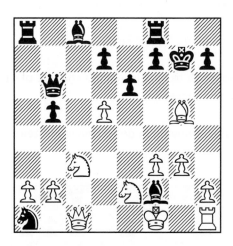

White goes for the weak dark squares around the black king, not pausing to pick off the errant knight which is doomed anyway.

17...f5!?

This is virtually a draw offer as White has a forced draw in hand after this. However, the move makes good sense as it:

1) Removes the e4-square from the white knight.

2) Frees the f7-square for the black king to escape to.

Alternatively, 17...e5 18 ♘e4 f5 19 ♘xf2 might be all right for Black in analysis, but under tournament conditions, it is very risky to allow White to keep the unopposed dark-squared bishop, while 17...♗b7 18 ♗h6+ ♔h8 19 ♗g7+ ♔xg7 20 ♕g5+ draws by perpetual check.

18 ♗h6+ ♔f7 19 ♗xf8 ♔xf8

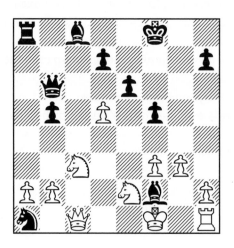

20 ♕xa1?!

With hindsight a dubious decision as now Black proceeds to play accurately right to the end. Rapport was banking on the porous black kingside to give him chances and thus rejected the outright draw. Indeed, he could have decided to split the point here with 20 ♕h6+ ♔g8 21 ♕g5+ ♔f7 22 ♕h5+ ♔e7 23 ♕g5+ ♔d6 24 ♕f4+, with perpetual check.

From personal experience, I know that grandmasters play on in positions which are drawish or sometimes even worse for them, but due to their practical strength, it pays off more often than not.

20...b4!

Booting away a defender of d5 and also clearing the a6-f1 diagonal for his own bishop. Most importantly, though, it denies White the opportunity to secure the c3-knight with b2-b4.

21 ♘d1

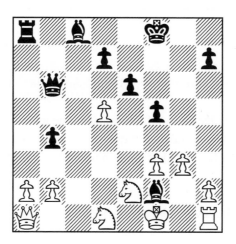

21...♗d4!?

> **Question:** Why didn't Black keep the bishop-pair with 21...♗c5?

Answer: He did not want to give white counterplay after 22 ♕c1 ♗a6 23 ♕h6+ ♔e8 24 ♕xh7 ♕b5 25 ♕g8+ ♔e7 26 ♕g5+ ♔d6 27 ♕f4+ ♔xd5 28 ♕d2+ ♔c6 29 h4, although the resulting position still looks pleasant for Black.

22 ♔g2

Black also doesn't mind the trade of the dark-squared bishop as it improves his queen's position: 22 ♘xd4 ♕xd4 23 ♔g2 (or 23 ♕c1 ♗b7 24 ♔g2 ♗xd5) 23...♗b7! 24 dxe6?? ♗xf3+!.

22...♗b7

Now that the white king has left f1, Black goes for the long light-square diagonal.

23 ♘xd4 ♕xd4

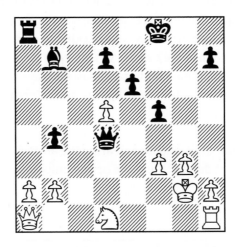

24 ♘f2?

> *Exercise:* You have just three seconds to calculate what happens after 24 dxe6.

Answer: 24...♗xf3+ 25 ♔xf3 ♕e4+ 26 ♔f2 ♕xh1 does the job.

However, White should have hurried to get his major pieces back into action after 24 ♕c1 ♗xd5 25 ♖e1 ♖xa2 26 ♖e2. Black is a pawn up, but it would be harder to White away in this line.

24...♕xd5

Material is even here, but every black piece is substantially stronger than its white counterpart.

25 ♕d1

Forced.

25...♖xa2 26 ♕e2 ♕b3

Pinning White down. The game is virtually over.

27 ♖b1 ♗c6

White is in zugzwang. Most knight moves are met by 28...♗xf3+ and 29...♕c2+ winning the rook, or if 28 ♘d3 ♗b5. White is almost reduced to pawn moves on the kingside which he will soon run out of.

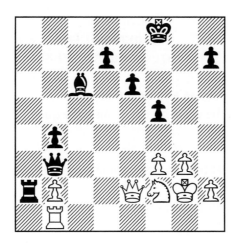

28 ♕d3 ♗d5 29 ♔h3

Trading queens is also futile: 29 ♕xb3 ♗xb3 30 ♘d1 ♗xd1 31 ♖xd1 ♖xb2+ 32 ♔g1 d5 is simply winning for Black.

29...♖xb2 30 ♖c1 ♕xd3 31 ♘xd3 ♖b3 32 ♘e5 ♔e7 33 f4 ♖c3 34 ♖a1 ♖c7 0-1

As previously mentioned, if 'hustle and flow' is not your style, here's a more sedate and positional approach against the Dlugy variation.

C) 5 f3 axb5 6 e4 ♕a5+

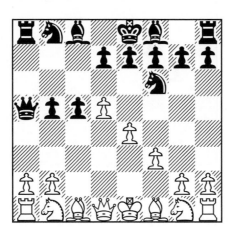

My first correspondence chess game with the Benko Gambit survived its baptism of fire against the Russian correspondence chess champion Sergey Romanov in this line. I would also like to acknowledge the contribution of Erik Kislik here, as he demonstrated to me how giving up the light-squared bishop in the 10 a3 line is fine for Black; a concept which I failed to grasp during my game against Romanov.

Game 30
S.Romanov-J.Tay
Correspondence 1999

1 d4 ♘f6 2 c4 c5 3 d5 b5 4 cxb5 a6 5 f3 axb5 6 e4 ♕a5+

Solving the problem of the weak b5-pawn. Also, the queen check nullifies the need to defend against e4-e5 for now.

7 ♗d2

The simplest way to meet the counter-gambit 7 b4!? is 7...♕xb4+ 8 ♗d2 ♕a4 when we have:

a) 9 ♕xa4 bxa4 10 ♘c3 d6 11 ♖b1 ♘fd7! 12 ♗b5 ♗a6! 13 ♗xa4 g6 with a comfortable game for Black.

b) 9 ♕c1 b4! 10 ♕xc5 ♘a6 11 ♗xa6 (if 11 ♕d4 e6!) 11...♗xa6 (11...e6!? 12 d6 jamming the black kingside was played in J.Lautier-I.Smirin, Cap d'Agde (rapid) 1996; I don't fancy Black's kingside development, although analysis of the resulting positions shows that Black is at least level) 12 ♕xb4 ♕xb4 13 ♗xb4 g6 14 ♘d2 ♗g7 15 ♖c1 d6 16 ♘e2 0-0 17 a3 ♘d7 and I prefer Black's pressure to White's extra pawn.

7...b4

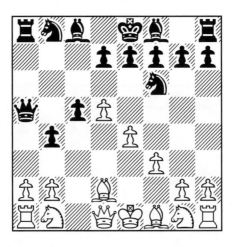

Exercise: Assess this position in terms of pros and cons.

Answer: The good news about this line is:

1) Black is not a pawn down, which is a big deal for a Benko Gambiteer.

2) White's pawn structure makes his development slightly cumbersome (there's no natural ♘f3 and ♘c3 development).

3) Black for now has more space on the queenside.

The bad news is:

1) White has the juicy c4-square for a knight.

2) He occupies the centre rather solidly.

3) He can play a2-a4 in good time to create an outside passed pawn, or a2-a3 to harass the b4-pawn.

8 ♘a3 d6 9 ♘c4 ♕d8!

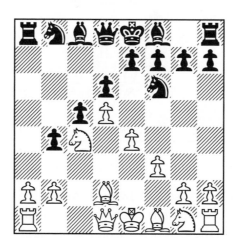

The slight advantage of 9...♕d8 over 9...♕a7 or 9...♕c7 is that the queen provides more support to the ...d6-d5 push after ...e7-e6; dxe6 ♗xe6.

10 ♗d3

Important alternatives are:

a) 10 ♘e2 e6 (once again, an immediate fight for d5; instead, after 10...g6 11 a3 bxa3 12 ♖xa3 ♖xa3 13 bxa3 ♗g7 14 ♕a4+ ♗d7 15 ♕a7 White's passed a-pawn gives him a slight edge, D.Paulsen-M.Trauth, Zurich 2000) 11 dxe6 fxe6! was J.Ulko-A.Fominyh, Nizhnij Novgorod 1998, where Black has a nice central presence and a potential central pawn advance, but 11...♗xe6 12 ♘f4 is pleasant for White according to Flear.

b) 10 a3 e6 11 dxe6 (after 11 axb4 ♖xa1 12 ♕xa1 exd5 13 exd5 ♘xd5 14 ♕a8 ♗e6 15 bxc5 dxc5 16 ♗a5 ♕c8 the game is level according to Schandorff) 11...♗xe6 12 ♘e3 (or 12 axb4 ♖xa1 13 ♕xa1 d5! and after 14 exd5 ♘xd5 15 b5 ♗e7 Black is at least equal according to analysis by Kislik, while after 14 ♘e5 dxe4 15 ♗b5+ ♘fd7 16 ♕a7 ♗d6 17 ♘c4?? ♗xc4 18 ♗xc4 e3 he won in M.Dlugy-A.Battey, Internet 2013) 12...d5 13 exd5 ♘xd5 14 ♗b5+ ♗d7 15 ♘xd5 ♗xb5 16 ♗g5 ♕d7 17 ♔f2 f6 18 ♗f4 ♔f7 19 ♘c7 ♖a5 20 ♘xb5 ♕xd1 21 ♖xd1 ♖xb5 and Black is fine here according to Kislik.

c) White can create a passed pawn with 10 a4, but Black has a comfortable game as shown by the Italian GM Belotti: 10...e6 11 dxe6 ♗xe6 12 ♘e3 ♗e7 13 ♘e2 0-0 14 ♘f4 ♘c6 15 ♗d3 ♘d4 16 ♘c4 ♘d7 17 0-0 ♘e5 18 ♘xe6 ♘xe6 19 ♗e3 ♗f6 20 ♘xe5 ♗xe5 21 ♖a2 ♕h4 22 g3 ♗xg3 23 hxg3 ♕xg3+ 24 ♔h1 ♕h3+ ½-½, I.Sokolov-B.Belotti, Moscow Olympiad 1994.

10...e6 11 dxe6 ♗xe6 12 ♘e2

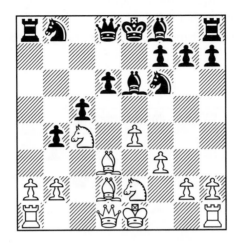

12...d5!?

Following 12...♘c6 13 ♘f4 (13 0-0 ♗e7 14 ♘f4 comes to the same thing) 13...♗e7 14 0-0 0-0 "Black has finished his development and has no meaningful pawn weaknesses. The position is roughly equal" in the view of Aveskulov. Kislik went on to analyse that 15 a4 d5 16 exd5 ♗xd5!? 17 ♘xd5 ♕xd5 18 ♗e2 ♖fd8 sees Black's space advantage nullify White's bishop-pair.

13 exd5 ♘xd5

Following the analysis session with Erik, I realized that Black could also reply with 13...♗xd5!? 14 ♘f4 (or 14 0-0 ♗e7 15 a4 bxa3 16 ♖xa3 ♖xa3 17 bxa3 ♘c6 18 ♗c3 0-0 and Black is not worse) 14...♗b7 15 0-0 ♗e7 16 ♕c2 0-0 17 ♖fd1 ♘c6. Even though White has the c4 blockade, Black has good central control (the d4-square and more space), and easy development for his pieces.

14 ♘f4

I think 14 0-0 ♗e7 15 ♕c2 is best met by 15...h6 as in W.Browne-J.Waitzkin, San Francisco 1995. Indeed, I feel that Black can equalize even though White has a nice outpost on c4: for example, 16 f4 (or 16 ♗f5 ♗xf5 17 ♕xf5 ♕d7 18 ♕xd7+ ♘xd7 19 ♖fc1 0-0 with equal chances; White's outpost is balanced by Black's pressure on the a-file) 16...0-0 17 f5 ♗c8 18 ♗e4 ♗b7 19 ♘f4 ♗f6 20 ♖fd1 ♘xf4 21 ♗xb7 ♘e2+ 22 ♔h1 ♖a7 23 ♗e4 ♘d4 with active play for Black.

14...♘xf4 15 ♗xf4 ♘d7?!

Better was the simple 15...♗e7 16 0-0 0-0 17 ♕c2 ♘c6! when Black can just sacrifice the h7-pawn for a space advantage: 18 ♗xh7+ ♔h8 19 ♗e4 (or 19 ♗d3 b3! threatening ...♘b4, and if 20 ♕e2 ♘b4 21 ♗e4 ♕d4+ 22 ♘e3 ♖xa2 when White is in serious trouble) 19...♘d4 20 ♕d3 ♖a7 and Black is already threatening ...f7-f5.

16 0-0 ♕f6

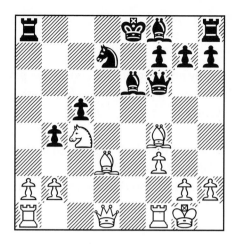

17 ♗g3!

This quiet move was a novelty and now I began to realize why Romanov was the Russian correspondence champion. Unlike in the Olafsson-Wang Zili game mentioned below, White frees his queen to hit h7 and mobilizes his rooks swiftly. Instead, Black had no problems after 17 ♕d2 ♗e7 18 ♗e4 ♗xc4! 19 ♗xa8 ♗xf1 20 ♖xf1 0-0 21 ♗e4 ♘b6 22 b3 ♖d8 23 ♕e3 ♘d5 24 ♗xd5 ♖xd5 25 ♖e1 ♗f8 26 ♗e5 ♕e6 27 ♕e2 h6 28 ♗f4 and ½-½ in H.Olafsson-Wang Zili, Moscow Olympiad 1994.

17...♗e7 18 ♕c2 h5!

Black feints a kingside attack to disrupt White's piece coordination. After 18...h6 19 a4! bxa3 20 ♖xa3 ♖xa3 21 bxa3 0-0 22 ♖e1 White is extremely solidly placed and Black can only wait passively as White slowly advances his a-pawn.

19 ♗f2 h4

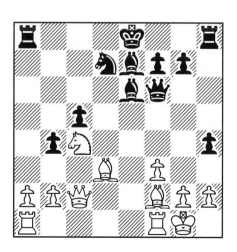

> *Question:* Should White be worried about Black's pawn rush?

20 ♖fe1!

Answer: Definitely not. White, by ignoring Black's aggressive pawn lunge, can concentrate on central pressure, which once again pays homage to the adage that a flank attack is best countered by action in the centre.

20...h3 21 ♗f5!

A neat way to take advantage of the black king being in the centre.

21...♗xf5 22 ♕xf5 ♕xf5 23 ♘d6+ ♔f8 24 ♘xf5

Now it's time for Black to take drastic measures to counter White's lead in development.

24...♗f6 25 ♖ad1!

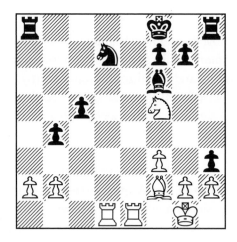

There's no rest for the wicked. Now Black must remain on the defensive, whereas 25 ♖e2 would have given me just enough time to complete my development and reach a level position after 25...g6 26 ♘g3 ♔g7 27 ♘e4 ♗d4.

25...♖a7 26 ♘d6 g6 27 a3!

A nice finesse by White. Now he obtains a passed a pawn for Black to worry with.

27...bxa3 28 bxa3 hxg2 29 ♔xg2 ♖h5

Defending c5 and also playing for exchanges with ...♖e5.

30 ♖e8+ ♔g7 31 ♘e4

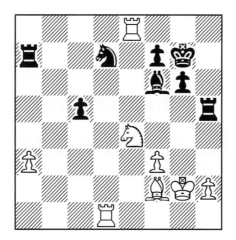

Black has a sombre position and does not even have time to eye the a3-pawn.

> *Exercise:* Can you find a way for Black to unravel?

Answer: 31...♖e5!

This pawn sacrifice frees Black from his defensive duties.

32 ♖xd7

Better is 32 ♖xe5 ♗xe5 33 ♘xc5 ♘xc5 34 ♗xc5 when White has an extra pawn, although Black has excellent drawing chances with his active pieces.

32...♖xe4 33 ♖xe4 ♖xd7 34 ♗xc5 ♖d2+ 35 ♔g3 g5!

This move secures the draw for Black who can remove enough wood to ensure the draw thanks to his mobile pawns, active rook and the precarious position of the white king.

36 ♗e7

Black can hold too after 36 a4 ♔g6 37 ♗e3 ♖a2 38 ♖c4 ♗e5+ 39 f4 ♖a3! 40 ♔f2 ♖a2+ 41 ♔f3 gxf4 42 ♗xf4 ♗xf4 43 ♖xf4 ♖xh2.

36...♗xe7 37 ♖xe7 ♔g6 38 ♖a7

Once again, 38 a4 is no problem: 38...f5 39 a5 f4+ 40 ♔h3 ♖f2 41 ♖c7 ♔h5! 42 ♖h7+ ♔g6 and a draw will result.

38...f5

Thanks to Black's more active king and rook, the draw is in the bag.

39 h4 f4+ 40 ♔h3 ♖f2 41 hxg5 ♔h5 42 ♖a5 ½-½

Chapter Five
The Safety Dance

1 d4 ♘f6 2 c4 c5 3 d5 b5 4 cxb5 a6 5 e3

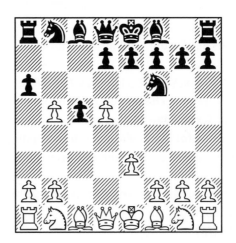

This line is termed the Modern Variation. White accepts the gambit pawn and plays to hold it without opening too many queenside files for Black. In an ideal state of affairs, he would like to play ♘c3, ♘f3, a2-a4, ♖a3 and gradually e3-e4. Hence, I term this line the 'Safety Dance' as White slowly attempts to keep control without compromising his classical pawn structure (knights on c3 and f3, pawns on d5 and e4). My recommendation against this line is once again to take immediate action in the centre with 5...e6!?.

In the Blumenfeld Gambit (1 d4 ♘f6 2 c4 e6 3 ♘f3 c5 4 d5 b5), I consider the positional continuation 5 ♗g5! the toughest for Black to meet as White keeps a grip on d5 pretty comfortably. Thus the recommended 5...e6!? reply to the Modern Variation is akin to White playing the insipid e2-e3 instead of ♗g5 against the Blumenfeld.

A) White plays in Blumenfeld Accepted style: 6 dxe6 fxe6 7 bxa6

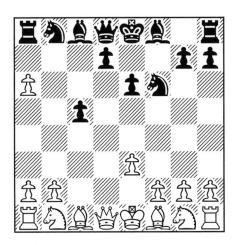

White trusts in his defensive skills as this line virtually gifts Black the whole centre and an open f-file to boot. In Samartsev-Ponkratov, White could not cope with Black's queenside pressure plus attack against his king. Probably White does better to develop his queenside first before castling so as not to provide Black with an early target, although the resulting positions are still satisfactory for Black.

Game 31
A.Samartsev-P.Ponkratov
Khanty-Mansiysk 2010

1 d4 ♞f6 2 c4 c5 3 d5 b5 4 cxb5 a6 5 e3 e6

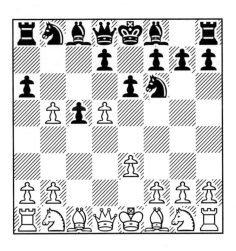

This move has not been recommended in recent Benko Gambit tomes. However, during my early correspondence chess days, I could not find anything wrong with the black set-up and 10 years later, after doing the research for this project, I still think that Black is holding his own.

6 dxe6

White decides to accept Black's gambit pawn and weather the storm. This brings us into Blumenfeld Gambit territory.

6...fxe6 7 bxa6

White might do better to concentrate on development:

a) 7 ♘c3 d5 8 ♘f3 c4 9 bxa6 ♘xa6 10 ♗e2 ♘c5 11 ♗d2 ♗e7 12 0-0 0-0 13 ♕c2 ♕b6 14 ♘d4 ♗d7 15 b3 cxb3 16 axb3 ♘ce4 17 ♘xe4 ♘xe4 18 ♖xa8 ♖xa8 and White's extra pawn is counterbalanced by Black's space advantage and ability to press on the b-pawn, J.Knudsen-A.De Groot, correspondence 1999.

b) 7 ♘f3 d5 8 b3 ♗d6 9 ♗b2 0-0 10 ♘bd2 ♘bd7 11 ♕c2 ♕b6 12 ♗d3 axb5 when I prefer Black's centre and free play to White's extra pawn, H.Gruenberg-R.Knaak, Plauen 1980.

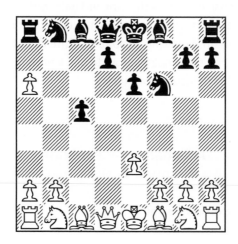

Question: Which piece should Black use to recapture a6?

Answer: None for now!

7...d5

There is no rush to retrieve the a6-pawn as Black unfurls his strong centre (some would call it an umbrella).

8 ♗b5+ ♘bd7 9 ♘e2?!

A rather strange square for the knight. 9 ♘f3 would be more natural.

9...♗d6 10 0-0 0-0 11 ♘g3

This is White's idea, to shield the d6-bishop with the knight.

11...♗xa6 12 ♗xa6 ♖xa6 13 ♘c3 ♕b8!

Black puts pressure on the b-file and also the h2-b8 diagonal simultaneously.

14 a4 ♕b4!

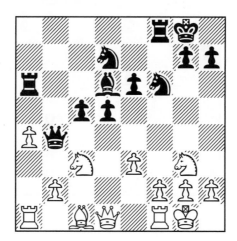

By threatening to shift the queen to h4, Black provokes a weakness from White.

15 f4 c4!

It was all a feint as GM Ponkratov merely wanted to weaken White's structure. Now b3 and d3 become juicy squares for Black's knights to plant themselves on.

16 f5

A desperate attempt to fight back as White tries to undermine the e6-d5-c4 pawn chain.

16...♗xg3

Taking the opportunity to weaken White's kingside pawns and earn a tempo for the queen to find its way nearer the king.

17 hxg3 ♕d6 18 ♘b5!

Giving up the g3-pawn in the hope that he can make use of e6 to create some threats.

18 fxe6 ♕xe6 19 g4 h6 20 ♕d4 also puts up a fight.

18...♕xg3

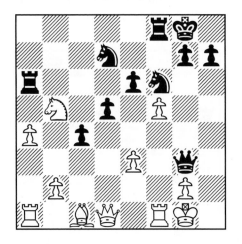

19 ♖f3?!

Although it looks logical for White to drive the queen from g3, there was a better way to do so.

> *Exercise:* After 19 e4! what is wrong with 19...♘xe4?

Answer: It allows White to take over the position after 20 ♗f4! ♕h4 21 fxe6 when Black is in trouble.

Instead, 19...♕b8! allows Black to retain the better game as 20 ♗f4 is met by 20...♕b6+ 21 ♔h1 e5.

19...♕b8 20 fxe6 ♖xe6 21 ♘d4 ♖e4

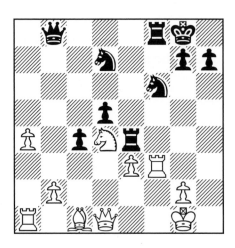

White is still cramped and there simply is no way to stop the marauding black pieces from making a beeline for the white king.

22 ♖f4

After 22 a5 ♘e5 23 ♖h3 ♘d3 24 a6 ♕b6 25 b3 ♘g4 White will not last long either.

22...♘e5 23 ♘e6 ♖e8

It's all over.

24 ♖xf6 gxf6 0-1

A possible finish could be 25 ♕xd5 ♘f3+ 26 ♔f2 (or 26 gxf3 ♕g3+ 27 ♔f1 ♕xf3+ 28 ♔e1 ♖xe3+ 29 ♗xe3 ♕xd5) 26...♖8xe6 27 gxf3 ♕h2+ with a whitewash.

B) 6 ♘c3 exd5 7 ♘xd5

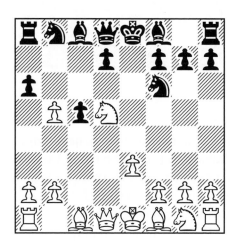

White temporarily occupies d5 in this line and gives it up to complete kingside castling. However, Black gets a truckload of space in return for the gambit pawn, as in our next game.

Game 32
K.Pecotic-M.Dos Santos
Correspondence 2006

---

1 d4 ♘f6 2 c4 c5 3 d5 b5 4 cxb5 a6 5 e3 e6 6 ♘c3

White keeps control of the d5-square.

6...exd5 7 ♘xd5 ♗b7

Removing the white knight with tempo while placing the bishop on the excellent long diagonal.

8 ♘xf6+ ♕xf6 9 ♘f3 ♗e7

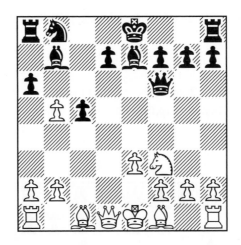

10 bxa6

Some other possibilities:

a) White can also play to lose a move in order to get his bishop to a more active square via 10 ♗c4 axb5 11 ♗xb5, but after 11...0-0 12 0-0 ♖d8 13 e4 ♕e6 (or 13...♗xe4 14 ♗g5 ♕xb2 15 ♗xe7 ♖e8 16 ♗xd7 ♖xe7 17 ♗f5 ♗c6 18 ♕d6 ♕f6 19 ♕xf6 gxf6 with equality, J.Rizzardi-M.Dos Santos, correspondence 2006) 14 ♗d3 ♖xa2 15 ♖xa2 ♕xa2 16 ♕c2 ♘c6 17 ♗c4 ♘b4 18 ♕c3 ♕a8 19 ♕e5 ♖e8 20 ♕h5 ♖f8 21 ♗g5 ♕e8 22 ♖e1 ♗xg5 23 ♘xg5 h6 24 ♘h3?! d5! and the e-pawn is toast, A.Pavlov-A.Fominyh, Perm 1998.

b) 10 ♕b3 0-0 11 bxa6? ♗xf3 12 gxf3 ♕xf3 13 ♖g1 ♗h4 14 ♕c2 ♘xa6 15 ♕e2 ♕f6 16 ♖g4 ♘b4 and despite having the bishop-pair, White is markedly worse as Black's pieces dominate the board, F.Portisch-R.Vaganian, Kecskemet 1979.

c) 10 ♗e2 0-0 11 0-0 d5 12 a4 axb5 13 ♗xb5 ♖d8 with a strong centre and easy piece play for the pawn, M.Lacrosse-D.Collas, Cappelle la Grande 1991.

d) White chose to return the pawn with 10 b6 in N.Zhukova-V.Golubenko, Khanty-Mansiysk 2010, and after 10...0-0 11 ♗e2 d5 12 0-0 ♕xb6 13 b3 ♗f6 14 ♖b1 ♘c6 15 ♗b2 d4 16 ♘d2 ♖ad8 17 ♗f3 dxe3 18 fxe3 Black had an excellent position, even though at this juncture a draw was agreed.

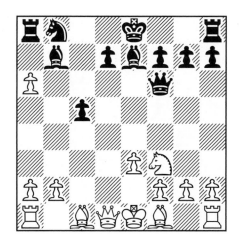

> **Question:** After 10 bxa6 how should Black recapture the pawn?

Answer: No tricks this time.

10...♘xa6!

Usually in the Benko Black wants to trade the light-squared bishops. Here it is more logical to capture with the knight, though:

1) Black has sacrificed a pawn for swift development. Thus it makes less sense for him to trade off White's bishop on f1 in one move, allowing White to castle swiftly.

2) The knight on a6 will soon be integral in creating threats on the queenside and in the centre, with the aid of the queen's rook and the queen.

Instead, after 10...♗xa6?! 11 ♗xa6 ♕xa6 12 ♕e2 ♗f6 13 a3 0-0 14 ♖b1 ♘c6 15 ♕xa6 ♖xa6 16 ♔e2 ♖b8 17 ♖d1 ♖xa3 18 ♖xd7 ♖a6 19 ♘d2 ♖e8 20 ♖d5 ♘d4+ 21 ♔f1 ♘e6 22 ♘e4 ♗e7 23 ♗d2 ♖a4 24 f3 f6 25 ♗c3 incredibly Black even managed to outplay White in the endgame after being a pawn and later the exchange down in D.Gordievsky-V.Zvjaginsev, Khanty-Mansiysk 2013.

11 ♗e2

After 11 ♗d2 ♕xb2 (forcing a queen trade; Black can play for more with 11...0-0 12 ♗e2 ♘c7 13 0-0 ♕g6 with attacking chances) 12 ♖b1 ♗xf3 13 ♖xb2 ♗xd1 14 ♔xd1 ♘c7 there are equal chances, T.Ghitescu-R.Knaak, Zinnowitz 1983.

11...♘b4

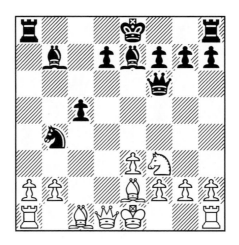

Immediately threatening a2. Note that Black has five pieces developed compared to White's two. However, there is no direct kingside attack and Black is playing more for space and pressure rather than a king hunt, unlike in, say, the Evans or Danish Gambit.

12 a3

Two quick draws occurred after 12 0-0 ♖xa2 13 ♖xa2 and ½-½ in V.Babula-J.Plachetka, Portoroz 1998, and 13...♘xa2 14 ♕b3 ♘b4 15 ♗d2 0-0 16 ♗xb4 cxb4 17 ♘d4 ♖c8 18 ♗f3 ♗xf3 ½-½, L.Renaze-C.Adrian, French League 2007. However, of course, Black can simply ignore the a2-pawn and complete development with 12...0-0.

12...0-0!

There's no need to move the knight as the a-pawn is pinned down. Less accurate are:

a) 12...♕g6?! 13 0-0 ♘c2 14 ♗d3 ♗e4 15 ♗xe4 ♕xe4 16 ♖b1 ♘e1 17 ♗d2 ♘xf3+ 18 ♕xf3 ♕xf3 19 gxf3 d5 20 ♗c3 was S.Halkias-A.Szieberth, Cappelle la Grande 2002, and, as Tisdall remarked on chesspublishing.com, "White has a long technical task ahead, but there can be little doubt that this is an extra pawn for not too much."

b) 12...♗e4 13 0-0 ♘c2? (13...0-0 transposes back to the game continuation) 14 ♘d2! ♘xa1 15 ♘xe4 ♕e6 16 ♘c3 c4 (if 16...♘b3 17 ♘d5! or 16...0-0 17 ♗f3 ♖ab8 18 ♗d5!) 17 ♘d5 ♖c8 18 ♘xe7 ♕xe7 19 ♗d2 ♘b3 20 ♗b4 and the bishop-pair rules.

13 0-0 ♗e4

Homing in on the c2-square.

14 ♘e1

Covering c2 and preparing in good time to advance in the centre with f2-f3 and e3-e4.

Note too the neat line 14 ♕xd7 ♘c2 15 ♖b1 ♘e1 16 ♖a1?! (if White decides to repeat, expecting ...♘c2 and ...♘e1, he'll be in for a big shock; instead, 16 ♖xe1 ♗xb1 gives equal chances) 16...♘xf3+ 17 ♗xf3 ♗xf3 18 gxf3 ♕xf3! 19 ♕xe7 ♖a6! 20 ♕h4 ♖g6+ 21 ♕g3 h5! 22 e4 h4 23 ♕xg6 fxg6 24 h3 ♕xh3 25 f4 g5! and White is crushed.

14...d5

Black mobilizes his strong central pawns.

15 ♘d3

White plans to exchange off the pesky b4-knight.

Instead, 15 f3 ♗g6 16 ♘d3 ♖fd8 17 ♘xb4 cxb4 18 ♗d3 bxa3 19 ♗xg6 hxg6 20 ♖a2 axb2 21 ♗xb2 ♕e6 22 ♖xa8 ♕xe3+ ½-½ was R.De Boer-R.Hendriks, correspondence 1994.

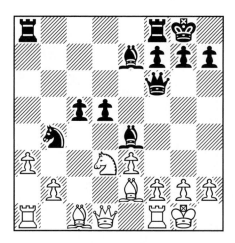

Answer: **15...♖fc8!**

Black envisages the opening of the c-file and the invasion of the rook on c2.

Also interesting is 15...♕g5!?. Previously, though, Black had played to prepare the ...d5-d4 push, but he could not do better than a level game: 15...♖fd8 16 ♘xb4 cxb4 17 f3 ♗f5 18 ♗d3 ♗xd3 19 ♕xd3 bxa3 20 ♖a2 d4 21 bxa3 ♕e6 22 ♖c2 ½-½ G.Timoscenko-V.Arbakov, Irkutsk 1983.

16 ♘xb4

Generally it's a good policy for the side with less space to exchange pieces. Black has a good game after 16 a4!? ♕g6 17 ♘f4 (or 17 ♘e1 ♖d8! with the idea of ...d5-d4) 17...♕h6 18 ♗f3 ♗d6 19 ♗xe4 dxe4 20 ♕e2 c4 21 ♗d2 ♘d3.

16...cxb4 17 a4

White manages to create a passed pawn and Black now proceeds to stop its advance.

17...♖c5 18 ♕b3?

Finally, White gets round to an active move, but the queen is required for defensive duties on the kingside and centre.

After the correct 18 f3! ♗c2 19 ♕d4 ♕xd4 20 exd4 ♖ca5 21 ♖e1 White has reached parity.

18...♗d6

Threatening to induce weaknesses in the kingside pawn structure with ...♕h6 or ...♕h4.

Even better would have been 18...♕g6! 19 f3 (after 19 g3 ♖c2 20 ♗d1 ♕c6! 21 ♗g4 ♖a5 22 ♖d1 (22 ♗h3 ♖a6 23 ♗g2 ♕e2 White has run out of moves) 22...♖xf2!!) 19...♖c2 20 ♖e1 (20 ♖f2 ♗h4) 20...♕h5 21 fxe4 ♖xe2 22 ♕d1 ♖xe1+ 23 ♕xe1 dxe4 when Black's huge space advantage is more significant than White's passed a-pawn.

19 f3 ♕h4 20 f4 ♖c2

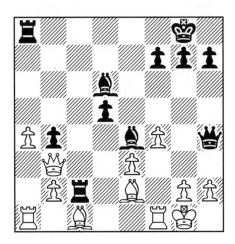

The point of 15...♖fc8 is realized. White is tied down to total defence.

21 ♗f3 ♕e7 22 ♖d1

White threatens 23 ♗xe4 ♕xe4 24 ♕xd5.

22...♖ac8!

Now White's plan is not possible because of his weak back rank.

23 ♗d2 ♕e6!

Black prepares to invade on the kingside after wrecking White's structure with a trade on f3 in good time.

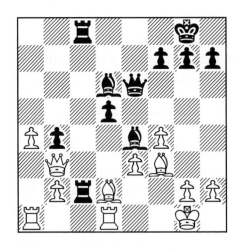

24 ♖ac1

Question: What is Black's best continuation if White ignores the threat with 24 a5?

Answer: 24...♗xf3 25 gxf3 ♕g6+ 26 ♔h1 ♕h5 27 ♔g2 ♖8c6! 28 ♕d3 ♗f8 29 ♕e2 d4! 30 exd4 ♖e6 31 ♕f2 ♖xb2 and the white pawn still cannot advance due to ...♕g6+ and ...♖xa6.

24...♖8c4!

This ties White down to play on the first three ranks only.

25 ♗xe4

A forced move as there was nothing else to play.

25...♕xe4 26 ♖xc2 ♖xc2 27 h3 h6?!

It's too bad this move is unnecessary. Usually creating a luft is a good idea, but time is of essence in this position and Black must make forcing moves for a winning attempt.

Santos could have considered 27...♗c5! (threatening ...♖xd2) 28 ♔h2! (28 ♔h1 only wastes a tempo compared to 28 ♔h2: 28...♕c4! 29 ♕xc4 dxc4 30 ♗c1 ♗f8 and Black's active pieces and advanced queenside pawns accord him a strong advantage) 28...♕c4! 29 ♕xc4 dxc4 30 ♗c1 ♔f8 31 ♔g3 ♔e7 32 ♔f3 b3 33 a5 c3 34 bxc3 b2 35 ♗xb2 ♖xb2 when Black has some winning chances.

28 a5!

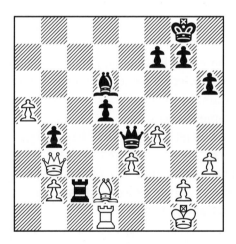

28...d4

Trying to force open the dark squares around the white king. Instead, after 28...♗c5 29 ♔h2 ♕c4 30 ♕xc4 dxc4 31 ♗c1 c3 32 bxc3 b3 33 ♔g3 b2 34 ♗xb2 ♖xb2 35 ♖d8+ ♔h7 36 ♖d5 ♗xe3 37 ♔f3 ♗a7 38 ♖d7 ♗c5 39 ♖d5 ♗f8 40 ♖d8 White draws comfortably.

29 ♔h1

Not 29 exd4?? ♖xd2 30 ♖xd2 ♕e1+ 31 ♔h2 ♗xf4+ 32 g3 ♕xd2+.

29...d3

Black creates his own passed pawn.

30 a6 ♗c5

Covering a7.

31 a7 ♗xa7 32 ♕xb4

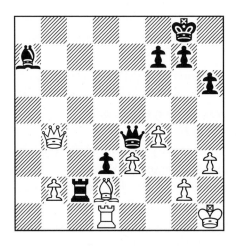

32...♕xb4?!

Black goes a pawn up in this ending, but White will hold firm to draw it.

> ***Exercise:*** Can you find a better way for Black to maintain the pressure on White?

Answer: 32...f5! is the last chance for Black to play for a win. He need not worry about 33 ♕xe4 as 33...fxe4 gives him a protected passed pawn and White's b-pawn cannot travel very far without getting caught by the black rook: 33 b3 h5! 34 ♕a4 ♗c5 35 ♔h2 h4 36 ♔h1 ♔h7 37 ♔h2 ♖b2 with winning chances.

33 ♗xb4 ♗xe3 34 ♖xd3 ♗xf4 35 g3 ♖xb2 36 ♗c3 ♖b1+ 37 ♔g2 ♗b8 38 ♖e3 ♖b7 39 ♔f3 f6 40 g4 ♔f7 41 ♗d4 ♖b4 42 ♗c5 ♖f4+ 43 ♔e2 ♗e5 44 ♖a3 ♖c4 45 ♗f2 ♔g6 46 ♔f3 h5 47 ♗e3 ♖c2 48 ♗f4 ♗xf4 49 ♔xf4 h4 50 ♔e4 ♖e2+ 51 ♔f3 ♖b2 52 ♔e4 ♖b4+ 53 ♔e3 ♔h6 54 ♔f3 g6 55 ♔f2 ♔g5 56 ♔g2 ♖b2+ 57 ♔g1 f5 58 gxf5 gxf5 59 ♖a8 ♖e2 60 ♔f1 ♖c2 61 ♔g1 ♖d2 62 ♖a3 ♔f4 63 ♖a4+ ♔f3 64 ♖a3+ ½-½

C) 6 ♘c3 exd5 7 ♘ge2 (or 7 ♘h3)

Now we'll see White temporarily giving up d5 only to secure it a bit later. In Grabuzova-Sterliagova, Black had to sacrifice the exchange to prevent White from consolidating her grip on d5 and she obtained superb compensation in the form of the opponent's shattered kingside. Indeed, it was a great pity that Black was unable to cap her wonderful play with a glorious finish.

Game 33
T.Grabuzova-T.Sterliagova
Dagomys 2008

1 d4 ♘f6 2 c4 c5 3 d5 b5 4 cxb5 a6 5 e3 e6 6 ♘c3 exd5 7 ♘ge2!?

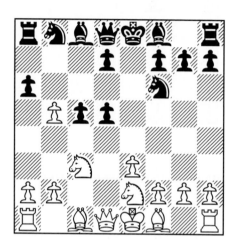

White plays to stick a knight on d5. 7 ♘h3 axb5 8 ♘f4 leads to the same position.
7...axb5 8 ♘f4

Black also has no problems after 8 ♘xb5 ♘a6 9 ♘ec3 ♗b7 10 ♗e2 ♘c7 11 0-0 ♘xb5 12 ♘xb5 ♗e7 13 b3 0-0 14 ♗b2 ♕b6 15 ♘c3 ♕e6 ½-½, V.Baikov-A.Poluljahov, Sochi 1996.
8...b4

Black once tried to force matters with 8...d4?!, but got nowhere after 9 exd4 ♘c6 10 dxc5 ♗xc5 11 ♗xb5 0-0 12 0-0 ♗b7 13 ♘h5! ♘xh5 14 ♕xh5 when White has excellent play, I.Khenkin-A.Koehler, Haarlem 1997.

9 ♘cxd5 ♗b7 10 ♗c4

White has temporarily won the fight for d5. However, she will find it hard to develop her queenside which is cramped by the half-open a-file and Black's queenside pawn configuration.

White can try to play for a d5-square squeeze with 10 ♘xf6+ ♕xf6 11 ♘d5, but 11...♕e5!? 12 ♗c4 ♕e4 13 ♘c7+ ♔d8 14 ♗d5 ♗xd5 15 ♕xd5 ♕xd5 16 ♘xd5 ♘c6 results in equal chances.

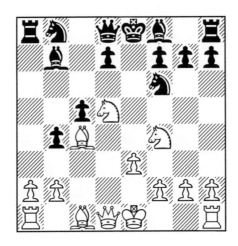

10...♗d6!?

An ultra-sharp continuation, leaving a loose bishop on d6. Black is just concentrating on swift development.

11 ♘xf6+!

White manages to find a continuation that can take advantage of the loose bishop.

After 11 0-0 0-0 12 h3 ♖e8 it's only a matter of time before White must take on f6 as there's really nothing else to do.

11...♕xf6 12 ♘h5 ♕g6 13 ♘xg7+ ♔e7 14 ♗d5 ♗xd5 15 ♕xd5 ♕xg7 16 ♕xa8

White has won the exchange, but at cost of woeful development and now it's Black's turn to attack.

16 ♕e4+ ♗e5 17 ♕xa8 ♘c6 18 ♕a6 ♕xg2 will lead to the same type of position as the game.

16...♘c6 17 ♕a6 ♕xg2 18 ♕f1 ♕f3 19 ♖g1 ♘e5

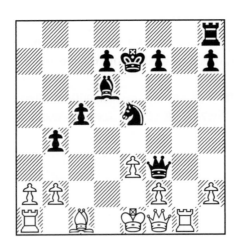

White is definitely suffering here as Black's pieces start swarming in.

20 ♕g2?

Even with the best defence 20 ♖g3, White is still suffering after 20...♕e4 21 f4 ♘d3+ 22 ♔d1 c4 23 ♕f3 ♕e6 24 e4 ♗c5 with fantastic compensation due to the superb knight on d3.

20...c4!

Activating the passed c-pawn and also keeping an iron grip on d3 for the knight.

21 ♗d2

White desperately tries to complete development. After 21 ♕g5+ ♔e6! 22 ♕h4 ♖c8! there is no defence against the coming ...c4-c3.

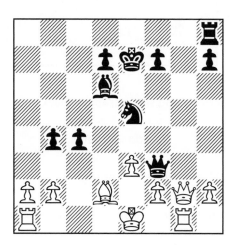

Exercise: It's Black to play and win.

21...♘d3+?

What a great pity. After such marvellous play, Black slips up at the critical juncture and White is back in the game.

Answer: 21...♖g8!! wins at least a rook as it is not possible to play 22 ♕xg8 because of 22...♘d3+ 23 ♔f1 ♕xf2#.

22 ♔f1 ♕xg2+ 23 ♖xg2 ♘xb2

Banking on the queenside pawns to supply some winning chances.

24 f3

White tries to defend along the second rank, utilising the position of the rook on g2. Instead, 24 ♖g4 c3 25 ♗e1 f5 26 ♖h4 h5 27 ♔e2 ♔e6 28 a3 ♖a8 29 ♖xh5 ♗e5 30 f4 ♗f6 31 ♖h6 ♔e7 32 ♖h7+ ♔e6 33 ♖h6 is an arcane draw.

24...♖a8

Trying to tie White down to defending a2 as well as preparing to hit the e3-pawn after ...♖a3.

25 ♖b1

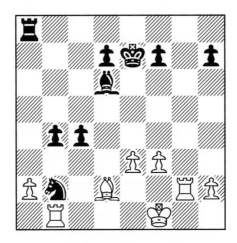

White chooses to play actively and sets a trap for Black.

Question: What is it?

Answer: 25...♖xa2?? 26 ♗xb4 and White is winning.

25...♘d3

With the intention of pushing the c-pawn. However the immediate 25...c3 26 ♗c1 ♘c4 would still have given Black good chances.

26 ♗e1

White has managed to set up her second rank defence, but still has to resist against Black's activity.

26...♗c5 27 ♖c2

A good counterattacking ploy.

27...d5 28 ♔e2 ♔e6 29 ♖d1

Hoping to return the exchange with ♖xd3 under favourable circumstances.

29...♖a3 30 ♗d2 ♗d6

The correct 30...f5 would have maintained Black's grip on the position.

31 e4!

After this, Black's winning chances are substantially reduced.

31...dxe4

If 31...f5 32 exd5+ ♔xd5 33 ♗c1! ♖a8 34 ♖xd3+ cxd3+ 35 ♔xd3 and White has saved her skin.

32 fxe4 ♘e5 33 ♗f4

To draw this comfortably, the c4-pawn must be eliminated, and, hence, its defender must go first.

33...♖h3

Also after 33...c3 34 ♗xe5 ♗xe5 35 ♖b1 ♗d6 36 ♔d3 White should be able to draw.

34 ♗xe5 ♗xe5 35 ♖xc4 ♖xh2+ 36 ♔f3 ♗c3 37 ♖c6+ ♔e7 38 ♖a6

After further adventures, a draw resulted:

38...♗d2 39 ♖g1 ♗c3 40 ♖g8 h6 41 ♖b8 ♖h3+ 42 ♔g4 ♖e3 43 ♔f4 ♖e1 44 ♖b7+ ♔f8 45 ♖aa7 ♔g8 46 ♖d7 ♖f1+ 47 ♔e3 ♔g7 48 ♖a6 ♖e1+ 49 ♔f3 ♖f1+ 50 ♔e3 ½-½

Chapter Six
Knight out on a Limb

1 d4 ♘f6 2 c4 c5 3 d5 b5 4 cxb5 a6 5 ♘c3

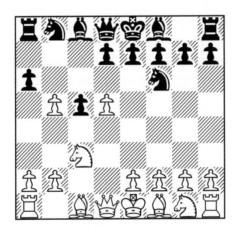

White temporarily accepts the pawn, but plans to give it back to send his queen's knight into no-man's land for an all-out attack.

5...axb5

Opening the a-file.

6 e4

Uncovering an attack on b5.

6...b4

Kicking the knight, a defender of e4, away.

7 ♘b5

Sending the knight to a very dangerous square where it can support tactics against d6 and c7.

7...d6

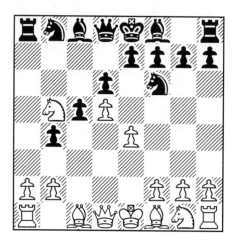

Stopping the e-pawn in its tracks for now. Of course, Black is not going to fall for 7...♘xe4? when 8 ♕e2! wins a piece as if the knight retreats, 9 ♘d6 is mate. Actually, according to my database, there are 16 victims in this line already.

A) The Nescafe Frappe Attack: 8 ♗c4

8 ♗c4 initiates the so-called 'Nescafe Frappe Attack'. On the surface, the bishop looks like it's just defending d5, but White intends to blast through in the centre with e4-e5 and d5-d6, clearing the bishop's diagonal.

Black does best to overprotect the e5-square with 8...♘bd7, as in Burgess-Beaumont, before he has the choice of going into utter chaos mode with Aveskulov's 9...♘xe4!?, Skytte's incredible 11...♘xe4 idea, or the safer and solid 11...♗g7.

> ### Game 34
> ### G.Burgess-C.Beaumont
> Aarhus 1990

1 d4 ♘f6 2 c4 c5 3 d5 b5 4 cxb5 a6 5 ♘c3 axb5 6 e4

6 ♘xb5 ♗a6 7 ♘c3 g6 just transposes back to 1 d4 ♘f6 2 c4 c5 3 d5 b5 4 cxb5 a6 5 bxa6 g6 6 ♘c3.

6...b4 7 ♘b5 d6 8 ♗c4

White intends to force the d5-pawn through to d6 and open the a2-g8 diagonal for his bishop. This line was christened the 'Nescafe Frappe Attack' by FM Graham Burgess, which is kind of whacky. I mean, we have openings named after players, countries and a certain river (the Volga), but a coffee product?

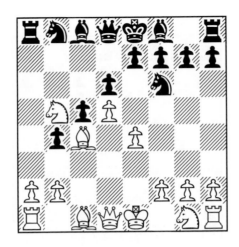

8...♘bd7!

Black restrains e4-e5 so that the b5-knight cannot make use of d5-d6 tricks.

White is playing for complications stemming from 8...g6 9 e5!? dxe5 10 d6 exd6 11 ♗g5 ♖a5.

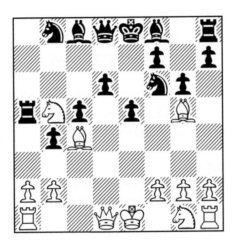

Although practical results favour Black, the position is very tough to defend at club level. In some instances, just to ease the defence, Black simply sacrifices the exchange with ...♖xb5, having two pawns in the bag already. However, play is ultra-theoretical and unless you are a calculating monster, it's best to stick to lines which are more positionally motivated. White develops easily with moves like ♕b3 (hitting f7), 0-0-0 and ♖d1 (ganging up on d6), whereas Black has to defend extremely carefully.

If the e-pawn looks too tempting to be true, it probably is as after 8...♘xe4?! 9 ♕e2 ♘f6 (otherwise, 9...♗f5 10 ♘f3 h6 11 0-0 ♕b6 12 ♖e1 ♘d7 13 a4! sees Black still suffering badly, while after 9...f5 10 f3 ♘f6 11 ♘h3 h6 12 ♘f4 g5 13 ♘e6 ♗xe6 14 ♕xe6 ♕d7 15 ♕e2 White has impressive compensation for his pawn) 10 ♗f4 ♖a6 11 ♘xd6+ ♖xd6 12 ♗b5+ ♖d7 13 ♗xb8 White gets to win the exchange.

9 ♘f3

Tempting Black to capture on e4 while preparing e4-e5.

9...♘b6

This is a safe option, which defuses White's aggressive intentions by removing or forcing the retreat of a strong central piece.

Instead, Aveskulov recommended 9...♘xe4!? 10 ♕e2 f5 11 g4!? ♘df6 12 gxf5 g6! 13 ♘h4! g5 14 f3 ♘d2! 15 ♗xd2 gxh4, but with the moves looking so irrational, I wonder how many of us could wend our way through the various continuations at each juncture.

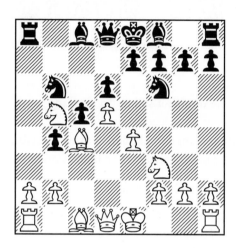

10 ♗d3 g6 11 b3

GM Simon Williams experimented with 11 a4 and got the worse of it after 11...♗g7 12 0-0 0-0 13 ♘d2?! e6 (even stronger is 13...♗d7! with the idea of ...♕b8 and the undermining ...e7-e6; indeed, White will be unable to deal with the multiple threats: for example, 14 ♕b3 ♕b8 15 ♖a2 e6! or 14 ♕c2 ♕b8 15 ♖a2 c4 16 ♗xc4 ♘xc4 17 ♕xc4 ♖c8 18 ♕b3 ♕b7 19 h3 ♕a6 20 ♘d4 ♘xe4 21 ♘xe4 ♗xd4 22 ♕xb4 ♕d3 23 ♘d2 ♖cb8 24 ♕c4 ♕xc4 25 ♘xc4 ♖xa4 when Black is on top) 14 ♘c4 ♘xc4 15 ♗xc4 e5 16 ♗d3 ♘e8 17 ♖a2 f5 18 exf5 gxf5 19 f4 e4, with a slight edge for Black, S.Williams-T.Chapman, British Championship, Sheffield 2011.

Instead, the pawn sacrifice 11 e5 should be dealt with by 11...dxe5! 12 ♘xe5 ♘bxd5 when White has insufficient compensation.

There's also this unfortunate miniature: 11 ♘d2 ♗g7 12 a4 ♗d7 (White is already in big trouble) 13 ♕e2 0-0 14 ♖a2??.

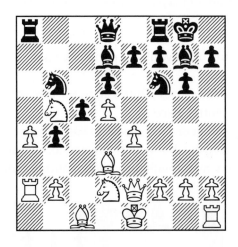

Exercise: It's Black to play and win!

Answer: After 14...c4! White resigned in J.Egger-J.Votava, Duisburg 1992, due to 15 ♗b1 b3! 16 ♖a3 ♗xb5 17 axb5 ♖xa3 18 bxa3 ♘fd7 when Black's queenside passed pawns are going to cost him at least a piece.

11...♗g7

Nicolai Pedersen pointed out the extremely innovative concept of IM Rasmus Skytte, a Benko expert, in *Play the Benko Gambit*, namely 11...♘xe4!?. After 12 ♗xe4 ♗g7 13 ♗d2 ♗xa1 14 ♕xa1 ♖g8 15 ♕b2 ♗f5! 16 ♗xf5 gxf5 17 0-0 ♕d7 18 a4 bxa3 19 ♘xa3 ♘xd5 20 ♘c4 f4 21 ♖a1 ♖xa1+ 22 ♕xa1 ♕c8 it's a right mess. *Houdini* seems to like White, while I would find it tough to play either position.

12 ♗b2 0-0

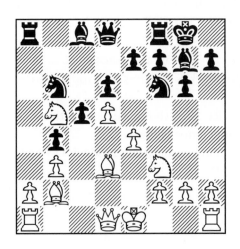

13 0-0

Question: Why not 13 ♕c2?

Answer: This is a huge mistake with the knight out on a limb, as 13...♗a6! nets Black at least a pawn: 14 a4 (or 14 0-0 ♘xe4 15 ♗xg7 ♔xg7 16 ♗xe4 ♗xb5) 14...bxa3 15 ♘xa3 (if 15 ♖xa3 ♗xb5 16 ♗xb5 ♖xa3 17 ♗xa3 ♕a8! with the idea of ...♕a5+ , and if 18 ♗a4 ♕a5+ 19 ♘d2 ♘xa4 20 bxa4 ♖a8) 15...♘fxd5 16 ♗xa6 ♘b4 17 ♕e2 ♗xb2 18 ♕xb2 ♖xa6 when Black has both the pawn and pressure.

13...♗a6

Not only the natural square for this bishop, but an attempt to force White to eventually play with a weak b-pawn after the forcing a2-a4 bxa3.

14 ♕e2 ♕d7

Once more, putting the question to the knight and forcing White to play his next move.

Black also obtained a comfortable position after 14...♘h5 15 ♗xg7 ♔xg7 16 g3 ♕d7 17 ♘d2 ♖fb8 (17...f5!?) 18 a4 bxa3 19 ♘xa3 ♗xd3 20 ♕xd3 ♕h3 in H.Van Riemsdijk-A.Ferrara, Vicente Lopez 2000.

15 a4 bxa3 16 ♖xa3 ♘h5!

A nice attempt to exploit the f4-square for the black knight. There are tactical chances here for Black based on removing White's dark-squared bishop. If it is removed from the board, White's a3-rook might be left en prise in the event of a combination.

Also, Simon Williams could not make headway after 16...♗b7 17 ♖fa1 ♖xa3 18 ♖xa3 ♖a8 19 ♖xa8+ ♘xa8 20 ♕e1 when Black has a typical, ideal Benko structure, although without rooks, it is difficult to exploit White's weak b3-pawn. Suddenly, though, a wild forcing line arose: 20...♘xd5!? 21 ♗xg7 ♘f4 22 ♗h6 ♘xd3 23 ♕c3 ♘e5 24 ♘xe5 dxe5 25 f3 ♘c7 26 ♕xe5 ♘e8? (missing 26...♘e6 with equality) 27 ♕xc5 and Black was in trouble, S.Williams-C.Jenks, Bournemouth 2012.

17 ♗xg7?!

White should keep his dark-squared bishop with 17 ♗c1! ♖fb8 18 h3, thereby retaining equal chances.

17...♔xg7 18 g3??

Most of us wouldn't think twice before playing this to deny Black the f4-square, but it's not good. Indeed, White had to settle for an exchange sacrifice: 18 ♖xa6 ♖xa6 19 ♘xd6 ♖aa8 20 ♘c4 ♘xc4 (if 20...♕c7 21 ♘xb6 ♕xb6 22 ♗c4) 21 ♗xc4 with Grünfeld-like compensation based on his strong central pawns.

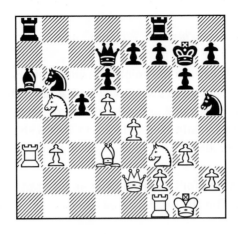

Answer: 18...♘f4!! 19 gxf4 ♕g4+ 20 ♔h1 ♗xb5 21 ♖xa8 ♗xd3 22 ♕xd3 ♖xa8

Material is even, but White's pawns are in a bad shape and need protection from his pieces. There's also the matter of the active black rook on a8 which threatens to invade down the file.

23 f5

A clever way of defending the pawn.

23...♘d7

Of course, not 23...gxf5?? 24 ♖g1.

24 ♕e3 ♘f6 25 ♘d2 ♖a2 26 ♖g1 ♕h5

26...♕h4 is also very strong, but IM Chris Beaumont is looking for an elegant solution...

27 f3

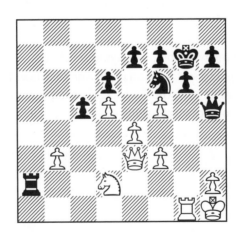

White's pawns look secure for the time being, but this was what Black was waiting for.

27...♖xd2!

An elegant solution, indeed.

28 ♕xd2 ♕xf3+ 29 ♕g2 ♕xe4!

Black elects to play an endgame with knight and two pawns against a rook. Simpler would have been 29...♕xb3 30 fxg6 hxg6 31 ♕e2 ♕b4 32 ♖e1 ♘g4 33 ♔g2 ♘e5 when White is still having a torrid time.

30 fxg6 hxg6 31 ♕xe4 ♘xe4 32 ♖e1 f5 33 h4!

If Black's g-pawn gets to advance, the game is as good as over.

33...♔f6 34 ♔g2

34 ♖e3 only delays the inevitable: 34...g5! 35 hxg5+ ♔xg5 36 ♔g2 ♔g4 37 ♖e1 ♔f4 38 ♖d1 ♘f6 39 ♖f1+ ♔e5 40 ♖e1+ ♘e4 41 ♖f1 ♘c3 42 ♖e1+ ♔f6 43 ♖e6+ ♔f7 44 ♔f3 ♘xd5 45 ♖h6 ♘f6 46 ♔f4 ♔e6 and the d-pawn will advance.

34...♘c3 0-1

The d-pawn is a goner and with it, the game. Exquisite play by Chris Beaumont.

B) 8 ♗f4

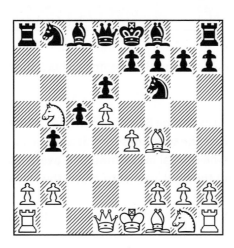

White invites Black to capture on e4, hoping to use the resulting half-open e-file to generate tactics based on ♘xd6 or ♗xd6. Of course, ♗f4 also sets up e4-e5 instantly. The main line has Black punting 8...g5 to exchange the e4-pawn for the g5 one. My take is to then regroup the kingside quickly with ...♘e4-f6 and castle swiftly, as in Hovhanisian-Daels. Note that a mere slight misplacement of the light-squared bishop allowed White to achieve his aim of blasting through the centre with a piece sacrifice on d6, although it was insufficient to win.

Game 35
M.Hovhanisian-M.Daels
Belgian Championship, Eupen 2008

1 d4 ♘f6 2 c4 c5 3 d5 b5 4 cxb5 a6 5 ♘c3 axb5 6 e4 b4 7 ♘b5 d6 8 ♗f4

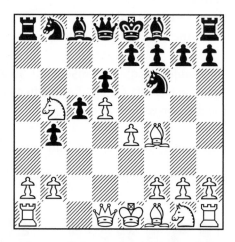

The most direct of White's options, threatening to blast through the centre with e4-e5 and d5-d6.

8...g5

It may seem foolhardy to exchange Black's g-pawn for White's e-pawn. However, there are a few factors that indicate the soundness of this approach:

1) White's e4-e5 and d5-d6 central breakthrough is averted and, hence, unless White has a tactical solution to hit the black pawn structure, the wayward knight on b5 is simply misplaced.

2) ...♘xe4 comes with a tempo by hitting g5 and thus there's not much loss of time involved for Black.

3) The weakened kingside is not easy for White to target because Black can generate pressure against d5 (which lacks pawn support) very quickly.

A typical blitz win would be 8...♘xe4 9 ♕e2 ♘f6?? (the position is actually playable after 9...g5 10 ♗e5 dxe5 11 ♕xe4 ♗g7 12 d6 ♖a5 13 ♖d1 0-0 14 ♘f3 ♘d7 15 ♘xg5 ♘f6 16 ♕h4 e6 with mutual chances, A.Dreev-.E.Bareev, Tilburg 1994) 10 ♘xd6+ ♔d7 11 ♕b5+ ♔c7 12 ♘e8#.

9 ♗xg5

Another popular line is 9 ♗e3!? when Black should develop sensibly with 9...♗g7 and then:

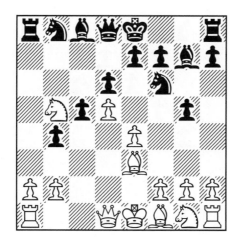

a) 10 ♗d3?! at this point gets White into massive trouble after 10...♕b6! 11 a4 (11 ♗xg5? ♖a5 wins material) 11...bxa3 12 ♖xa3 ♖xa3 13 bxa3 ♘g4! 14 ♕d2 (not 14 ♗xg5?? c4!) 14...♘xe3 15 ♕xe3 ♗d7 16 ♕e2 ♕a5+ 17 ♔f1 0-0 18 g3 c4 19 ♗xc4 ♖c8 when White is busted as he cannot prevent the loss of material after 20 ♔g2 ♖c5.

b) 10 e5 ♘g4! 11 ♗xg5 (after 11 e6? ♘xe3 12 fxe3 ♕a5! 13 exf7+ ♔d8 White has to defend against multiple threats on b5 and b2 and watch out for ...b4-b3+, J.Jolly-N.Tripoteau, French League 2009) 11...♘xe5 12 a4 bxa3 13 ♖xa3 ♖xa3 14 bxa3 0-0 with a comfortable game for Black..

c) 10 f3 h6 11 a4 bxa3 12 ♖xa3 ♖xa3 13 ♘xa3 ♘bd7 14 ♘e2 ♘h5 15 ♕d2 ♗a6 16 ♘c1 ♗xf1 17 ♖xf1 ♕b8 18 ♘d3 ♘e5 19 ♘xe5 ♗xe5 20 g4 ♘f4 when Black has good control of the dark squares and possesses the safer king, A.Potapov-J.Degraeve, Cappelle la Grande 2002.

9...♘xe4 10 ♗f4 ♘f6!

Putting pressure on d5 and returning the knight to the defence of the kingside. It is a good policy to keep Black's position as compact as possible to guard against tactical threats. Indeed, after 10...♗g7 11 ♕e2 ♘f6 12 ♘xd6+ ♔f8 13 ♘xc8 ♕xc8 Black must deal with the massive complications that arise after 14 d6 or 14 ♕f3.

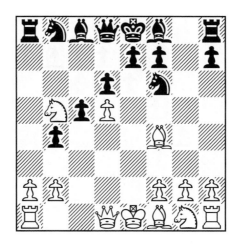

11 &c4

Defending d5 and a2, although the bishop seems better placed on d3 as White is play-ing more for swift development than to hold his pawns: 11 &d3 &g7 12 ♘f3 &b7! (Black does not even allow ♘xd6 or &xd6 tricks) 13 &c4 0-0 14 0-0 ♘bd7 15 ♕e2 ♘b6 16 ♖ad1 &xd5 and Black nabs the d-pawn when White does not have sufficient counterplay, I.Molnar-A.Forgacs, Hungarian League 2003, and here 16...♘xc4 17 ♕xc4 ♕d7, hitting b5 and d5, is even easier.

Instead, Glenn Flear pointed out that 11 ♕e2 can be met by 11...♖a6! when "the d-pawn is hanging", as in R.Dive-A.Ker, New Zealand 1991.

Since the text move also leaves the White d-pawn in trouble long-term, White might at-tempt to find other ways of playing the position. The sharpest try is 11 ♖c1 with the dard-stardly threat of ♖xc5 and ♘c7+, although this is refuted by 11...&g7!, and if 12 ♖xc5?? dxc5 13 ♘c7+ ♔f8 14 ♘xa8 ♕a5! 15 ♘c7 b3+ 16 ♔e2 bxa2 17 ♕a1 ♕a4 18 ♘h3 ♕c2+ 19 &d2 ♕b1 and Black wins.

11...&g7 12 ♘f3

Since d5 is more or less compromised, White just has to develop pronto while Black tries to surround d5.

Creating a passed pawn is too slow as after 12 a3 bxa3 13 ♖xa3 ♖xa3 14 bxa3 0-0 15 ♘e2 ♘bd7 16 0-0 ♘b6 17 ♕d3 &b7 18 ♘bc3 ♕a8 White must choose between losing d5 or a3, M.Michna-W.Ehrenfeucht, Krakow 1998, while 12 ♘e2 ♘bd7 13 ♘g3 ♘b6 14 b3 is re-futed by Aveskulov's excellent 14...h5, after which White doesn't even have a kingside tar-get to aim at.

12...0-0 13 ♕d2!

The best square for the queen with the idea of attacking the black king with &h6 and/or an h-pawn rush, while if Black plays ....&a6 or ....&b7, then ♘h4-f5 comes into con-sideration.

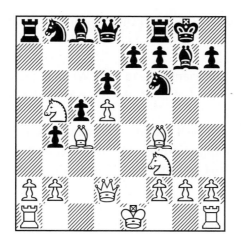

13...♔h8!

Nicely done with an eye to meet White's standard ♗f4-h6 (to remove a key black defender) with aggressive defence. Moreover, Black probably didn't like White getting frisky on the kingside after 13...♘bd7 14 ♗h6 ♗xh6 15 ♕xh6 ♔h8 16 ♘g5 ♘e5 17 b3 ♗f5 18 0-0 ♕d7 19 ♖fe1.

14 0-0

Black intends to meet 14 ♗h6 with 14...♖g8, after which the rook joins in the defence of the king and starts to put pressure on the white kingside.

14...♘bd7 15 ♖ae1

Going all in. White realizes that there is no point leaving the rook on a1 to play a2-a4, so he decides to go the whole hog in the centre and, in good time, on the kingside.

15...♘b6 16 b3

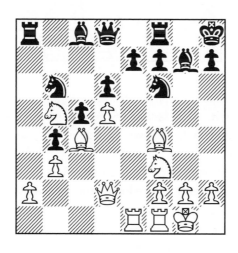

Exercise: A choice of bishop placement: to b7 or d7?

16...♗d7?!

Black reckons that there is sufficient time to force White to sacrifice yet another pawn with a2-a4 in order to meet the threat of ...♖a5. However, White has set up an insidious tactic to confuse the issue.

Answer: Black's pieces are very well placed to counterattack in the centre and after 16...♗b7! White's centre simply crumbles: 17 ♘h4 (or 17 a4 bxa3 18 ♘c3 a2 19 ♖a1 ♕d7 with the strong ideas of ...♕g4 and ...♕f5) 17...♘bxd5 18 ♘f5 ♕d7 and White has nothing to show for his pawn.

17 ♘xd6!

White should be applauded for putting the b5-knight to good use. Thus it turns out that the kingside gestures were merely a feint. Now Black must deal with the psychological impact of a sudden shift in the balance of the initiative and White threatens to win all Black's queenside pawns.

17...exd6 18 ♗xd6 ♖e8 19 ♗xc5

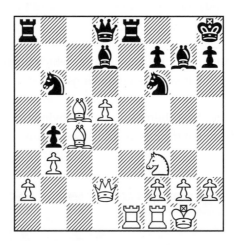

Question: In the face of losing yet another pawn to 20 ♗xb4 or 20 ♕xb4, what would a good rejoinder for Black be?

Answer: 19...♘xc4! 20 ♖xe8+ (if 20 bxc4 ♘e4) 20...♕xe8 21 bxc4 ♘e4 22 ♕xb4 ♖a4 23 ♕b6 ♖xc4 when Black's activity and extra piece look stronger than White's ability to use his three pawn advantage.

19...♘e4?!

This was exactly the reaction White wanted to provoke as now the key kingside defender gets lopped off at once.

20 ♖xe4! ♖xe4 21 ♘g5!

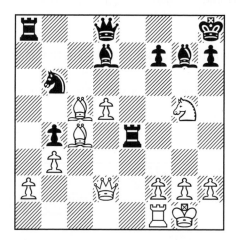

The point of the exchange sacrifice. Black is back-peddling now as White's pieces will just keep swarming in.

21...♘xc4 22 bxc4 ♖xa2

A very practical choice as Black decides to return material to ward off the attack.

Houdini actually demonstrates that Black could counterattack here with 22...♗c3! 23 ♘xf7+ ♔g8 24 ♕d3 ♕h4 25 ♘h6+ ♔h8 26 g3 ♖d4 27 ♕e3 ♕f6 28 ♘f7+ ♔g7 29 ♘e5 ♖xd5 when he is on top. Of course, for mere mortals like ourselves, it's a tall order to work out all those in-between moves.

23 ♘xf7+ ♔g8 24 ♕xa2 ♔xf7 25 ♗xb4 ♕c8

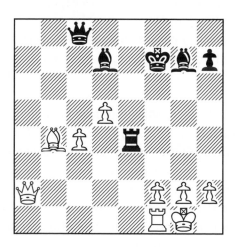

With four pawns for the piece, White seems to have more than ample compensation.

26 ♖c1

> *Question:* Can you suggest a good plan for Black?

Answer: **26...♗b5!**

All of a sudden, Black wrestles back the initiative with this criss-cross pin.

27 ♕b1?

27 d6 is parried by yet another criss-cross pin: 27...♕e6 and the c4-pawn won't run away.

27...♖xc4 28 ♖xc4

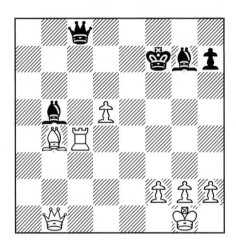

> *Exercise:* How should Black capture on c4?

Answer: Strongest is 28...♕xc4! 29 ♕f5+ ♔g8 30 ♕e6+ ♔h8 31 ♕e1 ♕xd5 32 ♗c3 when the exposed black king gives White good drawing chances, but there is no harm in making him sweat for it.

28...♗xc4?! 29 ♕xh7

By removing the last black pawn, White has done enough to draw the position.

29...♗xd5 30 ♕h5+ ♔f6 31 ♗d2 ♕c2 32 ♗g5+ ♔e6 33 h4 ♗c6 34 ♕g4+ ♔f7 35 h5 ♗e5 36 ♗f4 ♕e4 37 ♕g6+ ♕xg6 38 hxg6+ ♔f6 39 ♗xe5+ ♔xe5 40 g7 ♗d5 41 g8N ½-½

Herein lies the problem with the Zaitsev variation. White must at all cost, as Hovhanisian did, try to generate an attack based on his knight on b5 before Black consolidates and swallows up d5. Hence this line favours out-and-out attackers who think nothing of throwing even the kitchen sink for the initiative.

C) 8 ♘f3

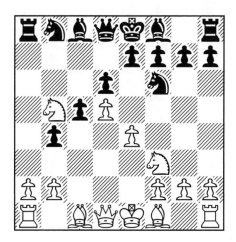

White makes an immediate attempt to push through e4-e5 and will later use his bishops to join in the fray with ♗c4 and ♗f4. In Minzer-Szmetan, Black had the option between grabbing the e4-pawn and Nisipeanu's safer 10...0-0, aiming to overprotect the e5-square with ...♘bd7. Once again, White must attack very precisely before his d5-pawn drops off.

Game 36
C.Minzer-J.Szmetan
Buenos Aires 1994

---

1 d4 ♘f6 2 c4 c5 3 d5 b5 4 cxb5 a6 5 ♘c3 axb5 6 e4 b4 7 ♘b5 d6 8 ♘f3

White chooses to develop his kingside pieces first.

8...g6 9 ♗c4

After 9 ♗f4 Black had no problems playing sensible developing moves with 9...♘h5!? 10 ♗g5 h6 11 ♗e3 ♗g7 12 ♗c4 0-0 13 0-0 ♘d7 14 ♕e2 ♘hf6 15 ♕c2 ♘g4 16 ♗d2 ♘b6 in G.Andre-S.Kasparov, Werther 2002.

Instead, 9 e5 usually transposes to the next note, but Black must be very careful with the following sacrificial line: 9...dxe5 10 d6?! exd6 11 ♗g5 ♗e7 12 ♗xf6 ♗xf6 13 ♘xd6+ ♔e7! 14 ♕d5 ♕xd6 15 ♕xa8 was M.Gerusel-O.Borik, Bad Pyrmont 1976, when Black should rely on his strong centre. After 15...♖d8 16 ♗e2 ♘c6 17 0-0 ♗e6 18 ♕b7+ ♔f8 19 ♖fd1 ♘d4 20 ♘xd4 exd4 21 b3 ♗d5 Black has a huge initiative for the exchange and pawn.

9...♗g7

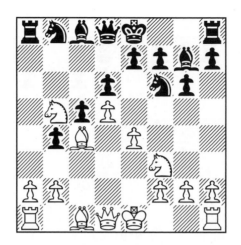

10 0-0

White can play for a quick central thrust, but as long as Black does not fall for any cheapos, he should be fine: 10 e5 dxe5 11 ♘xe5 (11 d6 is simply met by 11...0-0) 11...0-0 12 0-0 ♗a6! (this standard Benko move leads to the eventual win of a pawn by deflecting the c4-bishop away from d5; White does obtain compensation for it though, but not more) 13 ♖e1 (13 a4 leads to the same sort of position after 13...♗xb5 14 ♗xb5 ♕xd5) 13...♗xb5 14 ♗xb5 ♕xd5 15 ♕c2?! b3! 16 ♕e2 ♖xa2 and Black slowly but surely converted the win, B.Gulko-E.Vasiukov, Yerevan 1976.

10...♘xe4

A risky policy. Black plays to trade e4 for e7, rationalizing that the exchange favours him, because in order to win e7, White loses a defender of d5 (the queen).

Black can play more positionally with 10...0-0 11 ♖e1 ♘bd7 12 a4 bxa3 13 ♖xa3 ♖xa3, although after 14 ♘xa3?! (if 14 bxa3 ♘b6 15 ♗f1 ♗a6), Nisipeanu turned on the tactical tap with 14...♘g4 15 ♗f1 ♘de5 16 ♘d2?! ♘xf2! and blew Bacrot away: 17 ♔xf2 ♘g4+ 18 ♔e2 e6 19 ♕b3 exd5 20 h3? dxe4!! 21 ♘xe4? ♖e8 22 ♔d2 ♕a5+ 23 ♔c2 ♕xe1 0-1, E.Bacrot-L.Nisipeanu, Balatonbereny 1996.

11 ♖e1 ♘f6 12 ♕e2 ♗b7

The position is already critical for White as there's only one good way to proceed.

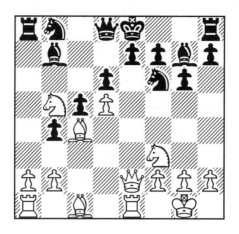

13 ♗f4?

Daring Black to castle and lose e7, and possibly d6.

However, White must play the exchange sacrifice starting with 13 ♕xe7+ ♕xe7 14 ♘xd6+ ♔d8 15 ♖xe7 ♔xe7 16 ♘xb7 with good compensation due to his hyperactive pieces and strong d-pawn: for example, 16...♘fd7 17 ♖b1 (or 17 ♗g5+ ♔f8 18 ♖e1 ♗xb2 19 ♗h6+ ♗g7 20 ♗e3 h6 21 ♘xc5 ♗c3 22 ♘xd7+ ♘xd7 23 ♖d1 ♔g7 when White's strong d-pawn might be just enough to hold the balance) 17...♖a7 18 ♗g5+ ♔f6 19 ♖e1+ ♔f8 20 ♗xf6 ♘xf6 21 ♘xc5 ♖c7 22 ♘e4 ♘xe4 23 ♖xe4 ♔g7 24 g3 ♖hc8 with equal chances.

13...0-0!

Welcoming the trades that are to come.

14 ♕xe7?

After 14 ♖ad1 ♖e8 White has insufficient compensation for the pawn. His pieces look active, but that's all to it.

14...♕xe7 15 ♖xe7

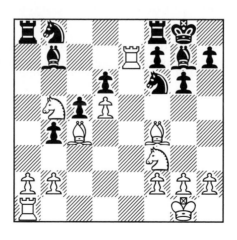

> ***Question:*** Can the d5-pawn be taken or is there a ♘c7 fork?

Answer: **15...♗xd5!**

Boom!

16 ♘c7 ♗xc4 17 ♘xa8 ♘d5

The sting in the tail. White cannot keep the exchange and has to return all the material garnered.

18 ♗xd6 ♘xe7 19 ♗xe7 ♖e8 20 ♗xc5

Two years later, White was also unsuccessful with 20 ♘b6 ♗xb2 21 ♖b1 ♖xe7 22 ♘xc4 ♗c3 and Black was winning in V.Yezersky-E.Kalegin, St Petersburg 1996.

20...♘d7

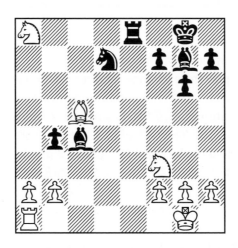

21 ♘b6

> ***Exercise:*** After 21 ♘c7 ♖c8 22 ♗d6 ♗xb2 23 ♖d1 can you find the win for Black?

Answer: 23...♗xa2! 24 ♖d2 ♗c3 and the b-pawn cannot be stopped.

21...♘xb6 22 ♗xb6 ♗xb2 23 ♖d1 ♖a8 24 ♗c5 ♗c3 25 h3 ♗xa2 0-1

Chapter Seven
Ignorance is Bliss

1 d4 ♘f6 2 c4 c5 3 d5 b5 4 ♘f3

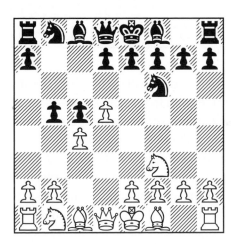

Here we'll see White decline the gambit pawn and develop sensibly with 4 ♘f3, 4 ♕c2, 4 ♘d2 and 4 ♗g5. In these lines, the Benko Gambiteer frequently does not obtain the open queenside files he enjoys in the main variations with automatic piece placements. Thus the ignorance of Black's pawn offer might appeal to white players who are not interested in a theoretical tussle and would rather test their ability to just simply play the positions that unfold.

On the surface, it looks like White is just ignoring the gambit pawn and passing up on the advantage. However, Black must be careful because nonchalant play will allow White to obtain a strong foothold in the centre: for example, 4 ♘f3 bxc4 5 ♘c3 d6 6 e4 g6 (6...♘bd7 7 ♗xc4 g6 8 0-0 ♗g7 9 ♖e1 0-0 10 h3 gives White a nice space advantage) 7 e5 dxe5 8 ♘xe5 ♗g7 9 ♗c4 and White's central play has already begin.

My proposed repertoire is to meet 4 ♘f3 with a queenside fianchetto: 4...♗b7 intending to strike back with ...e7-e6 if possible. Note that the immediate 4...e6 transposes to the Blumenfeld Gambit which I do not advocate as 5 ♗g5! gives White too an easy game in my opinion.

A) 4 ♘f3 ♗b7 5 a4

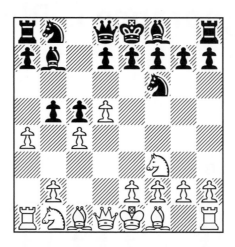

White's fifth move is aimed at forcing Black to clarify the situation in the centre. Black typically gives up the central tension to take queenside space after 5...♕a5+ (displacing White's queen's bishop to d2, instead of the better b2-square) 6 ♗d2 b4. Here Black can choose to play Aveskulov's recommended ...0-0 with ...♘h5 ideas, which I have put in the notes to Tunik-Terentjev, or the new-fangled ...h7-h6, ...g7-g5 and ...0-0-0 idea which has been essayed by young Russian masters in the past decade. In my opinion, this makes good logic as Black has annexed queenside space and, with that sector more or less locked up, he can play for a direct kingside attack without his king being there (unlike in the ...0-0 lines where both kings are often in peril after Black gets in ...f7-f5).

Game 37
G.Tunik-V.Terentjev
Kazan 2012

---

1 d4 ♘f6 2 c4 c5 3 d5 b5 4 ♘f3 ♗b7

Black immediately challenges the White centre and intends, if allowed, to undermine it with ...e7-e6.

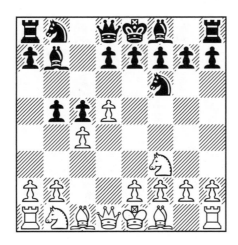

Answer: 4...e6 transposes to the Blumenfeld Gambit, and I consider 5 ♗g5! a strong riposte. For example, the game can go 5...exd5 6 cxd5 d6 7 e4 a6 8 ♘bd2 ♗e7 9 ♗f4 0-0 10 a4, as Ivanchuk played against Nisipeanu in Khanty-Mansiysk back in 2007.

5 a4

Forcing Black to decide immediately what he intends to do with the centre. White can also defend c4 with a knight:

a) 5 ♘bd2 e6 6 dxe6 (transposing to a type of Blumenfeld Gambit; 6 e4 exd5 7 cxd5 c4! 8 ♗e2 ♗c5 9 0-0 0-0 resembles our line against the Dlugy variation, but without Black sacrificing any pawns and here his position has great potential) 6...fxe6 7 cxb5 ♗e7 8 g3 0-0 9 ♗g2 ♕a5 10 a4 a6 11 bxa6 ♕xa6 12 b3 ♘c6 13 0-0 ♘a5 14 ♗a3 ♖ab8 15 ♖c1 ♖fc8 16 ♖e1 was B.Avrukh-B.Zueger, Elista Olympiad 1998, when Avrukh recommended 16...♗d5 17 ♖c3 ♕b7 18 ♘h4 ♗xg2 19 ♘xg2 d5 20 ♖e3 with unclear play.

b) 5 ♘fd2 e6 6 e4 bxc4 7 dxe6 (7 ♘c3 exd5 8 exd5 ♘xd5 9 ♘xd5 ♗xd5 10 ♘xc4 ♗e6! doesn't give White sufficient compensation) 7...dxe6 8 ♘c3 ♗e7 9 ♗xc4 0-0 10 0-0 ♘c6, as in R.Fyllingen-K.Lie, Oslo 2006, should be more than okay for Black, given his grip on d4. Indeed, Black has won the lion's share of games from this position in my databases.

5...♕a5+

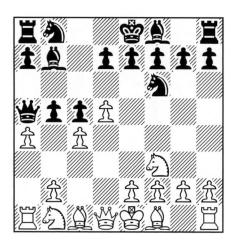

This move is aimed at:

1) Encouraging White to win a tempo by responding with 6 ♗d2. Given the nature of the pawn structure, White's dark-squared bishop ideally would be placed on b2.

2) Discouraging White from castling queenside for the time being with the black queen lurking in the vicinity.

> ***Question:*** Why not chip away at White's centre with 5...bxc4?

Answer: Theory considers White to have the better game after 6 ♘c3 e6 7 e4 exd5 (after 7...♘xe4 8 ♘xe4 exd5 9 ♘c3 d4 10 ♗xc4 dxc3 11 ♗xf7+ ♔xf7 12 ♕b3+ c4 13 ♕xb7 Black is in trouble, F.Hoelzl-G.Steiner, Austrian League 1994) 8 exd5. Following either 8...♗d6 or 8...d6, White retains a space advantage.

6 ♗d2

After 6 ♘bd2 bxc4 7 e4 ♘xe4 8 ♗xc4 ♘f6 9 0-0 e6 White's centre is crumbling, A.Indjic-D.Milanovic, Vrnjacka Banja 2012, as it is after 6 ♘fd2 bxc4 7 e4 ♘xe4 8 ♗xc4 e6 9 0-0 ♘d6, and if 10 ♘c3 ♗e7 11 ♕e2 0-0 with an easy game for Black.

6...b4 7 ♕c2

Helping to support e2-e4.

7...g6 8 e4 d6 9 ♗d3

The same sort of attacking ploy was played three months later when Black got himself a fine knight outpost after 9 ♗e2 ♗g7 10 0-0 ♘bd7 11 h3 ♕c7 12 ♗f4 h6 13 ♘bd2 g5 14 ♗h2 0-0-0 15 ♘e1 ♘e5 16 ♘d3 ♘xd3 17 ♕xd3 ♘d7 18 ♖ab1 ♘e5 19 ♕c2 ♔b8 20 f4 gxf4 21 ♖xf4 ♗f6, with a great game in D.Temirkanov-I.Popov, Tyumen 2012.

9...♗g7 10 0-0 ♘bd7 11 h3

Making a square for the dark-squared bishop in case Black goes ...♘h5.

If 11 ♗f4 Kiril Georgiev considers that Black has equal chances after 11...0-0 12 ♘bd2 ♘h5 13 ♗g5 ♖ae8 14 ♖ae1 e5 15 g3 ♗c8, as in K.Georgiev-P.Tregubov, Ohrid 2001.

11...h6!?

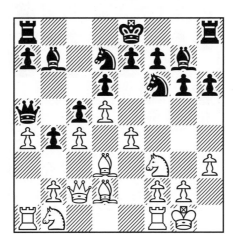

This is a recent idea. Black does not intend to castle on the kingside and prefers to make use of White's h2-h3 lever to play for a kingside attack. It makes perfect sense for Black to castle long since his king will be very safe there. Unlike in the 11...0-0 lines, Black does not intend to play ...e7-e5, but hopes to use that square for a knight or bishop at some point.

Some examples after 11...0-0 12 ♗e3:

a) 12 ♗f4 ♘h5 13 ♗h2 e5! 14 ♘bd2 (or 14 dxe6?! fxe6 when 15 ♘g5 is met by 15...♗h6 16 ♘xe6 ♖fe8, while after 15 ♗xd6 ♖xf3! 16 gxf3 ♗e5 17 ♗xe5 ♘xe5 18 ♗e2 ♘f4 White has no good way of stopping Black from invading the kingside with his queen) 14...♘f4 gives Black an excellent Czech Benoni or King's Indian with White unable to play on the queenside.

b) 12 ♗g5 ♖ae8 13 ♘bd2 e5 14 ♘h2 ♗c8 15 ♖ae1 h6 16 ♗e3 ♘h5 17 ♗e2 ♘f4 with a fine position for Black V.Milov-B.Zueger, Swiss League 2002.

c) Aveskulov's idea 12 ♗e3 ♘h5 gives Black equal chances after 13 ♘bd2 e5 14 ♖fe1 ♖ae8 15 ♗f1 ♗c8.

12 ♘h4

Discouraging Black from ...g6-g5 as it would provide White with an outpost on f5. This also prepares f2-f4 later.

In the game S.Volkov-V.Terentjev, Izhevsk 2011, White played for a quick e4-e5 with 12 ♖e1 0-0-0 13 e5 dxe5 14 ♘xe5 ♘xe5 15 ♖xe5 ♕c7 16 ♖e1 and here Black would have obtained a strong game after 16...e6! 17 dxe6 ♕d6! 18 ♗f1 fxe6. Despite the weak e- and g-pawns, Black's game is preferable with the two superb bishops on g7 and b7 raking the whole board.

12...0-0-0 13 ♗e3

Making way for the queen's knight to develop.

13...♖dg8

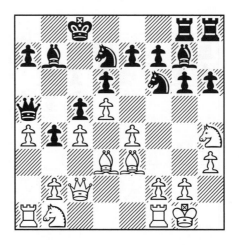

· Getting ready to lash out with ...g6-g5.

14 ♘d2 g5 15 ♘f5 ♗f8

Black's dark-squared bishop defends e7 for now and later will hold d6 when he boots away the knight with ...e7-e6.

16 ♘b3

Connecting the rooks.

16...♕c7 17 a5 a6

Stopping the a5-pawn in its tracks. Moreover, the pawn might prove a liability later in the game when White might be unable to defend it with a piece.

18 ♗d2

Making way for the knight as White anticipates ...e7-e6.

18...e6 19 ♘e3 ♘e5

A nice outpost for the knight. White, of course, will not want to play f2-f4 as it would now open the g-file for Black.

20 ♗e2 h5

Black's kingside assault is in full swing.

21 f3

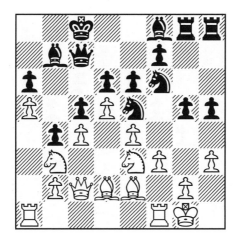

Overprotecting the g4-square.

21...♗h6

Placing the bishop on a strong diagonal in anticipation of ..g5-g4.

> ***Question:*** Why not immediately play 21...g4 as a pawn sacrifice?

Answer: Yes, it looks dangerous indeed. White can to try to win the g-pawn with 22 f4 (22 fxg4 ♕d8 gives Black a strong attack), but after 22...♘g6 (if 22...♘ed7 23 h4) 23 f5 exf5 24 ♖xf5 ♕e7 25 ♖af1 ♘xe4 26 ♖xf7 ♕e8 Black's attack looks very menacing. I guess Terentjev's attack was proceeding so well that he didn't even want to risk a pawn sacrifice to open lines.

22 ♖f2

Possibly preparing a second rank defence.

22...♕e7

Preparing ...g5-g4 as the f6-knight will need guarding after fxg4.

23 ♖af1

It turns out that the point of White's last was to prepare this move to deter ...g5-g4. This is a nice example of indirect overprotection of a square (g4).

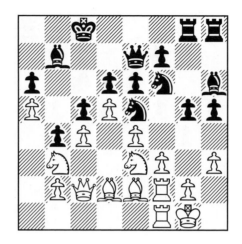

23...♖g6

Setting up the threat of ...g5-g4 once again by defending f6.

> ***Exercise:*** Instead of Black's move, can you find a
> way to force through ...g5-g4 as quickly as possible?

Answer: Since White is indirectly attacking the knight on f6, why not move it away first? There is no need to bother about having enough pieces to aid ...g5-g4 since the h6-bshop can remove the e3-knight (a defender of the g4-square): 23...♘fd7! 24 ♗d1 g4 25 fxg4 ♗xe3 26 ♗xe3 hxg4 and Black breaks through.

24 g4!?

A good defensive idea to prevent ...g5-g4 once and for all. However, it is not good enough as Black can change plans and head for the h-file instead.

24...♗g7

Paving the way for the doubling of rooks on the h-file.

25 ♖h2 ♖gh6

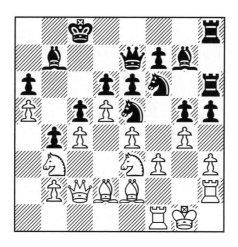

26 f4

White is not going down without a fight and plays to complicate by not allowing Black to open the h-file.

> **Question:** What if White defends h2 resolutely after 26 ♖ff2 ♘g6
> 27 ♘f1, attacking g5 in the process? How does Black continue the assault?

Answer: Black can nonchalantly sacrifice the exchange with 27...hxg4!! 28 ♗xg5 gxf3 29 ♗xh6 ♗xh6 30 ♗xf3 ♗f4 31 ♖h1 ♘d7 32 ♘bd2 ♘de5 33 ♗g4 ♕g5 34 ♕b3 ♕h6 35 ♗d1 f5!, with an irresistible attack.

26...gxf4 27 g5 ♖g6

Also strong is 27...fxe3 28 gxh6 ♗xh6 29 ♗e1 when despite being the exchange up, White's clustered pieces are no match for Black's hyperactive ones.

28 ♘g2 ♖xg5 29 ♗xf4 ♖g6 30 ♘xc5?

Desperation as Black remains in control. White could hold out longer after 30 ♔h1 ♘fd7 31 ♕d1.

30...dxc5 31 ♗xe5 exd5 32 ♗xf6 ♗xf6 33 exd5 ♗e5

The rest does not require commentary.

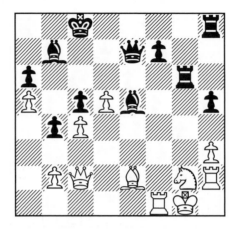

34 ♔h1 ♗xh2 35 ♔xh2 ♛e5+ 36 ♔h1 ♖hg8 37 ♘h4 ♖g3 0-1

B) Georgiev's 5 ♛c2

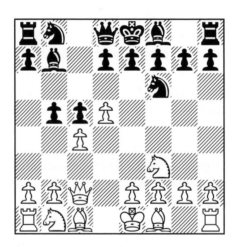

The Bulgarian Grandmaster Kiril Georgiev advocates 5 ♛c2 in his *Squeezing the Gambits*, introducing a dangerous pawn sacrifice on d5 after 5...bxc4 6 e4. My recommendation is to accept the pawn, complete development swiftly, castle safely and return the pawn quickly, as in Wagner-Milliet.

Game 38
C.Wagner-S.Milliet
French League 2012

1 d4 ♘f6 2 c4 c5 3 d5 b5 4 ♘f3 ♗b7 5 ♛c2

White, if unimpeded, will bolster the centre with e2-e4, but this requires a temporary pawn sacrifice on his part.

5...bxc4

Immediately whittling away at the centre.

6 e4 e6!

Black needs to attack the centre quickly or the b7-bishop will become a spectator. Indeed, after 6...d6 7 ♗xc4 g6 8 0-0 ♗g7 9 ♘c3 White has seamless development and the bishop is biting on granite.

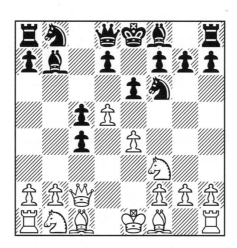

7 ♗xc4!

A temporary pawn sacrifice. White banks on the use of tactics on the e-file to win back the pawn.

Instead, 7 ♗g5 ♗e7 8 ♗xf6 (Aveskulov indicated that after 8 d6 Black can sacrifice a piece: 8...♗xd6 9 e5 ♗xf3 10 exf6 gxf6 11 ♕c3 ♗e5 12 ♕xe5 fxe5 13 ♗xd8 ♔xd8 14 gxf3 d5 – what a pawn chain!) 8...♗xf6 9 e5 ♗g5 10 dxe6 fxe6 11 ♘bd2 ♗xd2+ 12 ♘xd2 ♘c6 13 ♘xc4 0-0 gave Black a superb position in J.Szabolcsi-I.Salgado Lopez, Vienna 2012, while after 7 dxe6 fxe6 8 e5 ♘d5 9 ♗xc4 ♗e7 10 a3 0-0 Black has a comfortable game, J.Adler-B.Zueger, Swiss League 2004.

7...exd5 8 exd5 ♗xd5

Black accepts the proffered pawn.

If 8...d6 9 ♘c3 ♗e7 10 0-0 ♘bd7 11 b3 with a spatial plus for White, but an interesting try is 8...♕e7+ 9 ♔d2 ♕d6 10 ♖e1+ ♗e7 11 ♘c3. Here Black's best is probably to take a draw with 11...♕f4+ (11...♘xd5 12 ♘b5 ♕b6 13 ♘g5 is too dangerous a position to consider) 12 ♔d3 ♕f5+ 13 ♔d2 ♕f4+.

9 ♗xd5 ♘xd5 10 0-0 ♗e7 11 ♖e1

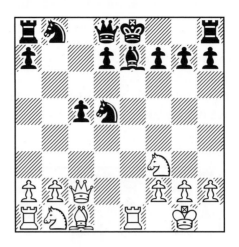

11...♘a6

This knight will defend the other via c7 and, if necessary, shield the e-file with ...♘e6.

White is slightly better after 11...♘b4 12 ♕e2! 0-0 (Georgiev demonstrated that after 12...♘8c6? 13 ♘c3 c4 14 ♕xc4 White has a great position) 13 ♘c3 ♗f6 14 a3 ♘4c6 15 ♗f4 d5 16 ♕b5 ♘d4 17 ♘xd4 ♗xd4 18 ♖ad1 ♕d7 19 ♕xd7 ♘xd7 20 ♘xd5 ♖fe8, as in A.Uberos Fernandez-F.Destruels Moreno, correspondence 2008.

> ***Question:*** What is wrong with moving the king to safety with 11...0-0?

Answer: The sneaky 12 ♕e4! nabs either the knight on d5 or the e7-bishop.

12 ♕c4

Winning back the pawn with the threatened fork.

If 12 ♕f5 ♘ac7 13 ♘g5 ♘f6 14 ♕xc5 ♘e6 15 ♕f5 h6 16 ♘xe6 dxe6 17 ♕b5+ ♕d7 18 ♕e2 with equality, H.Alvarez Villar-A.Satici, correspondence 2011, and 12 ♗g5 0-0 13 ♗xe7 ♘xe7 14 ♕c4 ♘c7 15 ♕xc5 ♘e6 16 ♕d6 ♖b8 17 b3 ♖b6 18 ♕d3 d5 was equal too in W.Kund-N.Bernal Varela, correspondence 2010.

12...♘ac7 13 ♕xc5 0-0 14 ♕c4 ♗f6

Activating the bishop on its best diagonal. Let's assess this position. Black has the more active pieces and is ahead in development. However, he has an isolated d-pawn which can later be subjected to attack by White's pieces. In return too, Black has two good open queenside files (the b- and c-files) to play on. All things considered, the position should be about equal.

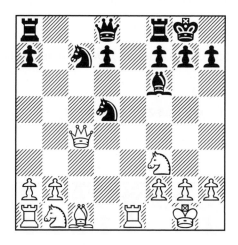

15 ♘c3?!

As Black will soon play ...♖b8 to put pressure on b2, White decides to remove the strong knight by accepting an isolated pawn of his own.

He does better with 15 ♘bd2 when 15...♖b8 16 ♖b1 ♘b6 17 ♕d3 d5 18 ♘b3 ♗e6 19 ♘bd4 ♘c5 20 ♕e2 is about level, Black's activity being counterbalanced by his isolated d-pawn.

15...♘xc3 16 bxc3 ♖c8

Immediately homing in on the c3 weakie.

17 ♗d2 ♘e6 18 ♕a4 ♕c7

Putting pressure on c3 as well as defending a7. The *Houdini* engine indicated that Black could instead sacrifice a7 with 18...d5! 19 ♕xa7 ♖a8 20 ♕b7 (20 ♕e3 ♖a3) 20...♘c5 21 ♕b5 ♘e4 22 ♕d3 ♖a3, exerting pressure in true Benko Gambit fashion.

19 ♖ab1 ♖b8 20 c4!

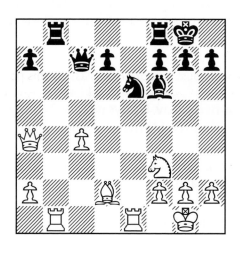

Seizing the chance to turn the isolani into an asset. White plans to exchange c4 for a7 and soon succeeds in doing so.

20...♖fc8 21 ♗e3

After this, the game peters out to a draw following mass exchanges.

21...h6 22 ♖xb8

Of course, not 22 ♗xa7?? ♖a8.

22...♖xb8 23 ♕xa7 ♕xa7 24 ♗xa7 ♖a8 25 ♗e3 ♖xa2 26 g3 ♖c2 27 ♖d1 ♖xc4 ½-½

C) 4 ♕c2

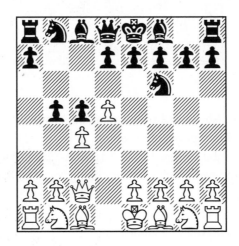

With the queen shifting ever so slightly to the next file, White supports the e2-e4 push and basically asks Black to clarify what he wants to do. My preference is to chip away at the White centre with 4...bxc4 5 e4 e6. The two games I'm giving, Mamedyarov-Nguyen Ngoc Truong Son and Gross-Nun, show that White can generate dangerous play in a relatively calm position due to his space advantage. Hence, in this line, make sure that you put your light-squared bishop on d7 unless you are a risk taker and prefer to take your chances with Aveskulov's risky ...♖b4 idea.

> *Game 39*
> **S.Mamedyarov-Nguyen Ngoc Truong Son**
> Khanty-Mansiysk (rapid) 2013

1 d4 ♘f6 2 c4 c5 3 d5 b5 4 ♕c2

The queen supports the e2-e4 push.

4...bxc4

Whittling away the support for the d5-pawn.

5 e4 e6

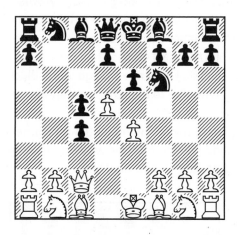

Further chipping away at the white centre.

6 ♘c3

Playing this before ♗xc4 allows White the possibility of playing into the complications seen in the next note. In any case, the move helps to support e4 and d5.

6 ♗xc4 exd5 7 exd5 d6 would normally lead to the same type of position as our main game.

6...♗e7!?

This avoids the gambit that Mamedyarov pulled on Bareev in the 2011 World Blitz Championship 2011: 6...exd5 7 e5!? (7 exd5 transposes back to the game continuation) 7...♘g4 8 ♘xd5 ♗b7? (Aveskulov showed that Black could sacrifice a knight with 8...♘xe5! for a truckload of pawns: 9 ♕e4 d6 10 f4 f5 11 ♕e3 ♗e6 12 ♘c3 ♘bc6 13 fxe5 d5 with a totally unclear position) 9 ♗xc4 ♘c6 10 ♘f3 ♗e7 11 ♕f5! Already with a winning position, S.Mamedyarov-E.Bareev, Moscow (blitz) 2009.

7 ♗xc4 0-0 8 ♘ge2!

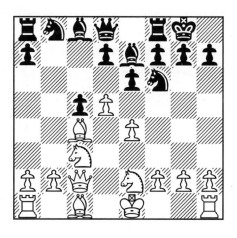

Recommended by John Watson in *A Strategic Chess Opening Repertoire for White* and, indeed, it is a strong idea. White plans to shift the knight to g3 where it has access to e4 or f5. His f-pawn is also free to advance if required.

8...exd5 9 exd5 d6 10 0-0 ♘bd7 11 ♘g3 ♘b6

Putting pressure on d5 and seeking an exchange on c4. Black is playing to trade pieces as he has less space to play with due to the pawn configuration.

12 b3 ♖e8

Please pay close attention to the following motifs recommended by Aveskulov. If Nguyen Ngoc Truong Son had known them, he wouldn't have been hacked as he was: 12...♘xc4 13 bxc4 ♖b8 14 ♖e1 ♖e8 15 ♗f4 ♖b4!?.

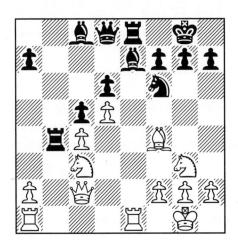

This is the key idea. After 16 ♘b5 (if 16 ♘ce4 ♘xe4 17 ♘xe4 ♗f5 with equality) 16...♖xb5 17 cxb5 ♘xd5 Black has full compensation in the form of a pawn for the exchange and the ability to use the two mobile central pawns in good time.

13 ♖e1 ♗f8

Black wants to trade off a pair of rooks to ease the congestion in his position.

14 ♗f4

A good square for the bishop, forcing Black to watch the d6-pawn.

14...♖xe1+ 15 ♖xe1 ♖b8 16 h3 ♘xc4 17 bxc4

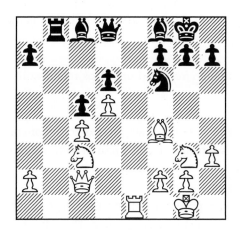

17...♕d7?!

Black is misplacing his light-squared bishop and queen with this move. It seems very natural to overprotect f5, but the queen's bishop is most comfortable on d7 in this variation to cover the rook on e8 and to keep the back rank connected. After 17...♗d7 if White attempts 18 ♘f5 Black can counter with 18...♘h5 (18...♖b4 is also good, and if 19 ♘xd6? ♕b8!) 19 ♗h2 ♕f6 20 ♘e3 when he is not worse.

Black can also try the audacious Aveskulov-like manoeuvre 17...♖b4!? 18 ♘b5 ♘xd5!? (18...♕a5 19 ♗d2 ♕a4 20 ♕xa4 ♖xa4 21 ♗c3 seems a bit too dangerous to contemplate) 19 ♗d2 ♖xb5 20 cxb5 ♘b6 21 ♗e3 ♗e6, although in this case, the central pawns are less mobile than in Aveskulov's example.

18 ♘ce4!

The awkward placement of the black queen allows White to centralize a knight and by now the Vietnamese GM was probably regretting his decision.

18...♘xe4 19 ♘xe4

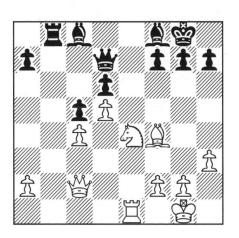

19...♗a6??

When it rains, it pours. That said, even after 19...♖b6 20 a4 a5 21 ♘c3 life is still tough for Black.

> ***Exercise:*** What did Black miss here?

Answer: 20 ♘xc5!

This hammer blow forces the win of a pawn, thanks to the pin on the d6-pawn and to compound matters, Black is forced to trade a pair of minor pieces, leading to an easily won endgame for White.

20...♕c8 21 ♘xa6 ♕xa6 22 c5!

And when it pours, it really pours in buckets. Everything clicks for Mamedyarov like clockwork as he fashions a protected passed pawn. There is no coming back for Nguyen from here.

22...♕a5 23 ♖d1 ♕b4 24 ♗g3 h5 25 c6 h4 26 ♗h2 ♖e8 27 ♔h1 ♕a5 28 f3 ♗e7 29 ♕e4 g6 30 ♗f4 ♖c8 31 ♕xe7 ♕a4 32 ♖b1 ♕xf4 33 ♕d7 ♖f8 34 c7 1-0

> *Game 40*
> **S.Gross-J.Nun**
> Trnava 1980

1 d4 ♘f6 2 c4 c5 3 d5 b5 4 ♕c2 bxc4 5 e4 e6 6 ♘c3 ♗e7 7 ♗xc4 exd5 8 exd5 0-0

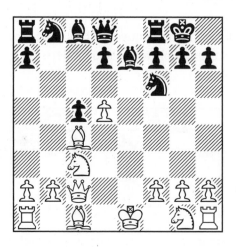

9 ♘ge2!

> ***Question:*** Why not 9 ♘f3 instead? Isn't it a better square for the knight?

Answer: Aveskulov demonstrated the following impressive antidote: 9...d6 10 0-0 ♘bd7 11 ♗f4 ♘b6 12 ♘d2 ♗b7 13 ♕d3 ♘h5 14 ♗e3 f5 when "Black has a pleasant position".

9...d6 10 0-0 ♘bd7 11 ♘g3 ♘b6

Putting pressure on d5 and seeking an exchange on c4.

12 b3 ♖b8

Anticipating ...♘xc4 when the rook will be useful on the b-file.

Alternatively, Black made use of the g4-square to ease his position by exchanging a piece after 12...♘xc4 13 bxc4 ♘g4 14 ♗f4 ♗f6 15 h3 (better was 15 ♖ab1! ♗e5 16 ♗xe5 ♘xe5 17 ♘d1 ♖e8 18 ♘e3 g6 with equal play) 15...♗e5 16 ♗xe5 ♘xe5 17 ♘ce4 f5! 18 f4 ♘xc4 19 ♕xc4 fxe4 by when he had an excellent game and the better pawn structure due to the weakness of the d5-pawn, L.Comas Fabrego-M.Llanes Hurtado, Sabadell 2011.

13 ♗d2!?

The f4-square seems a more natural square for the bishop as there it keeps an eye on Black's d-pawn, but White is playing for another piece configuration with a gradual king-side build-up.

13...♖e8 14 ♖ae1

White does not intend to contest the b-file as exchanges would ease Black's lack of space.

14...♘xc4 15 bxc4

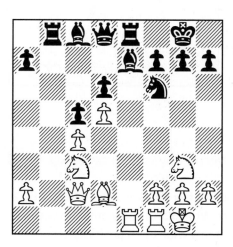

15...♕d7

Like in the previous game, Black intends to counterattack with ...♗a6, but this plan backfires spectacularly after some excellent play by White which is even more impressive than Mamedyarov's.

> **Exercise:** By now you should know that there
> are the two possible ideas for Black, which are?

Answer: 15...♗d7! 16 h3 ♗f8 with equal chances. Or, if you're a risk taker, 15...♖b4!? 16 ♘b5 (after 16 ♘ce4 ♘xe4 17 ♖xe4 ♖b8 18 ♖fe1 ♗d7 19 ♗c3 ♗f8 Black's bishop-pair counterbalances White's spatial advantage) 16...♖xb5 17 cxb5 ♘xd5 with compensation.

16 ♘d1

Planning to reroute the knight to e3. 16 ♘ce4 ♘xe4 17 ♘xe4 is not so dangerous with the bishop on d2 instead of f4.

16...♗a6

Black intends to sacrifice the minor exchange with ♘xd5; cxd5 ♗xf1 at a favourable time.

17 h3

Removing the possibility of ...♘g4-e5.

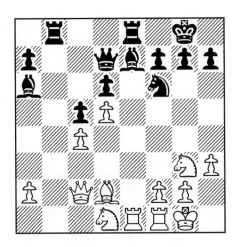

17...♗f8

> **Question:** Is 17...♘xd5 18 cxd5 ♗xf1 a good idea?

Answer: Unfortunately not, as after 19 ♖xf1 ♗f6 20 ♘e3! ♖b2 21 ♕d3 ♖xa2 22 ♘c4 ♕b5 23 ♖c1 Black is in trouble since White can simply build up with ♘f5 and ♗c3. The minor pieces are extremely potent in a wide open position.

18 ♗g5

White tests the waters first.

18...♗e7 19 ♗d2!

Gross plans to reroute this bishop to c3.

19...♗f8

Hoping for a trade of rooks.

20 ♘e3!

White declines.

20...g6

Played to prevent a menacing knight from appearing on f5.

21 ♗c3 ♗g7 22 ♕c1!!

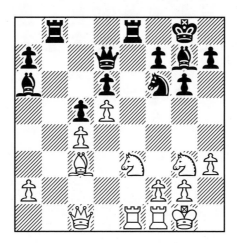

A beautiful concept. Black is crushed after this quiet move as there's amazingly no way to defend the position.

22...♕a4

It's hard to award this a question mark since the position was already lost, but Black now goes down without a fight. Moreover, in the other variations, White must find the ♘ef5 sacrifice to win: for example, 22...h5 23 ♘ef5!! ♗h8 24 ♘h6+ ♔h7 25 ♕g5 ♖e5 26 ♖xe5 dxe5 27 ♗xe5 ♖b6 28 d6 winning, 22...♕d8 23 ♘ef5!! gxf5 24 ♘xf5 ♘h5 25 ♖xe8+ ♕xe8 26 ♖e1 ♕f8 27 ♕g5 ♗xc4 (if 27...♗h8 28 ♖e3 ♗xc3 29 ♖xc3 ♕d8 30 ♕xh5 with a crushing attack) 28 ♖e3, or 22...♕c8 23 f4! (there's no satisfactory way to meet f4-f5xg6) 23...♕d8 24 f5 ♖f8 25 ♕a1 when Black is busted.

23 ♕a1 ♖e5

Hoping that White will settle for the exchange.

24 f4

But he doesn't.

24...♖xe3 25 ♖xe3 ♘e8 26 ♖xe8+ ♕xe8 27 ♗xg7 ♕e3+ 28 ♔h2 1-0

D) 4 ♘d2

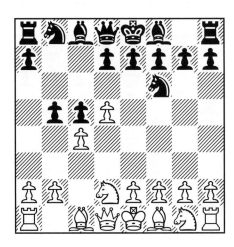

In this line, White is content to maintain his space advantage in the centre by supporting e2-e4. Proponents of this line include top GMs like Kramnik, Sasikiran, Dreev and Beliavsky. I propose that we adopt Leko's approach of capturing c4 followed by a swift counterstrike, as in Koch-Beukema. White does have a spatial plus, but by trading pieces Black can avoid being gradually squeezed.

Game 41
T.Koch-S.Beukema
European Club Cup, Eilat 2012

1 d4 ♘f6 2 c4 c5 3 d5 b5 4 ♘d2

This looks passive, but it has some high-powered adherents, such as Kramnik and Harikrishna. White aims to build a solid centre without being harassed by the traditional Benko queenside counterplay.

4...bxc4 5 e4 c3!?

The pawn is dead anyway, but by selling it on c3 the eventual placement of the bishop on g7 makes that square a target.

6 bxc3

6 ♘c4 ♘xe4?? would cost Black a piece in Zaitsev fashion after 7 ♕e2 because 7...♘f6 8 ♘d6# ends the game. Instead, 6...d6 7 bxc3 g6 transposes back to the Kramnik-Leko game shown below.

6...d6

6...g6 7 ♗d3 d6 transposes.

7 ♗d3

Alternatives:

a) 7 ♘c4 g6 8 ♗d3 ♗g7 9 ♘f3 0-0 10 0-0 ♘bd7 11 ♗d2 ♘b6 12 ♘a5? (better was 12 ♘xb6 axb6 13 a4 with equal chances) 12...c4! 13 ♗c2 (if 13 ♘xc4 ♘xc4 14 ♗xc4 ♘xe4) 13...♕c7! and White is worse already according to Leko in *Informant 73*, V.Kramnik-P.Leko, Dortmund 1998.

b) White can also play for a queenside fianchetto: 7 c4 g6 8 ♗b2 ♗g7 9 ♗d3 0-0 10 ♖b1 e5 11 ♘e2 ♘h5 with equal chances, A.Beliavsky-T.Fogarasi, Hungarian League 1999.

7...g6 8 ♘e2 ♗g7 9 ♖b1

Alexander Beliavsky considered this position to be slightly better for White. Personally, I think it's fine for Black. He might have a bit less space, but his pieces develop easily and White does not really have much to work with, compared to analogous lines in the Modern Benoni or King's Indian.

9...0-0 10 0-0 ♘bd7 11 f4

Not so much to start a central pawn storm as to secure e5 first. White must obtain appropriate squares for his knights before he can commence aggressive options.

11...♕c7

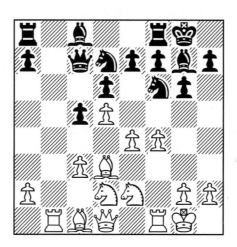

12 c4

Securing the centre.

> *Question:* How should Black meet 12 ♘c4 which makes use of c4 being an outpost?

Answer: Black should try to exchange pieces as he has less space: 12...♘b6 13 ♘e3 ♘g4. Here 12...♗a6 13 ♕a4 ♗xc4 14 ♕xc4 ♖ab8 is also fine as the bishop-pair doesn't exert much influence in this pawn structure.

12...♖b8

Contesting the b-file. Once again, Black should strive to exchange pieces to ease his more congested position.

13 ♖xb8

In an earlier game, after 13 ♖b3 Black erred by straightening out White's pawn structure with 13...♖xb3?! (13...♖b4!?) 14 axb3 and subsequently found himself unable to counter White's build-up on the kingside: 14...♘b8 15 h3 ♘a6 16 ♘f3 ♘d7 17 ♗d2 ♘b4 18 ♗b1 a5 19 ♗c3 ♗a6 20 ♗xg7 ♔xg7 21 ♘c3 ♘b6 22 ♘d2 f6 23 ♖e1 ♖a8 24 h4 and Black had to defend passively in A.Yuneev-D.Stojanovski, Wijk aan Zee 2000.

13...♕xb8 14 ♘b3

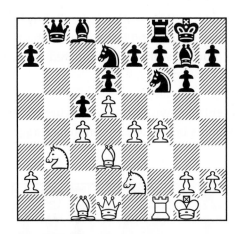

A rather strange square for the knight.

> **Question:** Can you provide a reason for White placing the knight here instead of the more natural f3-square?

Answer: He hopes for a possible invasion of the c6 outpost after ♘a5.

14...♗a6

Black focuses on the weak c-pawn.

15 ♗d2

White prevents the black queen from accessing b4 to hit c4 again. White can also proceed with 15 ♘a5 e6 16 ♘c6 ♕b6 17 ♘c3 ♖e8, with equal chances.

15...e6!

Finally, Black starts action against the imposing white centre.

16 dxe6

Not impressed with Black's undermining move, White exchanges on e6, rationalizing that Black has weakened b6 and g6.

After 16 ♗c3 exd5 17 exd5 Black can play a temporary knight sacrifice with 17...♘xd5 18 ♗xg7 ♔xg7 19 cxd5 and regain the piece after 19...c4.

16...fxe6

Now Black can very much feel his own central pawns which besides controlling good squares, also have the potential to be mobilized for a counterattack.

17 ♕c2

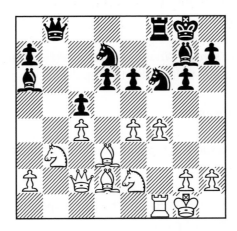

Lending protection to c4 as well as threatening e4-e5 at some point.

Question: How should Black respond to White's gradual build-up?

Answer: Black has placed all his pieces optimally for the key break, so:

17...d5! 18 e5

Trying to keep the position closed to contain Black's initiative.

Question: How would you meet 18 cxd5?

Answer: 18...c4! 19 ♗xc4 ♖c8 20 ♘a5 ♗xc4 21 ♘xc4 exd5 22 exd5 ♘b6 and Black picks up the knight.

Instead 18 exd5 exd5 19 f5 is well met by 19...♘e5.

18...♘g4 19 ♘a5?

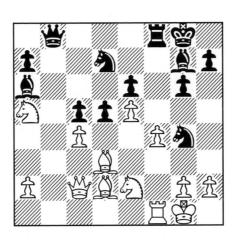

White adds another piece to the defence of c4 and threatens to win material after 20 cxd5, but Black is ready for this.

Exercise: What has Black worked out to overcome White's ploy to keep the position quiet?

Answer: He blows the centre apart:

19...♘dxe5!

A stunning blow. All of a sudden, the white build-up on the queenside looks sadly misplaced.

20 fxe5 ♖xf1+

20...♗xe5 21 g3 ♖xf1+ 22 ♔xf1 ♕f8+ 23 ♘f4 g5 transposes.

21 ♔xf1 ♕f8+ 22 ♘f4 ♗xe5 23 g3 g5

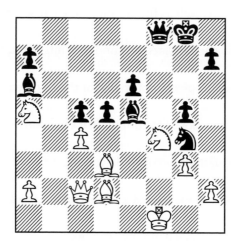

Black gets back his investment and with a dividend in the form of an extra pawn.

24 ♗xh7+ ♔h8

Frazzled by the turn of events, White now blunders.

25 ♗g8?

He could resist better with 25 ♕f5! exf5 26 ♘g6+ ♔xh7 27 ♘xf8+ ♔g8 28 ♘e6 ♗xc4+ 29 ♘xc4 dxc4 30 ♗xg5 ♘xh2+ 31 ♔g2 ♘g4 32 ♘xc5, with drawing chances.

25...♕xg8!

Of course, not 25...♔xg8? 26 ♕g6+ ♔h8 27 ♕h5+ ♘h6 28 ♕xg5.

26 ♘g6+ ♔g7 27 ♗xg5

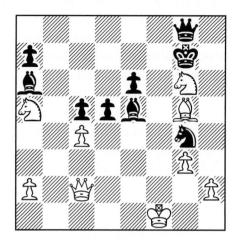

Question: Has White saved his piece?

Answer: Nope.

27...♕f7+ 28 ♔e1

White must have missed that 28 ♘f4 cuts across the e3-bishop's gaze, allowing a queen fork with 28...♘e3+.

28...♕xg6

The rest was a walk in the park for Black.

29 ♕xg6+ ♔xg6 30 ♗e7 ♗c3+ 0-1

E) 4 ♗g5

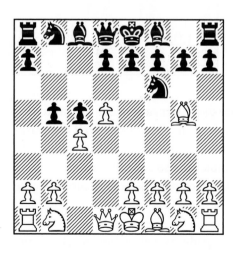

This bishop sally, akin to the Trompowsky, is unique in the sense that White cedes a lot of space to Black, hoping that he can gradually push him back and exploit the weak squares (usually light squares) created by Black's space-gaining ventures. The Greek Grandmaster Efstratios Grivas has written some excellent articles in *New In Chess Yearbook 103* and *104* detailing his adventures in this line, so I think it deserves to be called the Grivas variation, although I think the chap might prefer to call it something more esoteric given that his variations in the ...♕b6 Sicilian bear the names of Greek mythological figures.

We examine the most topical line in Kourousis-Tappyrov, where Black has the option of pausing with 7...♖g8, keeping the kingside pawn structure intact, or keeping White busy with the anti-positional 7...f6 (my preference), allowing a 'Swiss cheese' or V-formation structure.

Game 42
E.Kourousis-V.Tappyrov
Pardubice 2013

---

1 d4 ♘f6 2 c4 c5 3 d5 b5 4 ♗g5 ♘e4

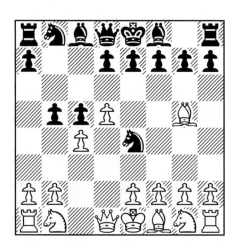

Gaining a tempo on the g5-bishop, a concept similar to the Trompowsky where White also lures the knight to e4, with the idea of kicking it back later.

5 ♗f4 ♕a5+

This position also resembles the so-called Vulture opening: 1 d4 ♘f6 2 c4 c5 3 d5 ♘e4. After 4 ♕c2, 4 f3 or 4 ♘bd2, Black plays 4...♕a5 to pin the piece on d2, with the idea of a quick ...b5 break.

6 ♘d2 g5

Gaining space on the kingside, as well as freeing g7 as a possible square for the dark-squared bishop.

7 ♗e5

White invites ...f7-f6, which has the effect of making the black kingside pawn structure look like a Swiss cheese as White can take over the h5-d8 diagonal after a future queen check on h5.

After 7 ♕c2 gxf4 8 ♕xe4 d6 9 ♘gf3 ♗g7 Black is already better, although a draw was agreed here in R.Damaso-E.Fernandez Romero, Santo Antonio 2002.

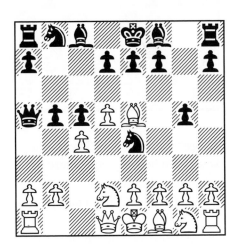

7...f6

Accepting the invitation to the Swiss cheese variation or, if you like this set-up, the V-formation structure (after Black gets in ...d7-d6). Incidentally, this pawn structure figures quite often in Sicilian Dragon endgames.

Aveskulov makes a case for 7...♖g8 8 ♘gf3 (after 8 b4 ♕xb4 9 ♘gf3 ♕a5! 10 ♖b1 a6 11 ♕c2 f5 12 e3 d6 13 ♗a1 g4 14 ♘h4 ♕xd2+ 15 ♕xd2 ♘xd2 16 ♔xd2 e5! 17 dxe6 ♗xe6 18 ♗d3 ♖g5 19 cxb5 ♖h5 20 g3 axb5 21 ♗xb5+ ♔d8 22 a4 ♗d5 Black is slightly better according to the Ukrainian GM, as he is after 8 ♕c2 ♕xd2+ 9 ♕xd2 ♘xd2 10 ♔xd2 d6 11 ♗g3 bxc4 12 e4 ♗g7 in the view of Grivas) 8...♘xd2 9 ♕xd2 ♕xd2+ 10 ♘xd2 d6 11 ♗g3 bxc4 12 e4 ♗g7 13 ♘xc4 ♗a6 14 ♖b1 ♗xc4 15 ♗xc4 ♘d7, with equality according to his analysis.

8 ♗g3

Aveskulov's preference for 7...♖g8 instead of 7...f6 stems from the resulting positions after 8 ♗c3 ♘xc3 9 bxc3. He noted that in this position, Black's "pawn structure looks miserable – Black's f8-bishop is closed in, the e8-h5 diagonal is weakened, while there is a problem with the b5-pawn." However, he did add a caveat that "of course, this position is playable for Black".

This position has occurred five times in my database and 9...bxc4, 9...♗xg7 and 9...d6 have all been played. However, I don't see anything wrong with 9...♕xc3!?.

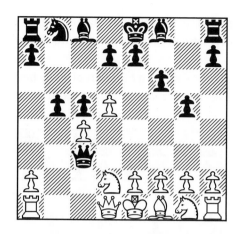

This continuation has also been suggested by Grivas as a possible line to investigate. It might seem foolhardy to take a pawn in a position where nothing else besides the queen is developed, but there are some plusses to this idea:

1) Black pins the d2-knight which can become a dangerous piece if, for example, it reaches c4.

2) The queen has no real purpose on a5 if not to clear the long diagonal.

3) The black king will most likely take a walk to d8, and maybe c7 anyway. Even in the 7...♖g8 line, the king is safer on the queenside.

4) White can hardly contemplate ♕h5+ ideas in the near future as his d2-knight will need guarding.

5) With ...d7-d6 coming soon, the position is closed and it is not difficult for Black to develop his queen's knight and bishop. As for the f8 chap, he can always activate it via ...f6-f5 and ...♗g7, or ...h7-h5, ...g5-g4 and ...♗h6.

The chess engines could not find a refutation to this idea after many hours of working on this line. Here are some sample lines:

a) 10 ♖c1 ♕a5 11 cxb5 d6! keeps the position closed instead of opening lines for White after 11...♕xb5 12 e4 a6 13 ♖b1 ♘d7 14 a4 ♘e5 15 ♘gf3 ♘xf3+ 16 gxf3 f5!, although even here the dark-squared bishop gets to g7.

b) 10 ♖b1 f5! (or 10...b4 11 ♖b3 ♕e5 12 e3 h5 13 ♘gf3 ♕c7 14 ♖b2 ♗g7 15 ♕b1 d6 16 ♕g6+ ♔f8 when the black king is safe even with the white queen lurking in the vicinity) 11 ♖xb5 (if 11 e3 d6 12 ♘h3 h6) 11...d6 12 e3 ♘d7 13 ♕h5+ ♔d8 14 ♘e2 (after 14 ♕xg5?! ♕c1+ 15 ♔e2 ♘f6 and White is in trouble already) 14...♕f6 15 ♘g3 ♘e5 and Black is fine.

c) 10 cxb5 d6 11 e3 (if 11 e4 ♘d7 12 ♖c1 ♕a5 13 ♕h5+ ♔d8 14 ♘gf3 a6!) 11...♘d7 12 ♖c1 (12 ♗c4 ♕a5 13 ♘e2 ♗g7 14 a4 is "unclear" according to Grivas, but after 14...0-0 15 0-0 f5 Black has a nice typical Benko position; though his kingside is kind of airy, White doesn't seem well placed to take advantage of it) 12...♕b4 13 ♕h5+ ♔d8 14 ♗e2 f5! 15 ♘gf3 ♘f6 16 ♕xg5 ♖g8 17 ♕h4 ♕xh4 18 ♘xh4 ♘xd5 19 ♗f3 ♗e6 20 ♘xf5 ♖b8 21 a4 ♘b4 and Black has good play.

8...bxc4

This is a suggestion of Grivas, who shared his vast experience of more than 20 years of this variation in *New in Chess Yearbook*.

9 e3

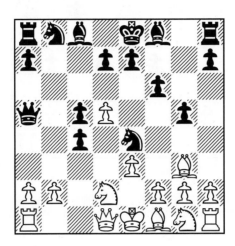

9...h5

Still following Grivas's suggestion. Ironically Black has more space than White on both sides of the board.

9...d6 is also strong as a check on h5 is just a waste of move because the queen would have to return to defend the pinned knight on d2, while after 10 f3 ♕xd2+ 11 ♕xd2 ♘xd2 12 ♔xd2 ♗a6 Black is better as he can soon play ...f6-f5 and obtain a great diagonal for his dark-squared bishop.

10 h4

Otherwise, 10 ♗c7 ♕xd2+ 11 ♕xd2 ♘xd2 12 ♔xd2 ♘a6 13 ♗a5 ♖b8 14 ♗c3 ♘c7 15 ♗xc4 ♘b5 gains the bishop-pair thus giving Black a slight edge, while Grivas analyzed 10 ♘gf3!? ♘a6 11 h3 with compensation for the material.

10...g4!?

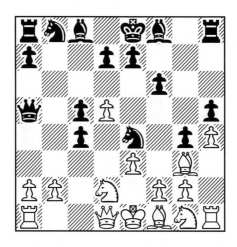

Answer: The pros are that Black gains space and denies White's knights the f3-square. Moreover, the dark-squared bishop enjoys a decent diagonal if it is deployed to h6. On the other hand, Black has given up the f4-square for now and a subsequent white knight there will cause inconvenience, as the h5-pawn is then hit and has been immobilized by the h4-pawn.

11 ♗xc4?!

Stronger is 11 ♘e2 ♗b7 (or 11...♗a6 12 ♕c2 ♕xd2+ 13 ♕xd2 ♘xd2 14 ♔xd2 e5 15 ♘c3 d6 when Black has a solid position) 12 ♘f4 ♗g7 13 ♗xc4 ♗a6! 14 ♖c1 f5 15 ♘d3 d6, although here Black is for choice as his pieces are the better placed and he has a handy space advantage.

Instead, the desperado move 11 ♗c7 is best met by a queen and knight trade: 11...♕xd2+ 12 ♕xd2 ♘xd2 13 ♔xd2 ♘a6 14 ♗a5 ♖b8 15 ♗c3 ♘c7 16 ♗xc4 ♗b7 17 e4 e6 18 ♗xf6 ♗h6+ 19 ♗g5 exd5 20 exd5 ♗xg5+ 21 hxg5 ♗xd5 22 ♗xd5 ♘xd5 23 b3 ♔f7 with the better ending for Black.

11...♗a6?!

Black missed a chance to fracture White's pawns: 11...♘xg3! 12 fxg3 ♗h6 13 ♔f2 d6 (Black is structurally better) 14 ♘e2 ♗f5 15 ♘f4 ♘d7 16 e4 ♗h7 17 ♖f1 ♘e5 18 ♔g1 ♖b8 when Black has a slight edge, but White's position is very solid and quite hard to breach.

12 ♖c1 d6

12...♗xc4 13 ♖xc4 ♘xg3 14 fxg3 ♕xa2 15 ♘e2 ♗h6 16 ♘f4 gives White compensation for the pawn as he will have some well-placed pieces.

13 ♘e2 ♗h6 14 ♕c2?!

This move merely allows Black to play what he intended all along and with an extra tempo, namely to trade down into a structurally better ending.

White should have secured the piece on f4 with 14 ♗f4!.

14...♘xd2 15 ♕xd2 ♕xd2+ 16 ♔xd2 ♗xc4 17 ♖xc4 ♘d7

Now that the smoke has cleared, we can see that Black is better because his pawns are compact and he has a nice target on d5 to take aim at.

18 ♖c2 ♘b6 19 ♘c3

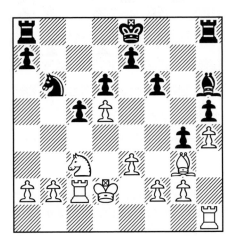

Question: Now that the knight is no longer going to f4, what should Black's plan be?

Answer: To open the long dark-squared diagonal for the bishop.

19...f5! 20 ♔c1

After 20 ♖d1 ♗g7 21 ♔e2 ♔f7 White is suffering and Black can further improve his position with ...♖fb8 and ...♗f6.

20...♗g7 21 ♖d1 ♗xc3!?

Black is anticipating White's attempt to play ♘e2-f4, so he lops off the steed. Moreover, the black knight is stronger than White's bishop in this closed position.

22 ♖xc3 ♔f7 23 e4?

White loses patience and tries to open up the position for his rooks to attack e7. However, this move also allows a black rook to attack d5 via f8-f5.

23...fxe4 24 ♖e3

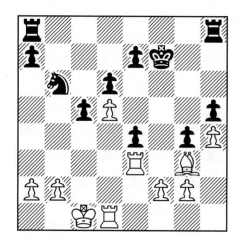

24...♖h6!?

> ***Exercise:*** Can you find a more economical way for a Black rook to get to f5?

Answer: 24...♔e8! 25 ♖xe4 ♔d7. This way, the rooks are connected and if White tries to trade an f5-rook, another one will appear there: for example, 26 ♖d3 ♖hf8 27 ♖f4 ♖xf4 28 ♗xf4 ♖f8 29 ♗e3 ♔c7 30 ♔c2 ♖f5.

25 ♖xe4 ♖f6 26 ♔c2 ♖f5

The problem with this idea is that only one rook can get to f5 so White trades it off.

27 ♖f4 ♖xf4

Activating the king with 27...♔g6! was perhaps stronger.

28 ♗xf4 a5!

Gaining queenside space.

29 ♖d3

29 b3 will also be met by 29...a4.

29...a4

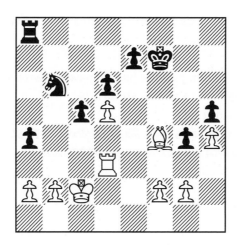

30 ♗d2

> *Question:* How would you deal with f2-f3,
> intending to create an outside passed pawn?

Answer: After 30...♖g8! Black has yet another target to aim at.

30...♔e8 31 f3 gxf3 32 ♖xf3!

Giving up d5 for active play. If 32 gxf3 ♔d7 and White has three weaknesses to defend (d5, f3 and f5).

32...♘xd5 33 ♖f5 ♘f6

White decides to go into a rook ending with a pawn deficit.

34 ♗c3 ♔f7 35 ♗xf6 exf6 36 ♖xh5 ♖g8 37 ♖h7+ ♔e6 38 ♖a7 ♖xg2+ 39 ♔c3 ♖g4 40 h5 ♖h4 41 h6 ♖xh6 42 ♖xa4 ♖h3+ 43 ♔c2 f5

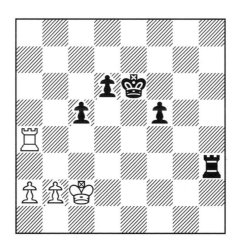

44 ♖f4?

Keeping the rook active with 44 ♖a8 with the idea of a2-a4 would provide much more resistance.

44...♔e5 45 ♖f1 f4

Now it's all over as the king nurses the passed pawn down the board.

46 a4 f3 47 ♔d3 ♔f4 48 a5 ♖h8 49 a6 ♖a8 50 ♖a1 d5

Simpler is 50...♔g3 51 ♖g1+ ♔f2.

51 a7 c4+ 52 ♔d4 f2 53 ♔xd5 ♔e3 54 ♖f1 ♖xa7 55 ♔xc4 ♖c7+ 56 ♔b4 ♖b7+ 57 ♔c3 ♔e2 58 ♖xf2+ ♔xf2 59 b4 ♔e3 60 ♔c4 ♔e4 61 ♔c5 ♔e5 62 b5 ♖c7+ 63 ♔b6 ♔d6 64 ♔a6 ♖c1 0-1

Chapter Eight
The Outsiders

1 d4 ♘f6 2 c4 c5 3 d5 b5

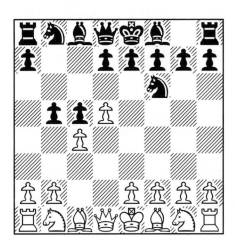

Here we will consider White's remaining if rare options, 4 f3, 4 a4, 4 b3 and 4 e4.

A) 4 f3
In this variation, White simply gets on with bolstering his centre with e2-e4. If Black undermines part of his centre with ...bxc4, he can choose to recapture either with the bishop or knight. Generally the resulting positions hold no danger for Black because essentially White is just slowly building up without having any quick plans to play for a central break or a kingside attack. However, in Munkhgal-Goh Wei Ming, Black's attempt to take the bull by the horns nearly backfired and he had to play the endgame very well to clinch the draw.

Game 43
G.Munkhgal-Goh Wei Ming
Asian Nations Cup, Zaozhuang 2012

1 d4 ♞f6 2 c4 c5 3 d5 b5 4 f3

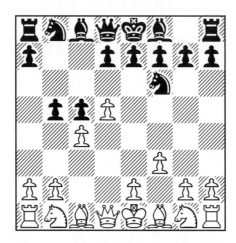

According to Wei Ming, he was relieved to see this move as he was happy with a non-theoretical game.

4...bxc4 5 e4 d6

In this case, I am not adverse to suggesting that we move back into standard Benoni/Benko waters because White's f2-f3 set-up is a tad slow and Black can mobilize easily.

There's nothing wrong either with 5...e6!? as Black should be able to get his pieces out easily: for example, 6 ♞c3 ♝b7 7 ♝xc4 ♞xd5!? 8 ♞xd5 (and not 8 exd5?? ♛h4+ 9 g3 ♛xc4) 8...exd5 9 ♝xd5 ♝xd5 10 ♛xd5 ♞c6 11 ♞e2 ♝e7 12 0-0 0-0 13 ♝e3 ♞b4 14 ♛d2 d5 with equal chances, J.Gilbert-M.Hannon, British League 1999.

6 ♝xc4

White reserves the c4-square for his knight with 6 ♞a3, but the time taken for him to develop in this fashion gives Black seamless Benko piece placement: 6...g6 7 ♞e2 ♝g7 8 ♞c3 0-0 9 ♞xc4 ♞bd7 10 ♝e2 ♜b8 11 0-0 ♝a6 12 ♜b1 ♞g4 13 ♛e1 ♝xc4 14 ♝xc4 ♞ge5 and Black has easy mobility, E.Montenegro-A.Ramirez, San Jose 2012.

6...g6 7 ♝d2!?

White intends to post his bishop on c3 to oppose the one on g7.

An interesting plan of Gareyev's in the standard Sämisch-type structure is to delay castling with 7 ♞c3 ♝g7 8 ♞ge2 ♞bd7 9 0-0 ♜b8. Indeed, there's no hurry to castle as White's structure isn't geared towards an e4-e5 break or a direct kingside attack. Only after the pieces had reached their desired squares with 10 ♜b1 ♞b6 11 ♝b5+ ♞fd7 12 b3 did he move his king to safety: 12...0-0 13 ♝d2 ♞e5 14 ♛c2 a6 15 ♝d3 e6! 16 dxe6 fxe6 17 ♞c1 d5 and White's pieces are bunched aimlessly on the queenside, R.Hungaski-T.Gareyev, Wheeling 2011.

7...♗g7 8 ♗c3 0-0 9 ♘e2

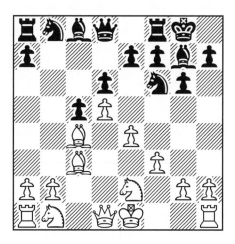

9...♘a6

Question: What is the purpose of this knight move?

Answer: The knight is heading for c7 where it supports the central ...e7-e6 break.

Exercise: Can you find another route for this knight?

Answer: Black can consider 9...♘bd7 10 0-0 ♘b6 11 ♘d2 ♖b8 12 b3, although White is very solidly placed: 12...♘xc4 13 ♘xc4 ♗a6 14 ♖b1 with absolute equality. Hence Black plays the other plan; with the knight on c7, at least the ...e7-e6 break is supported.

10 0-0 ♘c7 11 ♘d2 ♘d7

A risky move. Black hopes to go to e5 or b6 to hit the bishop on c4. However, this leaves the black king vulnerable without a key defender, the g7-bishop.

11...♖b8 12 b3 e6 at least adds some tension to the position.

12 ♗xg7 ♔xg7 13 f4!

Things are getting slightly dodgy for Black as White increases his central presence and threatens to start a kingside attack with f4-f5.

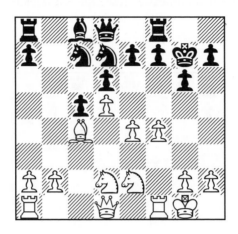

13...♘b6 14 b3 f5!?

Not just weakening White's hold on d5, but also jamming his attempt at a kingside attack. Perhaps 14...a5 was possible too and after 15 ♕c2 a4 16 bxa4 ♘xa4 17 f5 ♘e8! 18 ♖ab1 ♘f6 things are quite unclear.

15 ♘g3

Bolstering e4 and putting pressure on f5.

15...fxe4?!

Black embarks on a plan to completely wipe out White's centre by removing both d5 and e4. However, there is a snag. Moreover, Black's position was not so easy to puncture: for example 15...♖b8 16 exf5 ♗xf5 17 ♘xf5+ ♖xf5 18 g4 ♖f8 19 ♘e4 ♕d7 20 f5 gxf5 21 gxf5 ♔h8 22 ♘g3 ♘e8! 23 ♕d3 ♘f6 and Black is fine.

16 ♘dxe4 e6

Forcing White to capture, since the d5 pawn is attacked three times.

17 dxe6 d5

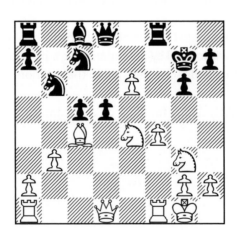

This is Black's big idea, taking over the centre and seemingly winning a piece.

> **Exercise:** As previously mentioned, there is a snag with this idea. What is it?

Answer: 18 f5!

It transpires that Black cannot meet the threat of f5-f6 satisfactorily. Wei Ming had seen this move in his calculations, but did not think much of it then.

18...♗xe6!

The only move and one that gives White a truckload of options. When one is in dire straits, it is often a good idea to keep the position complex and not give your opponent a forced line to find.

White wins easily after 18...dxe4?? 19 f6+! ♔h8 20 e7 or 18...♘xc4?? 19 f6+.

19 ♘xc5

Bagging a pawn. However, at this juncture, Wei Ming pulled up his socks and fought back brilliantly. Firstly, he played for a queenless ending a pawn down.

White should concentrate on keeping that passed e-pawn alive with 19 fxe6!, instead of snagging a pawn: 19...dxc4 20 ♕g4! cxb3 21 axb3 ♕d4+ 22 ♔h1 ♖ae8! 23 ♘h5+! (if 23 ♖xa7?! ♖xf1+ 24 ♘xf1 ♘bd5 and Black is back in the mix) 23...♔h8 24 e7 ♖f5 25 ♖fd1! ♕b2 26 ♘d6 and White wins. One topic in GM Boris Alterman's ICC lectures, namely that a passed pawn on the sixth rank might be worth a piece, certainly applies in this instance.

19...dxc4 20 ♕xd8 ♖axd8 21 fxe6 ♖xf1+ 22 ♖xf1 ♖f8! 23 ♖c1

White must keep the rook to maintain any winning chances. If 23 ♖xf8 ♔xf8 24 ♔f2 cxb3 25 axb3 ♔e7 with an easy draw.

23...cxb3 24 axb3 ♖e8 25 ♖e1 ♘c8!

The only way White can try to win this is to find a way to attack a7 with ♘e4-d6-c8. Hence Wei Ming immediately sets out to challenge the e4-square.

26 h4 ♘d6 27 ♘ge4 ♘xe4 28 ♖xe4 ♔f6 29 ♖a4

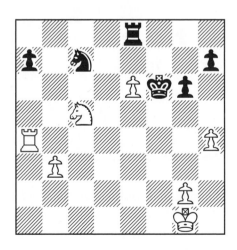

This is what White had been banking on, that in order to surround the e6-pawn, Black must give up a7. However, Wei Ming had worked out the draw already.

29...♞xe6! 30 ♞d7+

Making another attempt to win. After 30 ♞xe6 ♖xe6 31 ♖xa7 h5 32 ♖a4 ♖b6 33 ♖f4+ ♚e5 34 ♖f3 ♖b4 35 g3 ♖b5 36 ♚f2 ♚d4 37 ♚e2 g5! Black will soon draw.

30...♚g7 31 ♞e5

With the idea of tying the black rook to a8 or e7.

31...♞c7!

Black is prepared to give up the a-pawn to obtain a rook ending one pawn down.

32 ♖xa7 ♖xe5 33 ♖xc7+ ♚f6 34 ♖c4

Of course, 34 ♖xh7 ♖b5 is an even clearer draw.

34...♖e2 35 ♚h2 ♚e5 36 b4 ♖b2

Black obtains the desired draw. Usually in such endings, White's rook needs to be behind the passed pawn, instead of at the side or in front, in order for him to win by force. Moreover, the black king is extremely active here.

37 ♖g4 ♖b3 38 ♖c4 ♚d5 39 ♖c5+ ♚e4 40 ♖b5 ♚f4 41 h5 g5 42 ♖b7 h6 43 ♖b6 ♚g4 44 ♖xh6 ♖xb4 45 ♖h8 ♖b1 46 h6 ♖b6 ½-½

The intensity in this tussle between the board 2 players of their respective countries must have spurred them on as Munkhgal made his second IM norm and Wei Ming his second GM norm in this event.

B) 4 a4

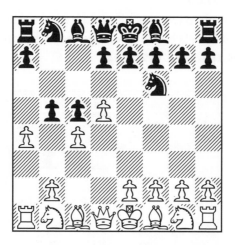

In rapid chess, FIDE-rated games and correspondence, the only time I have lost in the Benko Gambit was playing White in this line. Of course, the reason for my 'success' can be partly attributed to playing only one or two tournaments a year over the last 20 years and almost never outside Singapore. Anyway, 4 a4 and 4 b3 are attempts by White to keep the pawn structure intact, but Black should have no problems equalizing. Observe how I got taught a lesson in Tay-Bartsch after I played some stereotyped moves in a correspondence encounter.

Game 44
J.Tay-M.Bartsch
Correspondence 2001

1 d4 ♘f6 2 c4 c5 3 d5 b5 4 a4

White seeks to force Black to clarify his intentions. He can elect to gain space with ...b5-b4 or employ the game continuation.

After 4 b3 Black can immediately undermine White's centre with 4...e6! which was the choice of former FIDE World Champion Veselin Topalov: 5 dxe6 (after 5 ♘f3 ♗b7 White will have to give up the centre by exchanging on e6 sooner or later) 5...fxe6 6 ♘f3 d5!?, as in S.Sanchez Lopez-V.Topalov, Albox (rapid) 2005.

4...bxc4!?

With this capture, Black intends to steer the game into standard Benko territory and play on the b-file.

Those more inclined towards a Modern Benoni set-up can choose to gain space with 4...b4 and you can't go wrong with the Boss, Garry Kasparov, being the highest-rated exponent of this line: 5 ♘d2 (5 b3 e5 6 g3 d6 7 ♗g2 g6 8 e4 ♗g7 9 ♘e2 a5 gives equal chances, as in J.Markus-So.Polgar, Amsterdam 1995) 5...g6 6 e4 d6 7 ♘gf3 (or 7 f4 ♗g7 8 ♘gf3 0-0 9 ♗d3 e6 10 0-0 exd5 11 cxd5 ♖e8 with a satisfactory Benoni, C.Ward-J.Degraeve, Ghent 2005) 7...♗g7 8 g3 e6 9 ♗h3 exd5 10 ♗xc8 ♕xc8 11 cxd5 0-0 12 0-0 c4 and Black was already turning the screws on White in W.Schmidt-G.Kasparov, Dubai Olympiad 1986.

5 ♘c3 d6 6 e4 g6 7 ♗xc4 ♗g7 8 f4

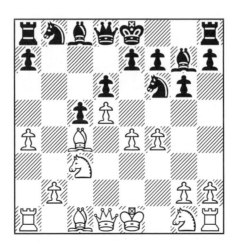

This looks pretty impressive for White, doesn't it? White establishes a Four Pawns Attack formation and with the bishop lurking on c4, it is difficult for Black to undermine that powerful-looking centre with ...e7-e6.

> *Exercise:* What's a good way to cross White's plan
> of ♗c4 and ♕e2 with the idea of an eventual f4-f5?

Answer: 8...♗a6!

Black should eliminate White's light-squared bishop, which also weakens his hold on d5 (for when he attempts e4-e5), and makes it easier for Black to achieve ...e7-e6 without having to worry about dxe6 fxe6; f4-f5 tricks.

I was trying to follow Chris Ward's game where he crushed world-class opposition in C.Ward-M.Adams, Hastings 1995: 8...0-0 9 ♘f3 ♗a6 10 ♗b5 ♘e8 11 0-0 ♘c7 12 f5!? ♗xb5 13 axb5 ♘d7 14 ♕e2 ♘b6 15 ♘g5 h6 16 ♘h3 ♘d7 17 ♖f3 (Black has no time to even contemplate queenside play having to keep on fending off the kingside marauders) 17...♘e5 18 ♖g3 ♕d7 19 ♘f2 ♖fb8 20 ♖a5 ♕e8 21 ♘g4 ♘xg4 22 ♕xg4 h5 23 ♕g5 ♔h7 24 e5! dxe5 25 d6! exd6 26 ♘e4 with a humongous attack.

9 ♗b5+ ♗xb5 10 axb5

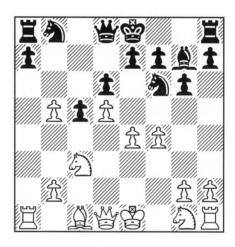

> *Question:* Is the b5-pawn a strength or weakness for White?

Answer: It's too early to tell at this stage. If White can issue sufficient threats against a7 or the kingside so that Black is unable to hit b5, then the pawn is a strength as it keeps Black hemmed in. However, if White is unable to put Black under such pressure, then the b5-pawn may become a liability, especially in the late middlegame or endgame where it will need guarding.

10...0-0 11 ♘f3 ♘bd7!

No more Ward-Adams stuff. Adams's plan of ...♘e8-c7 is too slow and allows White a free hand on the kingside.

12 0-0 ♘b6

Black plans to undermine White's centre with ...e7-e6. I underestimated this structure and had assumed that I already had the better game due to my strong b5-pawn and pressure down the a-file.

13 ♕e2?!

A pointless square for the queen. Either ♕e1-h4 or ♖e1 was more to the point, but I was still in Ward-Adams mode.

13...♕c7

Connecting the rooks and preparing to counter with ...e7-e6.

14 ♗d2

After 14 ♖d1 ♖ad8 15 ♖a6 ♖fe8 Black is ready to play ...e7-e6 and I didn't like the look of 14 f5 gxf5 15 ♘h4 e6 16 dxe6 fxe4 17 exf7+ ♖xf7 18 ♘f5 d5 as if my attack fizzled out, I would have to deal with that scary pawn mass in the centre.

14...♖fe8!

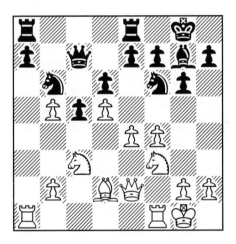

Playing the Benko Gambit does not mean that Black has to home in on the b-file at the first opportunity. Since White's centre is fluid and he might be able to generate kingside chances with f4-f5, Black first takes the time to undermine White's strong centre before it really becomes a threat.

15 ♖fe1

Anticipating that White will soon need to overprotect of e4.

15...♖ab8!

A good waiting move, encouraging White to gang up on a7. That said, the simple 15...e6 16 dxe6 ♖xe6 is, of course, a good alternative.

16 ♖a6 e6

Finally undermining the white centre.

17 dxe6 ♖xe6 18 ♖ea1?!

I got conned into seeking counterplay on the a-file. Likewise, after 18 ♕d1 ♖be8 19 ♕a1 ♖6e7 20 ♕a2 ♕b8 White's posturing on the queenside has come to a standstill.

18...♖b7

After 18 moves, I already found myself in serious trouble. I can no longer improve my position whereas Black has no problems finding useful moves such as ...♘fd7, ...c4 and ...♘c5-d3.

19 ♘g5

Played to transfer the queen to f3 and the knight to f2 to defend e4.

19...♖e7 20 ♕f3 ♕d7!

Heading for e8 where the queen contributes to putting pressure on e4 while keeping an eye on the b5-pawn. Observe how well the black rooks defend a7 sideways while actively harassing b5 and e4.

21 ♗e1

Hoping to transfer the bishop to g3 or h4 to issue some threats. White has exhausted his options and a waiting move like 21 ♔h1 just allows Black to improve his position further with 21...h6 22 ♘h3 ♘c4 23 ♗c1 ♘g4 when ...f7-f5 is lurking.

21...h6 22 ♘h3

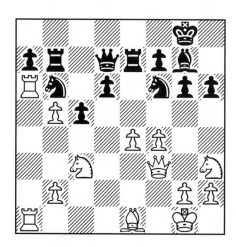

Exercise: How does Black exploit the lack of coordination among the white pieces?

Answer: Bartsch hit me with:

22...♘xe4! 23 ♘xe4 ♕e8

Now I have to return the piece with interest.

24 ♗c3 ♖xe4 25 ♘f2 ♖ee7

Hit and run. Now all Black has to do is to carefully mobilize his c- and d-pawns. There is also the matter of the en prise b5-pawn.

26 h3

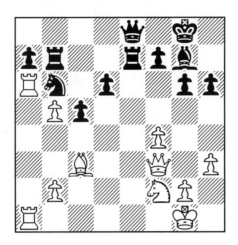

Avoiding any potential back-rank mate threats.

26...f5!

An excellent space grab. Now the b5-pawn is pronounced dead upon request unless White tries for more tricks.

Question: Why did Black not munch the seemingly free b5-pawn?

Answer: 26...♕xb5?! is met by 27 ♘e4! when 27...♕d7? (best is 27...♕b3 28 ♘xd6 ♖bd7 29 ♘e4 ♕d5 30 ♘f6+ ♗xf6 31 ♗xf6 ♕xf3 32 gxf3 ♖e6 33 ♗e5 with drawing chances for White) 28 ♗xg7 requires Black to sacrifice the exchange with 28...♖xe4 (not 28...♔xg7?? 29 ♕c3+) 29 ♕xe4 ♔xg7 and by now it is White who is playing for the win.

27 ♕c6 ♘c8!

Not an iota of counterplay will be granted. Black simply guards a7 and now proceeds to play against b5.

I was hoping for 27...♕xc6 28 bxc6 ♖bc7 when Black has to decide whether to lose a7 or let the c6-pawn survive.

28 ♖1a5 ♖b6!

Now Black starts to prepare for the conversion of his extra pawn by setting up exchanges.

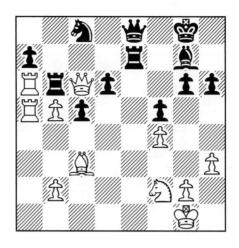

29 ♕d5+

After 29 ♕xe8+ ♖xe8 30 ♘d1 d5 White's rooks are still jammed on the a-file while Black has started rolling his extra pawn down the board.

29...♔h7 30 g4

A last-ditch attempt to denude the black king.

30...fxg4 31 hxg4 ♖f7

Black conveniently takes aim at yet another target.

32 ♖xb6 ♘xb6

If 32...axb6?! 33 ♖a8 and White is back in the mix.

33 ♕e4 ♕f8 34 f5

Still trying to smoke the black king out, but to no avail.

34...gxf5 35 gxf5 d5!

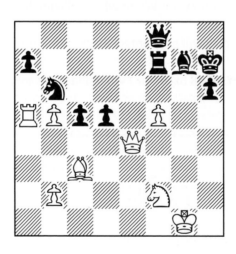

Finally, the pawns start their advance and the writing is on the wall.

36 ♕d3 c4 37 ♕c2 ♗xc3!

This looks dangerous, giving up such a good minor piece, but Black has worked it all out.

38 f6+ ♚h8 39 ♕xc3 ♕g8+ 40 ♚f1 ♕d8!

What a useful queen, hitting a5, g5 and threatening ...d5-d4.

41 ♕d4 ♚h7 42 ♚e2 ♕e8+ 43 ♚d1 ♕e6

With little queen moves, Black keeps improving his position ever so slightly.

44 ♖a3 ♕xf6

Finally cashing in.

45 ♕xf6 ♖xf6 46 ♖xa7+ ♚g6 47 ♘g4 ♖e6 0-1

In over-the-board play, maybe there are still some chances to survive, but not in correspondence chess, so I resigned.

C) 4 e4

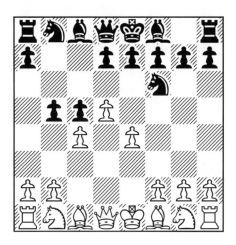

Finally we come to the belligerent 4 e4 where White sacrifices an important pawn to develop his queen to the aggressive f3-square. Black has to be careful with tactics based on d5-d6 and inaccurate play might leave him unable to develop his kingside, allowing White to obtain strong central pressure after a quick ♖e1. In Urcan-Koh, Black was certainly surprised and quite fortunate to escape when White overreacted in a strong position.

> *Game 45*
> **O.Urcan-J.Koh**
> Teck Ghee (rapid) 2013

1 d4 ♘f6 2 c4 c5 3 d5 b5 4 e4!? ♘xe4

I watched at this point with amusement as Olimpiu Urcan clutched his queen, hovered it over d3 hesitantly, shook his head and placed it on f3 with a sigh, a show of drama all for my sake. We had actually played two training blitz games from this position prior to this encounter.

5 ♕f3 ♕a5+

Check out this training game where I should have been slaughtered: 5...♘d6 6 ♗f4 (6 cxb5 should be met by 6...a6 as in a standard Benko) 6...♕a5+?! (6...♘a6! is correct and after 7 a3 ♘c7 8 ♘c3 ♗b7 Black has good play against the white centre, while after 7 cxb5 ♘b4 8 ♕d1 ♗b7 9 ♘c3 e6 10 dxe6 dxe6 11 ♘f3 ♕f6! 12 ♗g3 ♕f5 13 ♖c1 ♘e4 he has the better chances) 7 ♘d2 ♘xc4 8 ♗xc4 bxc4 9 ♘e2 d6 10 ♘c3 (I was aghast at how far behind in development I was after just 10 moves; hence I got desperate and decided to sacrifice a pawn to develop quickly) 10...g5 (10...g6 11 0-0 ♗g7 12 ♖fe1 just looks bad for Black) 11 ♗xg5 ♗g7 12 0-0 ♘d7 13 ♖fe1 ♘e5 (I saw the following sacrifice coming, but what could I do?) 14 ♖xe5!! ♗xe5 15 ♘xc4 ♕c7.

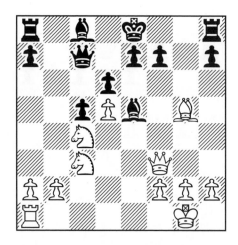

Exercise: What is the best way to deliver the coup de grâce?

Answer: 16 ♖e1! and there are no prizes for guessing where the rook is going. After 16...♖b8 17 ♖xe5!! dxe5 18 d6 ♕b7 19 ♕d3 f6 20 dxe7 fxg5 21 ♕d8+ ♔f7 22 ♘e4 it's total annihilation.

Instead, O.Urcan-J.Tay, Singapore (blitz) 2013, concluded 16 ♘b5 ♕b8 17 ♘xe5 (a sigh of relief as now the worst is over for Black; instead after 17 ♖e1!! ♗d7 18 ♗xe7 ♔xe7 19 ♘bxd6 Black gets smashed again and here 17...♕xb5 18 ♘xe5 dxe5 19 ♖xe5 0-0 20 ♗xe7 h6 21 ♕g3+ ♔h7 22 ♗xf8 is of no help either) 17...dxe5 18 d6 ♕xb5 19 ♕xa8 ♕b7 20 ♕xb7 ♗xb7 21 dxe7? (after 21 ♗xe7 ♔d7 Black has good drawing chances) 21...♖g8 22 ♗f6?? ♖xg2+ 23 ♔f1 ♖g6 24 ♗xe5 ♗a6+ 25 ♔e1 ♖g1+ 0-1.

6 ♘c3!?

Black is well placed after 6 ♘d2 ♘d6 7 b4!? ♕xb4! (White does have some compensation for the pawns after 7...cxb4 8 ♘b3 ♕a4 9 cxb5 ♘xb5 10 ♘h3; I will cop out with an unclear evaluation) 8 cxb5 ♗b7 9 ♗a3 ♕d4 10 ♖c1 ♕e5+ 11 ♘e2 e6!.

6...♘xc3 7 ♗d2

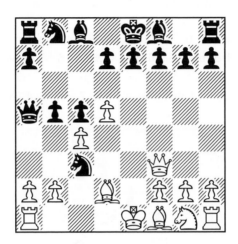

7...d6?!

The simplest way for Black to wend his way through the thicket of messy lines would be to quickly develop the kingside: 7...b4! 8 a3 (or 8 bxc3 g6! 9 cxb4 cxb4 10 ♗d3 ♗g7 11 ♖b1 ♘a6 12 ♘e2 0-0 when Black is doing well in terms of material and position) 8...♘a6! 9 bxc3 g6! 10 cxb4 cxb4 11 ♕b3 ♗g7 12 ♖a2 ♗c3! and White does not have enough for his pawn.

8 cxb5 a6?!

A reflex move for a Benko Gambit player. More circumspect would be to develop quickly with 8...♘d7 9 ♗xc3 ♕c7 10 ♘e2 ♗b7.

9 ♗xc3 ♕b6 10 a4 axb5 11 ♗xb5+ ♗d7 12 ♗xd7+ ♘xd7

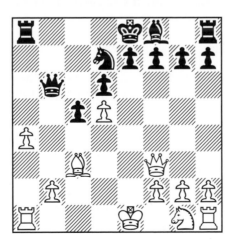

At this juncture, Olimpiu decided to play for a brilliancy. He went for an unsound ♘h3-

g5-e6 sacrifice but to no avail.

During the post mortem, he immediately pointed out that the prosaic 13 ♘e2! would win easily. Indeed, those present could not refute the continuation and even back home with the help of the engines, it transpired that Black is simply busted as the following variations show:

a) Also futile is 13...♕b3 14 0-0 ♖xa4 15 ♖xa4 ♕xa4 16 b4! and once the rook invades on the a-file, Black is in deep trouble. 16...f6 17 ♖a1 ♕b5 18 ♕e3 and the attack is bound to work.

b) 13...♘f6 14 0-0 ♕b3 15 ♘f4 ♖g8 16 ♖fe1 g5 17 ♖a3 ♕c4 18 ♗xf6 gxf4.

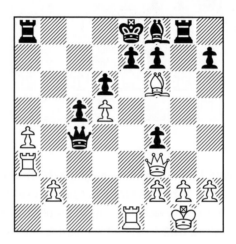

Exercise: Find a way for White to make inroads.

Answer: 19 ♖b3!! (once the rook invades, it's all over) 19...♔d8 20 ♗xe7+ ♗xe7 21 ♖b7 ♖e8 22 ♕g4 ♕xa4 23 b3 with a forced win.

Chapter Nine
Déjà Vu: Benko Gambit Motifs in Other Openings

In this chapter I will point out that Benko-type positions can occur in non-Benko openings. Here one's knowledge of the standard ideas in the Benko Gambit will help greatly in terms of confidence, the time taken to consider the resulting moves and, of course, the initial sacrifice of the b-pawn. In particular, if one's opponent is not a 1 d4 player and is facing a Benko-type counterattack, there is bound to be some disorientation.

Singapore's top player, GM Zhang Zhong, is an out-and-out 1 e4 player. According to my database, he has played 1 d4 less than 10% of the time. Moreover, there is not a single Benko Gambit game played by him with White or Black. As a former member of the Chinese national team, there is no doubt that he is familiar with Benko ideas, but in a National Rapid Championship game, albeit when he had already clinched the title, he let his guard down and Black created the biggest upset in Singapore chess history.

> *Game 46*
> **Zhang Zhong-Tin Jingyao**
> Singapore Rapid Championship 2011
> *c3 Sicilian*

1 e4 c5 2 c3 d6 3 d4 ♘f6 4 ♗d3 ♘c6 5 ♘f3 ♗g4 6 d5

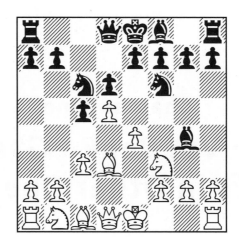

6...♗xf3

Question: What is wrong with 6...♘e5?

Answer: White can sacrifice his queen temporarily with 7 ♘xe5! ♗xd1 8 ♗b5+ ♘d7 9 ♗xd7+ ♕xd7 10 ♘xd7 when he goes a piece up.

7 ♕xf3 ♘e5 8 ♗b5+! ♘fd7 9 ♕e2 a6 10 ♗a4 b5 11 ♗c2

White has emerged with the better position, with the two bishops and the opportunity to probe Black's queenside.

11...g6 12 ♘d2

White might try 12 a4 c4 13 f4 and after 13...♘d3+ 14 ♗xd3 cxd3 15 ♕xd3 ♘c5 Black will get back his pawn, but the resulting positions are great for White, who is able to establish a clamp on the kingside while retaining the juicy option of ♘f3-d4-c6: for example, 16 ♕d4 f6 17 ♘d2 ♘xa4 (or 17...bxa4 18 0-0 ♗g7 19 ♕e3 0-0 20 f5 and Black is struggling) 18 ♘b3! ♗g7 19 0-0 0-0 20 f5 with a nice clamp for White.

12...♘b6 13 f4 ♘ed7 14 0-0 ♗g7 15 ♘f3 0-0 16 ♔h1 ♘c4 17 a4

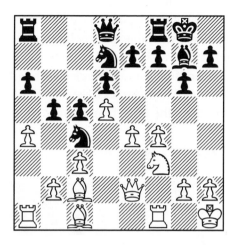

17...♘cb6!?

Question: Is this a dubious pawn sacrifice?

Answer: Having played the Benko Gambit for aeons, I am wont to see this as a bold bid to wrest the initiative. Moreover, the then 10-year-old Jingyao regularly essays the Benko too and, hence, is familiar with its motifs. Jingyao has worked out that trying to hold on to the b-pawn just gives White an easy game: for example, 17...♕b6 18 ♗d3 ♘a5 19 ♗e3 is good for White.

18 axb5 axb5 19 ♖xa8 ♕xa8 20 ♕xb5 ♖b8

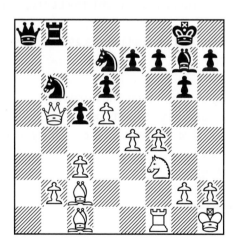

21 f5?

Inexplicable. Why weaken the position and give up the e5-square?

After 21 ♕e2 ♕a2 22 ♗d3 c4 23 ♗c2 ♘c5 Black has some Benko-like pressure. However, since Black's pieces are mostly messing about on the queenside, it's time for White to return material to go for the black king with 24 e5! ♘xd5 25 exd6 exd6 26 f5! (if 26 ♖d1 ♘f6 27 ♖xd6 ♖e8 28 ♕f1 ♘fe4 with considerable activity for the pawn) 26...♖f8! 27 ♕d1 ♕a8 28 ♘g5 and White has a strong attack.

Note that this e4-e5 pawn sacrifice, usually coupled with f4-f5, is a common feature in the Benoni and King's Indian Four Pawns Attacks. Usually it's played to clear the e4-square for a knight as well as to prise open the f-file, freeing the dark-squared bishop in the process.

21...♘e5 22 ♕e2 ♘bc4 23 ♘xe5 ♘xe5 24 ♕f2 ♕a6!

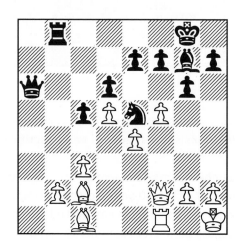

Seizing the key diagonal. This move comes naturally to a Benko Gambiteer. In the same year, Jingyao crushed a local National Master with the Benko, en route to winning the 2011 Cairnhill Open.

25 h3 ♕c4 26 ♔g1 ♗f6 27 ♗b1 ♘d3 28 ♗xd3 ♕xd3 29 ♖e1 ♗e5

With the threat of ...♗g3.

30 ♕e3?

And, finally, Zhang Zhong blunders away the b-pawn.

30...♕xe3+ 31 ♖xe3 ♗f4 32 ♖e1 ♗xc1 33 ♖xc1 ♖xb2

Any Benko text will tell you that the position is extremely hard for White to defend, with loose pawns on c3 and e4.

34 ♖e1 ♔g7 35 fxg6 hxg6 36 e5

Before the black king gets to e5 itself.

36...♖d2 37 c4 ♖d4 38 exd6 exd6

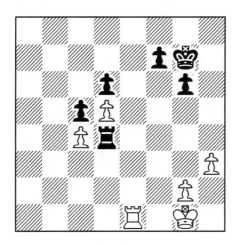

39 ♖e7

Probably Zhang Zhong did not want the black king to become too active after 39 ♖c1 ♔f6 40 ♔f2 ♖d2+ 41 ♔f3 ♔e5 42 ♖e1+ ♔d4 and life is still tough for White after 43 ♖e4+ ♔d3 44 ♖f4 g5! 45 ♖f6 ♔xc4 46 ♖xd6 ♖xd5.

39...♖xc4 40 ♖d7 ♔f6 41 ♖xd6+ ♔e5 42 ♖d7 f6 43 d6 ♖d4 44 ♖g7 g5 45 ♔f2 ♖xd6 46 ♖c7 ♔d4 47 ♔e2 c4 48 ♔d2 ♖d5 49 ♖f7 ♖f5 50 ♖d7+ ♔c5 51 ♔c3 ♖f2 52 ♖f7 ♖xg2 53 ♖xf6 ♖g3+ 54 ♔c2 ♖xh3 55 ♖f5+ ♔b4 56 ♖xg5 ♖h2+ 57 ♔b1 ♔b3 58 ♖b5+ ♔c3 59 ♖g5 ♖h1+ 60 ♔a2 ♖d1 61 ♖g3+ ♖d3 62 ♖g1 ♖d2+ 63 ♔b1??

Correct was 63 ♔a3 ♔c2 64 ♔b4 c3 65 ♔a3 ♖h2 66 ♖g7 when Black cannot make further progress.

63...♔b3 64 ♔c1 ♖a2 65 ♔b1 0-1

With ...c3-c2 looming, Zhang Zhong surrendered.

The next game was played in a correspondence tournament which I won with 5/6, mainly due to the Benko Gambit and its ideas. Two games were proper Benko encounters, but in the one we'll see here, it was my greater Benko understanding which played the key role when I had the white pieces.

Game 47
J.Tay-P.Lea
Correspondence 2002
English Opening

1 c4 ♘f6 2 g3 g6 3 ♗g2 ♗g7 4 ♘c3 c5 5 a3

White plans to expand on the queenside before deciding whether to put his knight on e2 or f3. This is a standard feature in the English Opening.

5...♘c6 6 ♖b1 0-0 7 b4 cxb4 8 axb4 a5 9 bxa5

9 b5?! only gives Black a passed a-pawn unnecessarily.

9...♖xa5

9...♕xa5, developing the queen, is more accurate.

10 d3!?

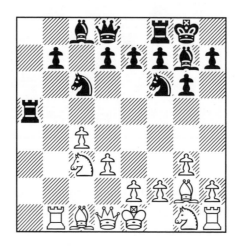

10...e6

In a later correspondence game, Black played a beautiful exchange sacrifice with 10...d5! 11 ♘xd5 ♘xd5 12 cxd5 ♖xd5 13 ♗xd5 ♕xd5 when he had full compensation due to White's weakened light squares and lack of development: 14 e4 ♕a5+ 15 ♔f1 ♕a6 16 ♔g2 ♖d8 17 ♕c2 ♖xd3 18 ♗b2 ♗xb2 19 ♖xb2 ♗g4 20 ♖b6 ♕a3 21 ♖xb7 ♖d1 22 ♕b3 ♕a1 23 h3 ♗xh3+ 24 ♔xh3 ♖xg1 25 ♖xg1 ♕xg1 26 ♕b1 ♕xf2 27 ♕b5 e5 28 ♕xc6 ♕f1+ ½-½, R.Pohjosmaki-F.Smit, correspondence 2008.

11 ♘f3 d5 12 ♘d2!

Freeing up White's fianchettoed bishop. I was also aiming to meet 12...dxc4 with 13 ♘xc4.

12...d4?!

On the surface, this looks like a useful space-gaining move, but now White obtains a good reversed Benko, with the same type of queenside pressure and without the pawn deficit.

13 ♘b5 e5 14 ♗a3!

There's no need to hurry to castle as there's no danger to White's king thanks to his firm control over e4.

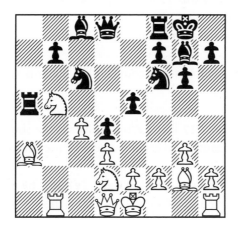

14...♖e8 15 ♗d6!

White is causing mayhem by utilizing the inverse of the d3-square, the d6-square.

15...♖a2 16 ♗c7 ♛e7 17 ♛b3?!

Too much finessing. Simply 17 0-0 ♗f5 18 c5!, annexing the d6-square for good, gives White an excellent game as Black cannot play the central break 18...e4?? because of 19 dxe4 ♘xe4 20 ♘xe4 ♗xe4 21 ♗xe4 ♛xe4 22 ♘d6, nabbing the exchange. Neither can Black really capture with 18...♛xc5 as White will obtain a fantastic grip on the position after 19 ♘c4!.

17...♖a6?!

Black had to complicate by parting with the exchange: 17...♖xd2! 18 ♔xd2 ♗h6+ 19 ♔d1 e4, with attacking chances.

18 ♗d6 ♛d8 19 0-0

Obviously White is having all the fun here. Black now tries to reduce the pieces, which is something that Benko exponents more than welcome.

19...♘a7 20 ♘xa7 ♖xa7 21 ♗c5 ♖a8 22 ♘e4

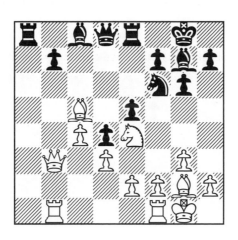

Forcing more exchanges by threatening to plonk the knight on d6.

22...♘xe4 23 ♗xe4 ♕c7 24 ♕b4

Increasing White's dark-square pressure.

24...♖a2

Finally obtaining some semblance of counterplay, but this will be insufficient as White just keeps building up.

25 ♕b5 ♖e6

After 25...♕d8 26 ♖b2 ♖xb2 27 ♕xb2 White still calls the shots. Now, however, comes a sequence of moves which leads to an ending where White can squeeze Black until the cows come home.

26 ♗d5 ♖a5 27 ♗b6 ♖xb5 28 ♗xc7 ♖xb1 29 ♖xb1 ♖e7 30 ♗b8 h6 31 ♖b5 ♔h7 32 ♖c5 1-0

The rook will invade on c7 and White will pick off either e5 or b7, winning.

Lastly, here's an interesting transposition from the French Defence to a reversed Benko type of position against a local FIDE Master, who is himself a Benko Gambit exponent. However, Mark Chan didn't look comfortable during this encounter.

Game 48
J.Tay-M.Chan
Cairnhill Open 2000
King's Indian Attack

1 e4 e6 2 d3 d5 3 ♘d2 c5 4 ♘gf3 ♘c6 5 g3 ♗d6

Not as common as 5...♘f6, but this bishop sally has been played by world-class players like Karpov, Tiviakov and P.Nikolic. Black's immediate aim is to overprotect the e5-square and make it extremely tough for White to effect his typical space-gaining e4-e5 push.

6 ♗g2 ♘ge7 7 0-0 f6 8 ♖e1 0-0

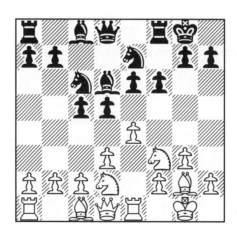

Here I had some problems finding a plan for White. The e5-square is well covered and opening the e-file doesn't seem to achieve much. 9 c3 would suffice, but after 9...d4 we get a sort of reversed King's Indian where White's rook is asking itself what it is doing on e1 instead of f1.

9 a3!?

A non-committal move, but I already had some semblance of what would transpire. Moreover, I didn't like the look of 9 c3 d4 10 ♘c4 e5 when Black has achieved a very solid reversed Sämisch position with equal chances.

9...♕c7 10 exd5! exd5

Black can also choose 10...♘xd5, but 11 ♘e4 gives White a pleasant if temporary outpost on e4 and the opportunity to play for the c2-c4 and b2-b4 breaks.

11 c4!

Making good use of the weakened central light squares to extend the range of the bishop on g2.

11...d4?!

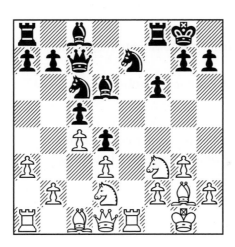

> **Exercise:** If you don't know what White's next move
> is, maybe you should play the QGD or the Slav...

Answer: **12 b4!**

Of course.

12...cxb4 13 ♕b3

Threatening to win a piece with c4-c5 as well as putting immediate pressure on the b-file.

13...♔h8 14 axb4

White has a superb Benko-style position.

14...♗xb4

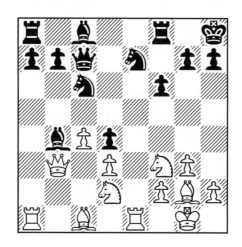

15 ♗a3?!

Too stereotyped.

> ***Question:*** This looks thematic, but what was better?

Answer: After 15 ♘xd4! Black cannot recapture as 15...♘xd4?? 16 ♕xb4 ♘c2 17 ♖xe7 wins material.

15...♗c3 16 ♖ab1

White has typical Benko-like pressure for the pawn. Unfortunately I couldn't reconstruct the rest of the game which later ended in a draw.

Chapter Ten
Benko Dojo Time

We're now approaching the end of this book. Here I've included 40 exercises, mostly from recent tournament praxis and my own Internet blitz games. These demonstrate standard Benko motifs that frequently occur and once you are familiar with them, you will be in good stead when you reach out to sacrifice your b-pawn on move 3 with that glint in your eye. Solutions follow at the end.

1) P.Deniau-D.Le Goff
Rennes 2012

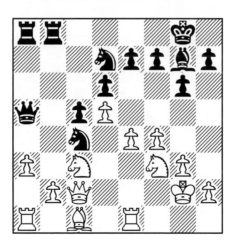

Black to play

Every Benko Gambit player knows this stock sacrifice and will play it in a flash.

2) M.Bluebaum-J.Tay
Internet (blitz) 2013

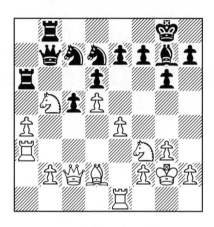

White to play

After the eviction of the knight on b5, Black will obtain tremendous pressure on the b2-pawn. How can White deal with this?

3) K.Troff-J.Xiong
Saint Louis 2013

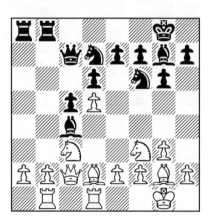

White to play

Black is poised to win the d5- or a2-pawn. Can you find a way for White to deal with the threat while improving his piece placement?

4) S.Bekker Jensen-S.Johansen
Oslo 2013

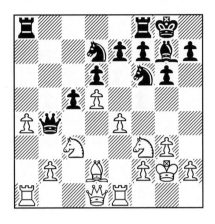

Black to play

Is ...c5-c4, with the idea of ...♘c5-d3, a good move here?

5) I.Lysyj-D.Gordievsky
Ekaterinburg 2013

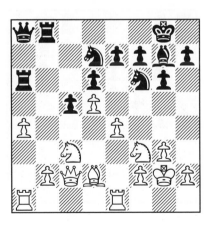

Black to play

Is ...c5-c4 playable here?

6) A.Riazantsev-J.Prizant
Ekaterinburg 2013

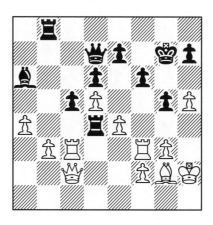

White to play

The position is getting critical as Black threatens ...♛g4, hitting h5. What can White do?

7) S.Mamedyarov-F.Caruana
Moscow (blitz) 2013

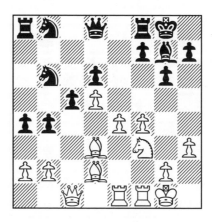

White to play

Black will soon complete development with ...♞8d7. Can White exploit this factor to gain a huge advantage?

8) S.Collins-J.Tay
Internet (blitz) 2013

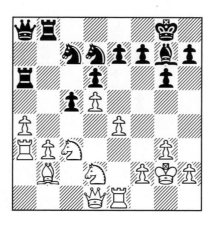

Black to play

White will soon be establishing a queenside bind with ♕c2 and ♘c4. What can Black do about it?

9) A.Szeberenyi-Li Bo
Budapest 2013

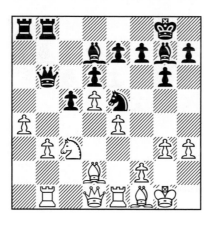

Black to play

How does Black seize the initiative?

10) F.Levin-D.Collutiis
Ortisei 2013

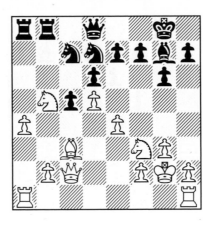

White to play

White has managed to get his queen's knight and bishop to their ideal squares. How does he make use of this to further improve his position?

11) A.Moiseenko-D.Dubov
Khanty-Mansiysk (rapid) 2013

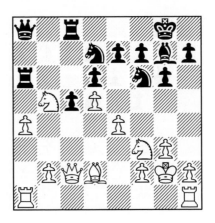

Black to play

Can ...c5-c4 be played here?

12) Tran Tuan Minh-N.Mariano
Manila 2013

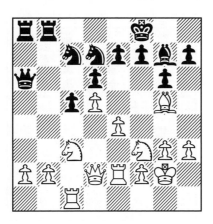

Black to play

After a standard move like ...♖b7, White intends to exchange the dark-squared bishops with ♗h6 and start a kingside attack. How does Black divert his attention to the queenside?

13) V.Daskevich-J.Tay
Internet (blitz) 2013

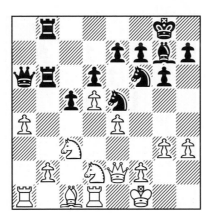

White to play

Black's queenside play is in full swing. How can White repel the attack?

14) R.Kropff-E.Iturrizaga
Cochabamba 2013

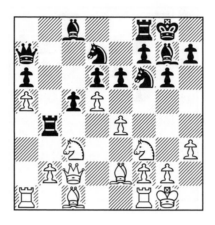

White to play

White is under pressure on the queenside and in the centre. What is his best plan here?

15) M.Narciso Dublan-R.Alonso Garcia
Catalan League 2013

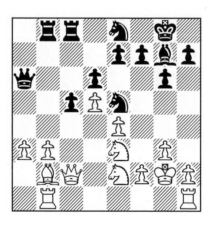

Black to play

Can 1...c5-c4 with the idea of exploiting the c-file with 2 b4 c3 be played?

16) J.Houska-B.Byklum
Norwegian League 2013

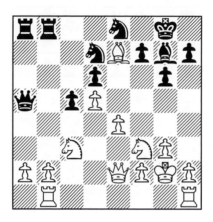

Black to play

Black can play to trap the white bishop, but how to best do this?

17) Li Chao-D.Castor
Sydney 2013

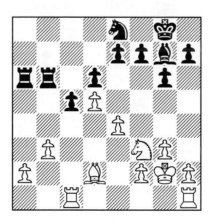

White to play

How does the first player seize the initiative?

18) V.Barnaure-J.Tay
Internet (blitz) 2013

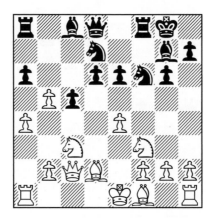

White to play

Can White seize the initiative?

19) T.Baron-D.Raznikov
Petach Tikva 2010

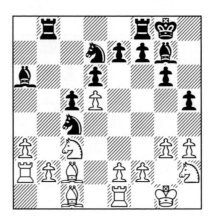

Black to play

Black is exerting strong pressure against b2, but White seems to have enough to hold it. Or does he?

20) C.Wichmann-J.Tay
Internet (blitz) 2013

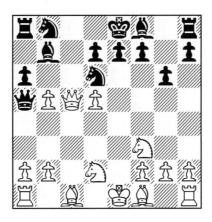

White to play

How can White exploit the dark-square weaknesses that Black has?

21) D.Baramidze-S.Petrosian
German League 2013

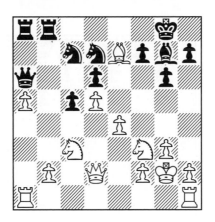

Black to play

Black has sacrificed his e-pawn and threatens to trap the bishop on e7. Which is better: 17...f6 or 17...h6?

22) R.Kasmir-J.Tay
Internet (blitz) 2013

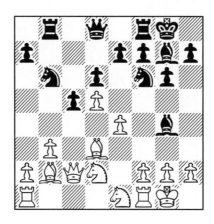

Black to play

White's set-up seems solid enough, but Black can make use of the long diagonal to set up a hit. How?

23) T.Radjabov-D.Andreikin
Astana (blitz) 2012

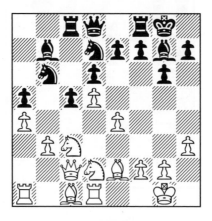

Black to play

White is poised to play ♘c4 establishing a queenside bind. How should Black counter?

24) M.Bosiocic-L.Van Wely
Aix-les-Bains 2012

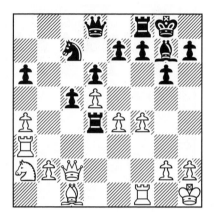

Black to play

The Dutch maestro virtually ends the contest here with a typical Benko idea. What is it?

25) K.Troff-Y.Wang
Maribor 2012

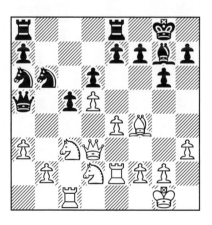

Black to play

White is poised to play ♘b3, trapping the black queen. How should Black respond?

26) K.Tancik-J.Tay
Internet (blitz) 2013

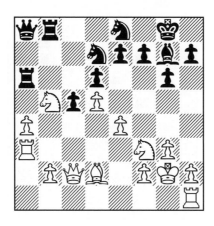

Black to play

Is it a good idea for Black to play ...e7-e6, undermining White's centre?

27) E.Kislik-J.Tay
Internet (blitz) 2013

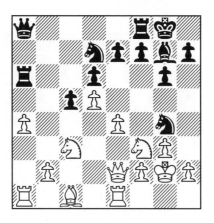

White to play

Black's last move, 14...♘g4 intending ...♘ge5, was a lemon. Can you find a continuation that allows White to gain a huge initiative?

28) A.Zatonskih-A.Tate
Gibraltar 2013

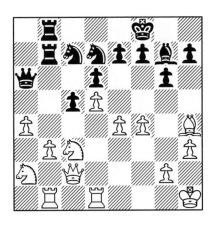

White to play

White has already fully consolidated her queenside and has built up an imposing centre. How did she press home her advantage?

29) S.Gligoric-T.Nyback
Stockholm 2004

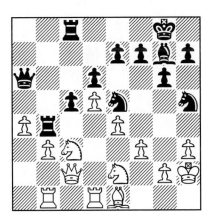

Black to play

How can Black blow up the white position?

30) V.Korchmar-J.Tay
Internet (blitz) 2013

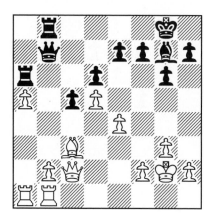

White to play

White is having some problems trying to convert his extra pawn as Black is resisting strongly on the b-file. How can White cut the Gordian knot?

31) E.Paciencia-J.Tay
Singapore 2012

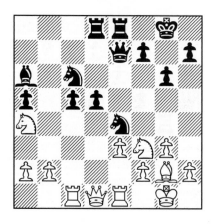

Black to play

Paciencia's last move, 18 e3, missed my threat. What was it?

32) F.Larcheveque-C.Navrotescu
Creon 2009

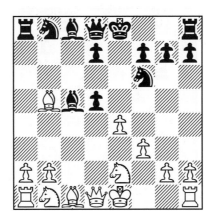

Black to play

What is your opinion of Black's last move, 9...exd5?

33) S.Popov-D.Milanovic
Serbian Team Championship 2010

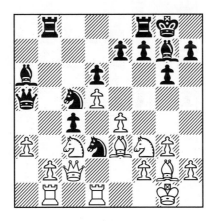

Black to play

How does Black deliver a bombshell?

34) V.Schoder-J.Scheider
Dortmund 2013

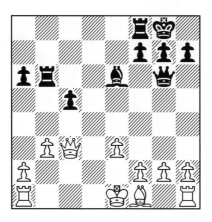

Black to play

White is a pawn up, but is way behind in development. Find an efficient line for Black.

35) A.Rychagov-M.Pap
Rethymnon 2013

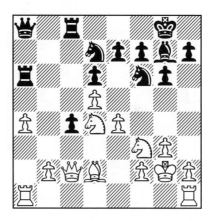

Black to play

White is poised to jam Black's queenside with ♘c6, but Black had already anticipated this move. What was his rejoinder?

36) Huang Qian-N.Pogonina
St Petersburg (rapid) 2012

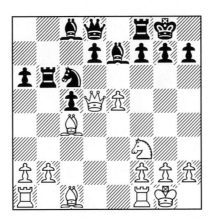

Black to play

White's e4-e5 advance seems a tad premature. Can you find a way for Black to aggressively mobilize her queenside pieces?

37) M.Hadolias-I.Tetepoulidis
Greek Team Championship 2013

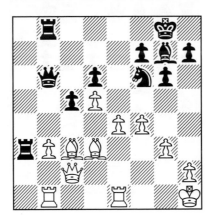

White to play

White is a pawn up and has a strong bishop-pair. Should he now go b3-b4?

38) M.Rodshtein-I.Nepomniachtchi
Kirishi 2004

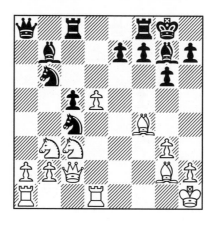

Black to play

How should Black clean up?

39) M.Richter-J.Tay
Internet (blitz) 2013

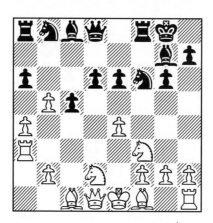

White to play

Black is attempting to take advantage of the lack of kingside development by White to strike in the centre. What can White do about it?

40) M.Godard-N.Short
Gibraltar 2013

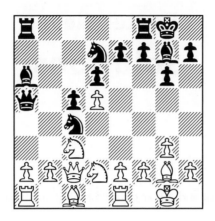

Black to play

White wants to exchange off the c4-knight to ease the pressure on his queenside. How should Black counter this idea?

Chapter Eleven
Solutions

1) Deniau-Le Goff

17...♘xb2! 18 ♗xb2 ♖xb2 19 ♕xb2 ♗xc3 with a highly advantageous position for Black.

2) Bluebaum-Tay

The German IM swiftly got his queenside pawns moving: **18 ♘xc7 ♕xc7 19 b4!** ♕a7 20 **bxc5 ♘xc5 21 a5** with a large advantage for White due to the protected a-pawn.

3) Troff-Xiong

The World U-14 Champion played the cool retreat **15 ♗c1!**, allowing Black to capture with **15...♗xa2 16 ♘xa2 ♖xa2** because he had the shot **17 ♘d4! ♖c8 18 ♘c6 ♘b8 19 ♕c4 ♖a8** and then another one: **20 b4! ♘xc6 21 dxc6** with advantage to White.

4) Bekker Jensen-Johansen

In this case **14...c4?** is a lemon because White has **15 ♘b5!** ♕c5 (and not 15...♕xb2?? 16 ♗c3) **16 ♗c3! ♘g4 17 ♘fd4 ♘ge5 18 ♖e2 ♖ae8** (or 18...♘d3 19 ♘c6 and White is on top) **19 ♕d2** (19 b4 is also strong) **19...♖a8 20 f4** with a winning advantage.

5) Lysyj-Gordievsky

Yes! The tactics work for Black: **15...c4! 16 ♘d1** (if 16 ♘d4 ♘c5 17 ♘c6 Black can sacrifice the exchange with 17...♖xc6! 18 dxc6 ♕xc6, with excellent compensation) **16...♖c8 17 ♗c3** (or 17 ♘d4 ♘xd5), and now **17...♘c5** would give Black an excellent game.

6) Riazantsev-Prizant

31 e5!. In fact Black is now the one who must be vigilant and capture correctly: **31...dxe5** (and not 31...fxe5?? 32 ♖f7+! ♔xf7 33 ♕xh7+ ♔f8 34 ♖f3+, winning) **32 ♖xc5 ♕g4 33 ♖c7 ♕xh5+ 34 ♔g1** and White is out of the woods.

7) Mamedyarov-Caruana

17 e5! ♖a7 (17...♘xd5 18 ♗e4 is quite painful) **18 e6 ♘xd5? 19 exf7+ ♔h8 20 ♘g5** with a huge advantage for White.

8) Collins-Tay

I should have spotted the weakness of the a3-rook and played **17...♗xc3! 18 ♖xc3 ♘b5!** when White has to sacrifice the exchange with **19 ♘b1 ♘xa3 20 ♘xa3** and Black is quite all right.

9) Szeberenyi-Li Bo

19...c4! (an outstanding temporary sacrifice) **20 ♘b5** (alternatively, 20 ♗xc4 ♕d4 21 ♔g2 ♘xc4 22 bxc4 ♕xc4 with good play for Black, 20 bxc4 ♕d4 21 ♔g2 ♘xc4 22 ♗xc4 ♕xc4 when Black is fine, or 20 b4 ♗xa4 21 ♘xa4 ♖xa4 22 ♕xa4 ♘f3+ 23 ♔g2 ♘xd2 24 ♖bd1 ♘xf1 25 ♖xf1 ♕xb4 26 ♕xb4 ♖xb4 and Black's passed pawn maintains the balance) **20...♗xb5 21 axb5 ♕d4 22 ♗e3 ♕xe4 23 ♗g2 ♕d3 24 f4?! ♕xd1 25 ♖exd1 c3! 26 ♖bc1 ♘d7 27 ♗d4 ♖xb5 28 ♖xc3 ♘c5 29 ♗xg7 ♔xg7** with winning chances for Black.

10) Levin-Collutiis

17 ♘xc7! ♖xc7 18 ♗xg7 ♔xg7 19 ♘d4! and the knight gets to anchor itself on b5 to secure the queenside once again: **19...♖b7 20 ♘b5 ♕a5 21 b3 ♕b4 22 ♖ac1 ♘b6 23 h4 c4 24 bxc4 ♖xa4 25 h5 ♘xc4?? 26 h6+ ♔f8 27 ♖b1 ♕a5 28 ♘a3** and White wins.

11) Moiseenko-Dubov

A resounding 'Yes!' as White's attempt to put a knight on the c6 outpost is rebuffed tactically: **15...c4! 16 ♘fd4?! ♘xd5! 17 exd5 ♗xd4 18 ♘xd4 ♕xd5+ 19 f3** (or 19 ♘f3 ♘e5 20 ♕c3 ♘xf3 21 ♕xf3 ♕xd2 with good chances for Black to win) **19...♕xd4** and Black is better since the dark-squared bishop can be easily blunted after ♗c3 with ...e7-e5 or ...f7-f6.

12) Tran Tuan Minh-Mariano

18...♗xc3! (a frequent motif in the Benko, although Black must weigh the consequences of this capture carefully; instead, after 18...♖b7 19 ♗h6! White has a slight pull) **19 ♖xc3** (or 19 bxc3 f6 20 ♗h6+ ♔g8 with equal chances) **19...f6** (19...♕xa2 20 e5 ♘xd5 21 exd6 e6 looks very dangerous, but *Houdini* claims that Black is okay) **20 ♗h6+ ♔f7 21 b3 ♖b4** and Black is still in the mix as it is difficult for White to undertake anything active.

13) Daskevich-Tay

White should have played **18 a5!** when Black's pieces will be repelled: **18...♕a8** (if 18...♘ed7 19 ♖a4 ♕xe2+ 20 ♔xe2 ♖a6 21 ♘c4 or 18...♕xe2+ 19 ♔xe2 ♖a6 20 f4 ♘ed7 21 ♘c4 with a dominant position for White) **19 f4 ♘ed7 20 ♘c4** and Black is suffering badly.

14) Kropff-Iturrizaga

White should attempt 15 dxe6! fxe6 16 e5!, and if 16...dxe5 17 ♘g5 when he has the better game thanks to Black's split pawns. Instead, he played **15 ♖a2 exd5 16 exd5 ♖e8** and Black was better.

15) Narciso Dublan-Alonso Garcia

Not this time as it only helps White to roll his passed pawns: **18...c4? 19 b4! c3 20 ♘xc3 ♘d3?? 21 b5! ♕a5 22 ♕xd3 ♗xc3 23 ♘c4 ♖xc4** (or 23...♕a4 24 ♕xc3 with winning chances for White) **24 ♕xc4 ♗xb2 25 ♖xb2 ♕xa3 26 ♖a2 1-0**

16) Houska-Byklum

After 15...h6! 16 g4! (giving the bishop access to h4 and later g3) 16...♗xc3 17 bxc3 ♕xc3 the position remains unclear. Instead, Black played **15...f6?! 16 e5! dxe5 17 ♘d2 ♕a6 18 ♕xa6 ♖xa6** and White kept her advantage.

17) Li Chao-Castor

19 b4! ♖xa2 (after 19...cxb4 20 ♖c8 ♔f8 21 ♖hc1 Black is in trouble as if 21...♖xa2?? 22 ♖d8 when he cannot prevent the deadly threat of 23 ♖cc8) **20 bxc5 dxc5 21 ♖xc5** with good winning chances.

18) Barnaure-Tay

White could sacrifice a pawn to split Black's centre pawns and jam in the dark-squared bishop: 12 e5! ♘xe5 13 ♘xe5 dxe5 14 ♗e3 ♕c7 15 ♗c4 with a dominant position. Instead he played **12 bxa6?! d5 13 ♗b5 d4 14 ♘e2 ♗xa6** and Black had good counterplay.

19) Baron-Raznikov

22...♘xb2! 23 ♗xb2 ♗c4! (Did you miss this in-between move? After 23...♖xb2 24 ♖xb2 ♗xc3 25 ♖eb1 ♗xb2 26 ♖xb2 although Black is better, the win is still far off.) **24 ♖ea1 ♖xb2 25 ♖xb2 ♗xc3 26 ♖b7** (if 26 ♖bb1 ♗xd5 and the a1-rook will still not run away) **26...♗xa1 27 ♖xd7 ♗f6** and Black calls the shots with his awesome bishops and soon-to-be rampant rook.

20) Wichmann-Tay

10 b4! ♕a4 11 ♗b2 f6 and now 12 b6! gives White a huge advantage.

21) Baramidze-Petrosian

Correct was 17...h6! 18 ♕f4 ♘e5 19 ♘xe5 ♗xe5 20 ♕xh6 ♖xb2 with equal chances. Instead, Black chose **17...f6? 18 ♕f4! ♘e8 19 ♕g4 ♕c8 20 ♕e6+ ♔h8 21 h4! h5 22 e5! dxe5 23 ♕f7 ♔h7 24 ♘e4 ♖a6 25 ♖ac1 ♖xb2 26 ♗xc5 ♘xc5 27 ♘xc5 ♘d6 28 ♘xa6** and White was winning.

22) Kasmir-Tay

13...♞a4! (tactics based on b2 are very common in the Benko; that's not surprising considering the frequent placement of a rook on b8 and the dark-squared bishop on g7 being ever ready to spring out) **14 ♗xf6** (I was hoping for 14 bxa4 ♖xb2 15 ♕xb2 ♞xe4 16 ♕xg7+ ♚xg7 17 ♞xe4 when Black should be better) **14...♗xf6 15 bxa4??** (15 ♖c1 ♞c3 16 ♞c4 ♞b5 17 h3 ♞d4 only gives Black an edge) **15...♗xa1** and Black soon won.

23) Radjabov-Andreikin

There are two possible breaks, the first being **16...f5! 17 ♗b2 fxe4 18 ♞dxe4 c4** with good counterplay for Black, and the second, 16...c4! 17 bxc4 ♗a6 18 ♕b3 ♞c5 19 ♕c2 ♞cxa4 20 ♖xa4 ♗xc3 21 ♖a2 ♗b4 with fine play for Black.

24) Bosiocic-Van Wely

Undermining is the name of the game. **20...f5! 21 ♖d3** (if 21 exf5 ♖xf5 and the d-pawn drops) **21...♖xe4 22 ♞c3 ♖b4 23 ♖e1 ♗f6 24 ♞d1 ♕d7 25 b3 c4! 26 bxc4 ♕xa4** and Black is on top.

25) Troff-Wang

21...c4! (a stunning riposte) **22 ♞xc4** (if 22 ♕c2 ♞c5 with strong pressure on the queenside) **22...♞c5! 23 ♕g3 ♞xc4 24 b4 ♕xa3 25 bxc5 ♕xc5** with an extra pawn for Black and a passed a-pawn for that matter.

26) Tancik-Tay

After **16...e6?** (better is 16...♞b6 17 ♖ha1 ♖b7 18 ♚g1 ♕b8 with threats against a4) **17 dxe6 fxe6 18 ♗c3** Black has only worsened his position, since White retains his iron grip on the queenside and will soon exert pressure in the centre as well.

27) Kislik-Tay

I had missed the sidestepping 15 ♞d2! ♗xc3 (Black has to admit that he has erred with 15...♞gf6 16 ♞c4, which is a dream position for White) 16 bxc3 ♞gf6 17 c4 ♖xa4 (after 17...♖b8 18 f4 White's central breakthrough cannot be prevented) 18 ♗b2 with a superb bishop on the long diagonal. Indeed, after 18...♖xa1 19 ♖xa1 ♕b7 20 ♗c3 Black is suffering. Instead, the game went **15 h3?! ♞ge5 16 ♞d2?!** (a trifle too late; White is trying to exploit the awkward position of the knight on e5, but the black knights are heading to the queenside in any case) **16...♞b6 17 f4 ♞ed7** and Black was well placed.

28) Zatonskih-Tate

There's no stopping White's assault: **34 e5! dxe5 35 ♗xe7+! ♚xe7 36 d6+ ♚f8 37 dxc7 ♖xc7 38 ♞b5 ♖cb7 39 ♖d6 ♕a5 40 f5** (or 40 b4! cxb4 41 ♞xb4) **40...♚g8 41 ♖f1 ♗f8? 42 fxg6** with a winning advantage.

29) Gligoric-Nyback

20...c4! 21 bxc4 ⬛bxc4 and in his haste to get out of the pin, White blundered with **22 ♕b3??** allowing Black to end with a flourish: **22...⬛xc3!! 23 ♞xc3 ♞xf3+ 24 gxf3 ♕f1 0-1**

30) Korchmar-Tay

23 b4!! ♝xc3 24 bxc5 ♝b4 25 c6? (unfortunately for White, he missed his way here; the key move is 25 cxd6! ♕a7 26 ⬛xb4! ⬛xb4 27 ♕c8+ ♚g7 28 dxe7 ♕xe7 29 ♕xa6 ♕xe4+ 30 ♚g1 ♕xd5 31 ♕f1 with a clear extra pawn) **25...♕c7 26 ♕c4 ⬛xa5 27 ⬛xa5 ♝xa5** and Black escaped to win later.

31) Paciencia-Tay

18...♞b4! (heading for the juicy-d3 square; White now has no choice but to shed the a2-pawn) **19 ♝f1** (if 19 ⬛a1 ♞d3 20 ⬛e2 ♞dxf2 with a crushing attack) **19...♝xf1 20 ⬛xf1 ♞xa2 21 ⬛a1 ♞b4** and one pawn to the good with an awesome centre to boot, Black had no problems converting to the point.

32) Larcheveque-Navrotescu

It's a losing move. Simply 10 e5! ♞h5 11 ♕xd5 wins. However, what transpired was **10 exd5? 0-0 11 ♚f1 ♕b6** and Black consolidated to win later.

33) Popov-Milanovic

22...♞xb2! (22...⬛xb2! 23 ⬛xb2 ♞xb2 works too) **23 ⬛xb2 ⬛xb2 24 ♕xb2 ♞xe4 25 ♝d4 ♞xc3 26 ♕d2 ♕xa3** and Black is two pawns to the good.

34) Schoder-Scheider

20...c4! (a hammer blow) **21 b4** (and not 21 bxc4?? ⬛b1+ 22 ⬛xb1 ♕xb1+ 23 ♚e2 ⬛d8 when it's a case of hasta la vista baby) **21...a5! 22 a3 h6 23 f3 axb4 24 axb4 ⬛fb8 25 ♚f2 ⬛xb4** with a won game thanks to the huge passed c-pawn and that White's king is not out of the woods yet.

35) Rychagov-Pap

16...♞xd5! 17 ⬛he1 (or 17 exd5 ♝xd4 18 ♞xd4 ♕xd5+ 19 ♞f3 ♞e5 20 ♕c3 ♞xf3 21 ♕xf3 ♕xd2 with the better position for Black as his rooks are very active) **17...♞5f6** (a knight is bound to land on d3 so White is virtually lost) **18 ♝b4 ♞g4 19 ⬛a3 ♞de5 20 ♞xe5 ♞xe5 21 ♝c3 ♞d3 22 ⬛e3 ♞c5 23 a5 f5 24 f3 e5 0-1**

36) Huang Qian-Pogonina

13...♝b7 (okay, this one was expected) **14 ♕d2 ♕c7 15 ⬛e1 ♞d8!?** (the point of this move is to swing the rook to the kingside; instead, *Houdini* pointed out 15...d5! 16 exd6 ♝xd6 17 ♝d5 ♞d4 18 ♝xb7 ⬛xb7 19 ♞xd4 cxd4 20 ♕xd4 ⬛b4 21 ♕c3 ♝xh2+ 22 ♚f1 ♕b8) **16 ♝d5 ⬛g6 17 ♝e4 ♝xe4 18 ⬛xe4 ♞e6** (completing the reorganization of queenside pieces to the other sector) **19 ♕e2 ♕c6** (White did not read Black's motives well here and now fell for a tactic) **20 ♗c4?! ♘d4!** (winning the exchange) **21 ♖xd4 cxd4** and Black later won.

37) Hadolias-Tetepoulidis
29 b4 seemingly allowed Black to obtain counterplay after **29...♖xc3 30 ♕xc3 ♘xd5**, but here White missed **31 bxc5! ♗xc3 32 cxb6 ♗xe1 33 exd5 ♗f2 34 b7 ♚f8 35 f5 ♚e7 36 ♗f1! ♚d8 37 ♗h3 g5 38 f6** when **♗c8** would win for him. So, yes, 29 b4 is a good move. Instead, after **31 ♕b3?! ♘xb4** Black had compensation for the exchange.

38) Rodshtein-Nepomniachtchi
24...♘xb2! 25 ♕xb2 ♘a4 and White has no good answer.

39) Richter-Tay
11 e5! (a pawn sacrifice to wreck Black's once proud centre) **11...dxe5 12 ♗c4** with an easy game for White. Instead, **11 ♗e2** was played and after **11...d5** Black had fighting chances with his strong centre.

40) Godard-Short
15...♘a3! (by nudging the queen off c2, Black exerts tremendous pressure on the queenside and White now had to keep making concessions to deal with the constant threats) **16 ♕d1** (after 16 bxa3 ♕xc3 17 ♕xc3 ♗xc3 18 ♖b1 Black's passed c-pawn would have had a wonderful career, but White's troubles on the queenside are not yet over) **16...♖fb8 17 ♘b3 ♕d8 18 ♕d2 ♘b5 19 ♕c2?** (this time when White moves the queen back, he gets hit by a standard advance) **19...c4!** (Black obtains the c5-square for his knight) **20 ♘d2 ♘xc3 21 bxc3 ♕a5 22 ♘b1 ♘c5 23 a4 ♗b5! 24 ♖a3 ♗xa4** saw Black regain his pawn and retain his huge queenside initiative.

Index of Variations

The King Takes a Stroll

1 d4 ♘f6 2 c4 c5 3 d5 b5 4 cxb5 a6 5 bxa6 g6 6 ♘c3 ♗xa6 7 e4 ♗xf1 8 ♔xf1 d6 9 ♘f3

> 9 g4 – 81

9...♘bd7

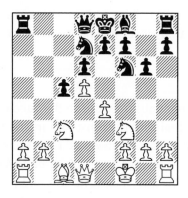

10 g3

> 10 h3 ♗g7 11 ♔g1 0-0 12 ♔h2
>> 12...♘b6 – 72
>> 12...♕a5 – 77

10...♗g7 11 ♔g2 0-0

> 11...♘a6 – 39

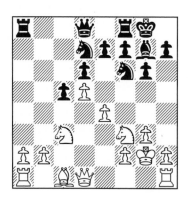

12 a4

    12 h3 ♕b6 – 47

    12 ♖e1 ♕c7 (12...♖a6 – 53; 12...♕a5 – 58)

        13 h3 – 61

        13 ♖e2 – 67

12...♕b6

    12...♕b8 – 34

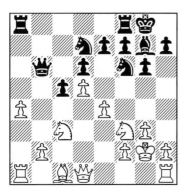

13 ♕e2

    13 ♖a3 – 28

13...♖fb8 – 18

    13...e6 – 31

Flummoxing the Fianchetto Variation

1 d4 ♘f6 2 c4 c5 3 d5 b5 4 cxb5 a6 5 bxa6 g6 6 ♘c3 ♗xa6 7 g3 ♗g7

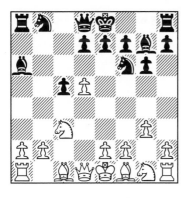

8 ♗g2

    8 ♘h3 – 126

    8 ♘f3 d6

        9 ♗h3 – 137

9 h4 – 143

8...d6 9 ♘f3

9 ♘h3 – 133

9...♘fd7

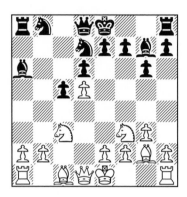

10 0-0

10 ♗d2 ♘b6

11 b3 – 87

11 ♕c1 – 121

10 ♖b1 – 94

10 ♕c2 – 102

10...♘b6 11 ♕c2 ♘8d7 12 ♖d1 0-0

13 ♖b1 – 111

13 b3 – 115

Benko Schmenko

1 d4 ♘f6 2 c4 c5 3 d5 b5 4 cxb5 a6 5 b6 e6 6 ♘c3 ♘xd5 7 ♘xd5 exd5 8 ♕xd5 ♘c6

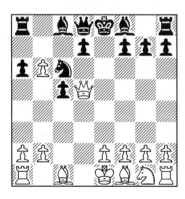

9 e4

9 ♗g5 – 155

Hustle and Flow

1 d4 ♘f6 2 c4 c5 3 d5 b5 4 cxb5 a6 5 f3

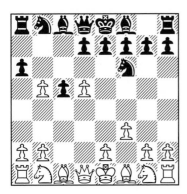

The Safety Dance

1 d4 ♘f6 2 c4 c5 3 d5 b5 4 cxb5 a6 5 e3 e6

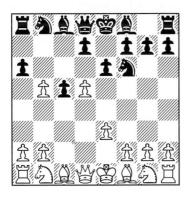

7 ♘xd5 – 207

7 ♘ge2 – 215

Knight out on a Limb

1 d4 ♘f6 2 c4 c5 3 d5 b5 4 cxb5 a6 5 ♘c3 axb5 6 e4 b4 7 ♘b5 d6

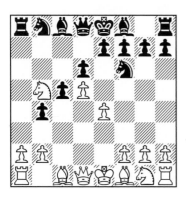

8 ♗c4 – 221

8 ♗f4 – 228

8 ♘f3 – 235

Ignorance is Bliss

1 d4 ♘f6 2 c4 c5 3 d5 b5 4 ♘f3

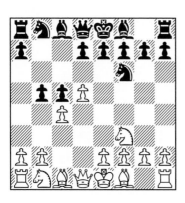

4 ♕c2 bxc4 5 e4 e6 6 ♘c3 ♗e7 7 ♗xc4 0-0 8 ♘ge2 exd5 9 exd5 d6 10 0-0 ♘bd7 11 ♘g3 ♘b6 12 b3

12...♖e8 – 252

12...♘xc4 – 256

4 ♘d2 – 260

4 ♗g5 – 266

4...♗b7

The Outsiders
1 d4 ♘f6 2 c4 c5 3 d5 b5

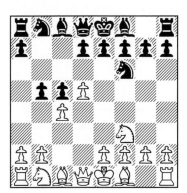

Index of Complete Games